Canada Learns To Play:
The Emergence of Organized Sport, 1807-1914

Alan Metcalfe

McClelland and Stewart

Cover photograph: New Westminster Salmonbellies vs. Vancouver at Brockton Point, Vancouver, 1914. Courtesy Vancouver City Archives.

Canadian Cataloguing in Publication Data

Metcalfe, Alan
  Canada learns to play

(The Canadian social history series)
Includes bibliographical references and index.
ISBN 0-7710-5870-5

1. Sports - Canada - History. 2. Canada - Social
life and customs - History. I. Title. II. Series.

GV585.M48 1987   796'.0971   C86-094106-X

This book has been published with the help of a grant from the Social Science Federation of Canada, using funds provided by the Social Sciences and Humanities Research Council of Canada.

Printed and bound in Canada by Webcom Ltd.

McClelland and Stewart Limited
The Canadian Publishers
481 University Avenue
Toronto, Ontario
M5G 2E9

Contents

Acknowledgements 7

Introduction 9

1 The Roots of Organized Sport:
Sport in British North America, 1807-1867 15

2 The Growth of Social Sporting Clubs in
Canada, 1867-1914 32

3 The Emergence of Organized Team Sport,
1867-1914 47

4 The Growth of Organizations and the
Development of Amateurism 99

5 The Growth of Professional and Commercial Sport 133

6 The History of Organized Sport:
A Case Study of Lacrosse, 1834-1914 181

7 Conclusion: Of Sport and Canada 219

Bibliographic Note 225

Notes 228

Index 240

DEDICATED TO

Heather, Alisa, and Karen

Acknowledgements

It is impossible to acknowledge everyone who has contributed to the publication of this book, thus I will recognize only those who have had a direct impact on its writing. In several instances they will not even be aware of their input. My whole approach to the history of sport is rooted in my graduate education at the University of Wisconsin, and in particular to Professors G. Kenyon and J.F.C. Harrison. Many of the ideas were first discussed in graduate classes at the University of Windsor. I learned much from my interactions with Ted Laurendeau, John Purcell, Howard Christie, George Short, Marian Pitters, Sheila Mitchell, Bill Myrer, Vicky Paraschak, Cathy Macdonald, David Norwood, John Key, John Byl, Tina Parratt, and Michel Vigneault. Over the years several sport historians and sport sociologists have deepened my understanding of sport and sport history. To Dick Gruneau I owe a very great debt. Don Morrow has been a continuing source of ideas and encouragement. Bruce Kidd, Max Howell, Gerry Redmond, Larry Fielding, Ron Smith, Mel Adelman, Steven Hardy, and Jack Berryman will each recognize parts of the book as reflecting their ideas.

In the preparation of the manuscript for publication I am indebted to Greg Kealey for his patience and encouragement during a long and arduous process. The comments of several reviewers were most helpful. In particular I wish to thank Morris Mott, whose forthrightness and openness have been very much appreciated. To Pat Baldwin, the secretary par excellence, who never once complained about the numerous drafts she typed, I owe a debt of gratitude.

Finally, my wife and two daughters have helped to keep my manuscript in the proper perspective while at the appropriate time giving much needed encouragement. Words cannot express my thanks to them.

Introduction

In 1963, in a brilliantly insightful book, *Beyond a Boundary*, West Indian historian C.L.R. James stated:

> A famous Liberal historian [G.M. Trevelyan] can write the social history of England in the nineteenth century, and two famous Socialists [Raymond Postgate and G.D.H. Cole] can write what they declared to be the history of the common people of England, and between them never once mention the man who was the best known Englishman of his time [Dr. W.G. Grace].[1]

Substitute Canada for England, Canadian historians for Englishmen, and rower Ned Hanlan for cricket player W.G. Grace and we have an accurate view of Canadian historical writing in 1986. Few Canadian historians have regarded sport as an integral part of the social history of Canada. What little sport history there is has come from Departments of Physical Education, not from Departments of History. Thus, the focus has tended to be on sport *per se* rather than on viewing it as an integral part of social history. The historiography of sport in Canada therefore has not reflected the changes that have transformed Canadian social history over the past twenty years. Although the few social historians who have recognized the existence of sport have treated it as ancillary to more "important" themes, their works demonstrate the potential sport has for furthering our understanding of Canadian social history. Examples of these works include small portions of S.F. Wise and D. Fisher's *Canada's Sporting Heroes* (1976) and, more important in placing sport within the framework of social history, Wise's "Sport and Class Values in Old Ontario and Quebec."[2] Bryan Palmer's brief reference to the importance of baseball in working-class culture in Hamilton during the nineteenth century placed baseball within the broader context of working-class life.[3] The most sustained and complete integration of sport and the broader context by historians in Canadian universities is to be found in the works of Peter Bailey, Keith Sandiford, and Morris Mott at the University of Manitoba.[4]

The limited works of these Canadian social and sport historians reveal that an immense gap remains between social historians and sport historians. Social historians address sport in the context of wider social issues, while sport historians view the subject outside the context of major social concerns. The underlying objective of this book is to sketch the outline of a bridge between the two different approaches. In all probability this will mean that social historians will find it wanting because too little attention is paid to sport's relationship to social variables, while sport historians will find it wanting because too little attention is paid to sport itself. My focus leads to a particular approach, one that emphasizes certain factors, briefly mentions others, and excludes others completely. More than anything this book is about Canada, not about Ontario or New Brunswick or Alberta. Thus, specific regional events will impinge only to the degree that they reflected or changed the nature of Canada, Canadian sport, and Canadian society.

The dominant influences on Canadian society to be considered are the changing demography, the ethnic composition of the population, the population distribution, the economy, the relationship of Canada and Canadians to Britain and the United States, and, in particular, the dominant role of the anglophone middle classes of Canada's urban areas. These concerns are necessary ingredients to any understanding of Canadian sport. Focusing on these elements, however, serves to exclude others. For example, the emphasis on the role of the anglophone middle classes moves other groups – French Canadians, native Canadians, workers, and women – to the periphery. These groups, while entering the account at various times, do so only insofar as they add to our understanding of the growth of organized sport. Each is quite deserving of separate treatment, but because they were peripheral to the development of organized sport I leave them for treatment elsewhere. Similarly, the relationship of sport to education and religion will be addressed only to the extent that they influenced the growth of organized sport.

What, then, is the focus of this book? It is primarily the history of the emergence of new sport forms within Canada as a direct consequence of the immense changes taking place within the country during the nineteenth and early twentieth centuries. Therefore, the development of organized sport will be viewed within the context of the physical expansion of Canada, the shifting distribution of population, the growth of cities, and the emergence of industrial capitalism. These variables created a changing framework within which Canadians created their identity. At the same time, people created sport, adapted it to the new environment, and articulated its ideology. Their social characteristics will provide the framework or context for our examination of the growth of organized sport in Canada.

The term "organized sport" instead of "sport" or "modern sport" is used to focus on particular aspects of sport and to delineate clearly the boundaries of the book. It narrows the focus by excluding a vast array of activities that are often encompassed by the term "sport" – informal games, children's play, fishing, etc. "Modern sport," on the other hand, carries with it the idea of modernization and the denial of human agency.[5] Even though organized sport developed within a particular context, it was created by men with their traditions, beliefs, attitudes, and values. Thus I have chosen to adopt the term "organized sport" with its implications of organization for participants and spectators. Four criteria are used to define organized sport: the form of the game, the structure of competition, the extent of participation, and, perhaps most important of all, the growth of organizations to codify rules, organize competition, and control sport.

With each of these aspects of organized sport, significant changes took place during the course of the nineteenth century that entailed the creation of something completely new. The form and structure of games changed from ill-defined time-and-space boundaries and a prevalence of local playing rules to far more clearly defined boundaries and standardized rules. For example, early lacrosse and football were played on large, open fields with the dimensions of the field of play being determined only by the size of the available playing area or the proximity of spectators. The outcome of these contests was determined by the winner of the best three out of five games; this meant a match could be over in four or five minutes or continue interminably. In addition, there was no standardized set of rules. For example, football was characterized by a variety of rules in different parts of Canada. Before any game, the captains met to agree on rules to be used in that particular game. The second half of the century witnessed the establishment of standardized rules, the development of generally accepted boundaries, and the creation of games of a determined duration.

The second major characteristic was the change in the structure of competition. Without exception, lacrosse, cricket, and curling matches in the year of Confederation were either exhibitions or challenges where one team would challenge another to a friendly competition. These games had no degree of regularity, with some teams playing only one or two inter-club games a year. The first hint of change had come one year earlier, in 1866, when the first championship game between the Caughnawaga Indians and the Montreal Lacrosse Club was played. This was very much a part of the old system in that such games were infrequent and because challenges were accepted or rejected at the whim of the champion. In the years to come organized sport was to emerge with the gradual increase in schedules and finally the creation of leagues. Within lacrosse the critical jump into the world of organized sport occurred in 1885, when the National Amateur Lacrosse Association adopted a series system for the championship matches, creating what was in effect a league. No longer was the championship decided by one game but by a series of games throughout the summer between the five or six leading teams. League structure is the critical variable that differentiates pre-industrial from contemporary sport. Very simply, the creation of a league is based on the assumption that the players and spectators have time off at the same time for a certain number of weeks into the future. Thus, the creation of leagues is the most important single variable in defining organized sport.

The third identifying characteristic of organized sport is its mass nature. It is not restricted to a select social group, but is available to all levels of society either as participants or as spectators. The development of mass sport has two dimensions: first, the growth of mass participation, which includes the growth of age-group sport, the expansion of sport into a wide variety of social groups, and the development of commercial recreation; second, the development of spectator sport, which in turn is related to the commercial exploitation of sport. Thus, the emergence of mass sport includes several criteria.

Finally, organizations emerged to codify rules and administer and control sport. Organization of sport prior to 1867 was limited to local clubs that served to organize limited intra- and inter-club competition. The formation of the National Lacrosse Association in 1867 ushered in the move toward bureaucratization. By 1914 Canadian sport was characterized by a mass of local, provincial, and national organizations. Central to nearly all these organizations was the ideology of amateurism. Amateurism supplied sport with its meaning and provides the focal point for the history of sport.

It is important to emphasize that organized sport is a composite of the aforementioned characteristics and that all were related to the growth of urban-industrial society. However, *few* sports attained *all* these characteristics. In other words, there were varying degrees of change from one sport to another.

Even a cursory examination of sport in 1867 and 1914 reveals significant differences in its form, structure, and popularity. Perhaps more important than an account of the historical development is an analysis of the reasons why it changed. While it is impossible to give definitive answers, it is possible to provide tentative hypotheses. First, although the development of urban-industrial society, itself created by men, provided the necessary conditions for the growth of organized sport, it was not in itself a sufficient condition. Organized sport, and particularly amateur sport, was created by a small group of men who made an impact on sport out of all proportion to their numerical size. Amateur sport was created by the anglophone mercantile, commercial, and professional middle class of Montreal and Toronto, and to a lesser extent in other urban centres with a significant commercial, mercantile, and professional middle class. In particular, amateur sport was to be found in the cities of central Canada. As the century progressed, amateur sport spread to the larger towns across Canada, for the most part restricted to one or two towns in each province. From these central points amateur sport spread to surrounding communities. While Canadian sport reflected the characteristics of sport recognized throughout the industrial world, its own unique features were in part borrowed. For ideology the Canadians turned to Britain, but in the real world of sport the practical answers most often given were akin to those being given in the United States. Finally, the contradictory aspects of sport were most clearly seen in the amateur/professional question. It is an analysis and understanding of this relationship that, in the end, provides the clearest and most accurate view of the development of organized sport.

Sport is not peripheral to society; indeed it is central to life and reflects the dominant social and political concerns. In modern society, sport is a visible and pervasive social system that has become an important institution for the transmission of cultural characteristics. In fact, sport is one of the sub-systems of culture that transcends socio-economic, educational, ethnic, and religious barriers. As well, it has the advantage of being a free-time activity, regarded as "frivolous" and thus "not important." As a result, these activities reflect the attitudes and values an individual holds rather than those one is "expected" to hold. In other words, it is when one is free from the constraints of work and social obligations in the "unimportant" world of play that an individual acts out his/her own reality. Therefore, the patterns of behaviour, attitudes, and values implicit within sport will be an excellent indication of basic cultural values.[6]

At the moment the gap between what research exists and what should exist is so great that much of what follows is tentative. This book is a first exploratory step toward a fuller understanding of the relationship between sport and society. It attempts to provide a clear outline of the emergence of organized sport within the context of basic social parameters, namely the changing patterns of population distribution, industrialization, ethnicity, and the domination of the anglophone urban middle class. Within this context each chapter addresses particular issues that are central to the history of sport.

Chapter One explores organized sport in pre-Confederation British North America. These roots had a profound impact on the subsequent development of Canadian sport. Chapter Two examines the seed from which all organized sport developed and in particular highlights the creation of a network of select social sporting clubs that were the forerunners of the exclusive, private clubs of the modern day. Organized sport, in its fullest sense, was related to the development of mass team sport. Chapter Three outlines the origins and spread of participant team sport across Canada. Particular attention is paid to the distinctive Canadian elements and their relationship to Britain and the United States. Providing a unifying theme across Canada was the ideology of amateurism. The genesis of this ideology, the groups that promoted it, and the creation of organizations to administer and control sport are the subject of Chapter Four. Chapter Five focuses on the important role of money in all sport, amateur, professional, and commercial. In particular it traces the growth of professionalism and commercialism. Finally, Chapter Six brings all these elements together and provides a composite view of the growth of organized sport in Canada. This is done through a case study of lacrosse, arguably the most popular Canadian summer game during the period under consideration.

1

The Roots of Organized Sport:
Sport in British North America,
1807–1867

On July 1, 1867, the inhabitants of British North America celebrated the birth of a new country. Invariably the celebrations held in towns and villages throughout the new Dominion included an array of sporting activities: horseracing, running and jumping, cricket, and a variety of other competitions. None of these had acquired *all* the characteristics of organized sport – organized competition, formally constituted clubs, specialized facilities, and codified rules. Some sports, however, in particular cricket and curling, had acquired some of these attributes. Thus the years prior to Confederation were important because the foundations laid determined the patterns of development of Canadian sport, in particular the central role of British games and ideals, the dominant position of the larger towns, and the centrality of certain social groups in the development of organized sport. It was created by people whose formative years were rooted in a pre-industrial non-North American environment. Therefore, the powerful forces of tradition played an important role in shaping the new sport forms. During the pre-Confederation years, when British North America was more British than it would ever be again, these forces of tradition were at their strongest.[1]

THE BRITISH INFLUENCE

Among the traditions the British immigrants brought with them was a wide variety of games. These games had a long history in British life and had been played on various festive and communal occasions for many generations. They were an essential part of the communal celebrations that punctuated the never-ending round

15

of dawn-to-dusk work that was the lot of the majority of Englishmen.[2] Life in British North America was even more restrictive; the harsh climate and the physical conditions of the frontier made survival the primary concern of many inhabitants. Even in these conditions the people took every opportunity, in their infrequent free time, to enjoy life. Central to these occasions were games, sports, and competitions. Coon hunts, cock fights, rifle matches, wrestling, and fisticuffs were common throughout British North America. However, it would be erroneous to equate these with the more organized sports beginning to develop in the larger urban areas.

> In the so-called backwoods settlements, like Richmond, Perth and Bytown, horse races were much less aristocratic events, and commonly resulted in fights and brawls; while in all parts of the province gambling and drunkenness were characteristic of such sporting activities.[3]

Contemporary accounts by upper- and middle-class observers attest to the lack of sophistication and the roughness of many of the "sports" played in the backwoods.[4] The same activities and attitudes were relevant among the majority of British North Americans, whether in the emerging towns or on the frontier. The games reflected the harshness of their environment and were used as a vehicle to gain momentary escape from a life of hardship and toil. At the same time, the games played on the frontier reflected two important factors: first, the way in which groups adapted to the new environment; second, the importance of traditional games in helping people adapt. This was to be seen not only in the backwoods settlements, but also in the towns where organized sport began to develop.

Organized sport developed in distinct locations and under certain conditions. It first saw light of day in the larger towns with a strong British presence, in particular colonial government and/or military garrisons.[5] The British influence was particularly important in terms of the games played and the ideology adopted. The games and ideology were combined in two institutions, the military garrisons and Upper Canada College (1829). These two institutions played pivotal roles in the organization and development of cricket.

Without doubt the most popular summer sport of the pre-1867 era was one that was pre-industrial in nature and remained so throughout the nineteenth century. Its continued existence and history illustrated the powerful forces of tradition and the way in which dominant social groups perpetuated their way of life in the face of massive social change. It also serves as a caveat against an overly simplistic view of the impact of urban industrial society on the lives of Canadians. Cricket was English in origin and orientation and was promoted and played by the English. It was played by immigrants, garrison teams, and native-born subjects imbued with the British sporting ideology at the prestigious private schools, such as Upper Canada College. As the *Toronto Patriot* stated on July 13, 1836:

British feelings cannot flow into the breasts of our Canadian boys through a more delightful or untainted channel than that of British sports. A Cricketer as a matter of course, detests democracy and is staunch in his allegiance to his King.[6]

Glorified by the colonial aristocracy and the educated elite as the game that surpassed all in its test of manhood and its gentlemanly qualities, the success or failure of cricket was one of the most accurate indications of the independence of Canadian culture from the constraints of the mother country. Its protracted battle for survival throughout the nineteenth century and its existence in small enclaves to the present day attest to its persistence and the pervasive influence of Britain in the history of Canadian sport.

Cricket was an Upper Canadian phenomenon, first taking root in Toronto, then spreading throughout the province. There were subsidiary areas of enthusiasm but these only developed under two conditions: an urban centre and a military garrison. Montreal, Halifax, Quebec City, Ottawa, Saint John, and later Victoria were all military garrisons and all outposts of cricket. However, despite its pervasiveness in the widespread outposts of British North America, the history of cricket was very much the history of Upper Canada. Even before the small village of York changed its name to Toronto, cricket was being played. There is evidence that games were contested in the 1820's; certainly this was the case after the foundation of Upper Canada College in 1829, where the first headmaster was an old Etonian and an ardent exponent of the game.[7] Upper Canada College thus took the lead in the development of cricket, which it was not to relinquish prior to Confederation. By 1836, the college team, including masters and old boys, played a Toronto eleven comprised of the social elite of the city.[8] From the outset, inter-town games were played between Toronto and teams from Guelph (1830) and Hamilton (1835). In 1840, a team of American cricketers arrived to play against Toronto; unfortunately, the Toronto team was unaware of the arrangements. The Toronto team graciously agreed to play an informal game against their American opponents for fifty pounds a side. As a result of the contacts established in 1840 the first international cricket match, not between England and Australia but between Canada and the United States, was held on September 24-25, 1844; the result – a victory for the Canadians. Thus, international competition alternating between Philadelphia and, for the most part, Toronto continued in 1845 and 1846, then, after a break of several years, in 1853 it became an annual competition. Cricket had gained a firm foothold among upper-class Canadians who were to perpetuate the game through the private schools. Cricket's longevity and persistence were directly related to its position within the highest levels of Canadian society.

Cricket experienced steady growth in the 1840's and 1850's. By 1848 there were at least eighteen clubs in Upper Canada playing primarily a variety of intra-club games. Inter-club competition, one of the hallmarks of organized sport, was given a boost with the construction of the railway network in the 1850's. By the early 1850's the number of clubs in Upper Canada had increased to thirty-one. Their distribution reflected what was to become the identifying characteristics of Ontario and Canadian sport; the domination of Toronto and its immediate hinterland. Eighteen of the clubs were either in the city or within thirty miles. Four of the others were in Hamilton, two in Ottawa, and the other seven were on the railway line. By 1858, the number of clubs had risen to fifty-eight.[9] Perhaps its popularity among recent immigrants was most vividly exemplified in the existence of ten teams within forty miles of Sarnia. These bore the names of such villages as Oil Springs, Florence, and Wyoming – surely a vivid example of the popularity of cricket. In fact, some historians claim that the 1850's were the halcyon days of cricket.[10] If this was the case it certainly reflected the weakness of its support among "Canadians." Cricket remained an English game rooted in pre-industrial England.

Cricket reached its heyday in the early 1860's. The tour of Parr and Lillywhite's team from England in 1859 ushered in an apparent explosion of interest in Canadian cricket. Stimulated by the influx of British troops, there was a surge of interest in

Curling on Fish Creek, Alberta, c. 1895. Courtesy Glenbow Archives, Calgary / NA-2560-4.

the game in Montreal and Toronto. In the latter, eleven new teams were formed between 1860 and 1863, as teams of shoemakers, tailors, bandsmen, and Hibernian and Caledonian societies took to the cricket squares to test their mettle.[11] The year 1863 was perhaps the high point of these dizzy days when the Toronto team hired a professional from England. The season concluded with a "Cricketiana," a week devoted to a series of games. These days were not, as many cricketers believed, an omen for the future when cricket would become the national game of Canada, but rather a peak that was never to be attained again. Looming on the horizon in rival Montreal to challenge for the title of Canada's national and most popular game was lacrosse, the game that was rooted in Canadian soil.

The significance of cricket lay in its relationship to a British influence. Its claim to be the most popular game in the colony certainly appeared to be well founded because of the apparent expansion in numbers and competitive opportunities. However, the healthy state of cricket was illusory. The foundations were weak. The only relatively permanent clubs were located in the cities and were supported by the social elite. In the rural areas cricket was dependent on the replenishment of players, and these were not forthcoming. Cricket remained dependent for its existence on a supply of English immigrants and thus became a vestigial remnant of the lifestyle of the English.

Curling, the other pre-industrial game, drew its support from a different segment of the community – the Scots. Throughout the nineteenth century it remained closely tied to Scotland and things Scottish. It was particularly popular among the business section of the community, and despite claims to the contrary it was essentially a game for the more affluent members of society. Informal games had been played in British North America since the mid-eighteenth century with the arrival of Scottish regiments.[12] The first curling club in British North America, the Montreal Curling Club, was the first organized sporting club in British North America, founded by a group of Scottish merchants who met at Gillies Tavern in Montreal on January 22, 1807.[13] The club met on an irregular basis for the first thirteen years before becoming a permanent fixture in the 1820's.[14] During the 1820's Scots also formed clubs in Kingston (1820), Quebec City (1821), and Halifax (1824-25).[15] The game spread into Upper Canada with the formation of the Fergus Curling Club in 1834. This was followed by clubs in various Upper Canadian towns. Perhaps more important to the development of the game was the first inter-club match between Montreal and Quebec played at Trois-Rivières in 1837.[16] By the early 1850's curling clubs were well established in Nova Scotia and Lower and Upper Canada. Curling had become the winter game wherever Scots settled. This Scottish connection, which dominated Canadian curling well into the twentieth century, was cemented in 1852. In two separate initiatives the curlers of Montreal and Nova Scotia created two Canadian branches of the Royal Caledonian Curling Club of Scotland. Until 1935 and the formation of a national organization, curling in Canada remained subject to the jurisdiction of a "foreign" organization. In many respects curling, although more appropriate to Canadian climes, remained a Scottish game. Thus, the game of middle-class Canadians perpetuated the colonial status of Canada.

MONTREAL AND THE EMERGENCE OF ORGANIZED SPORT

Throughout the nineteenth century cricket and curling remained tied to their pre-industrial origins. They continued to be identified with the old country and were recognized as "alien" games. At the same time they were not immune to the winds of change, which thrust sport into a new era with new forms of competition, new organizations, and new rules. The initial expansion of the 1830's and 1840's was due to the tide of British immigrants flowing into British North America. However, the changes of the 1850's provided the necessary conditions for the emergence of organized sport, and it was during this period that both cricket and curling witnessed an expansion of inter-city contests, the growth in clubs, and, in the case of curling, the development of umbrella organizations. Central to these changes was the development of the network of railways that served to link the cities, towns, and villages of British North America. Although the first railways were built in the 1840's, real expansion took place during the 1850's and 1860's, and the railways created the cords that were to tie the parts of British North America together. A second factor for change was initiated in Montreal in 1847 with the building of factories along the Lachine Canal. Industrialization, which created the necessary conditions for organized sport, extended from Montreal to Toronto, Hamilton, and the towns of western Ontario in the 1850's and 1860's. It was these areas that were to witness the development of organized sport. A third related change was the escalation of urbanization, the process of masses of people moving into urban areas. By 1861 there were sixteen towns with populations of over 5,000, and these towns and cities led the way in the development of sports, nine in Upper Canada, four in Lower Canada, two in New Brunswick, and one in Nova Scotia. Organized sport was unequivocally an urban creation. Because only 13.1 per cent of the population lived in urban areas in 1851, sport was the exclusive preserve of a relatively small proportion of the population. Organized sport, therefore, was first associated with the larger towns of British North America: Montreal, Quebec, Toronto, Hamilton, Halifax, and Saint John. Pre-eminent among these in size and location of industry was Montreal.

It is no accident that Montreal can be called the birthplace of Canadian sport. Montreal witnessed many firsts: the first organized club, the Montreal Curling Club (1807); the first cricket and hunt clubs in the 1820's; the first demonstration of lacrosse in 1834; the first Montreal Olympic Games in 1844; the first specialized sporting facilities in the 1840's and 1850's; the first lacrosse club (1856); and the first golf club (1873). Montreal was central to the growth of Canadian sport. In addition, it typified the experiences of the larger towns of Canada and its history was to be repeated with local variations throughout the nineteenth century.

Prior to the 1840's sport in Montreal was occasional, pre-industrial in form, and limited to certain social groups. Throughout the early period it was strongly influenced by the anglophone segment of the city. The earliest evidence of organized sport was the formation of the Montreal Curling Club. However, it was not until the 1820's that there was evidence of further organization when short-lived cricket and hunt clubs were organized by officers of the garrison.[17] The 1830's witnessed a growing interest in sporting activities among officers of the garrison and the mercantile and commercial section of the community – exhibition lacrosse, racquets, and rowing all surfaced for brief periods of time. Only cricket and curling had any degree of permanence. It must be emphasized that sporting opportunities were characterized by their lack of continuity and impermanence.

On Saturday afternoons in the winter of 1840, a group of twelve Montrealers embarked on "constitutional tramps" into the wilds around Montreal. This was the inauspicious beginning of the prestigious Montreal Snow Shoe Club (MSSC) and the first concrete example of a rising interest in sport. In 1842, 241 leading citizens formed the Montreal Olympic Athletic Club. The membership included officers from the military garrison, Scottish merchants, and a variety of professional and political figures, both French and British. This club joined the Montreal Curling Club and the newly formed Thistle Curling Club (1842) in providing social and competitive opportunities for the social elite. Intra-club activities were the *raison d'être* of the clubs. From 1846 to 1849, the main activities of the snowshoers centred on the weekly tramps, with only one race being held every year.[18] During the winters, six to ten members of the MSSC tramped across Mount Royal on Tuesday evenings and explored the surrounding countryside on Saturday afternoons, in each instance ending up at Dolly's

Chop House for a "convivial" evening. Competition had not yet moved to centre stage. For the curlers, competition was always central and the year revolved around a series of intra-club competitions for medals and trophies. Often, after the game, the rinks would adjourn to Compains for dinner.[19] In reality, these clubs were the forerunners of the prestigious social sporting clubs that were to become one of the cornerstones of the social life of the urban elite in the latter part of the century.[20]

At the same time the clubs did promote competition. For the curlers the competition remained within the boundaries of the mercantile and commercial segments of the community. The Olympic Athletic Club, however, promoted competition among a wider segment of society by promoting track and field, regattas, and, in 1844, the Montreal Olympic Games. In this they reflected the traditions of the old country, where different segments of society were allowed to compete together, albeit in clearly defined roles. The efforts of the Olympic Athletic Club were greeted with strong support by the *Montreal Transcript* on August 20, 1844.

> It is very gratifying to see a taste for the old English sports springing up in this country, and to find that the spirit which animated our forefathers, and gave strength and vigor to their arms, is not extinct.... The encouragement given to cricket and the establishment of regattas and Olympic Games, are as many proofs of this feeling.[21]

In these competitions club members competed against men from all walks of life. The first snowshoe races in 1843 were won by Deroche, a voyageur, in competition with Nicholas Hughes and five Indians. Races at the Olympic Games were won by Sergeant McGillvary of the garrison; Tarisonkwan, an Indian; E. Burroughs, a lawyer; and "Evergreen" Hughes.[22] However, such competitions were few and were to disappear by the 1870's. Social differences were recognized in the provision of a choice of prizes; for instance, at the Montreal Olympic Games, "The Victors of the principal prizes will receive silver medals or the value of them in money at their option."[23] The differences were to be made more explicit as the century progressed. These competitions were rooted in the past, not in the future.

It was in curling that the basic patterns of organized sport first developed. The Montreal club was joined by the Thistle (1842) and Caledonian (1850), which resulted in regular inter-club competition. The expansion of competitive opportunities in curling parallelled significant changes in the economic structure of Montreal. The establishment of mills on the Lachine Canal in 1847 signalled the beginning of the industrial era. This, in conjunction with the opening of the Montreal Telegraph Company in 1847 and the establishment of a rail link with Toronto in 1856, resulted in a change in the established patterns of work and leisure and a breakdown of the physical isolation that was a reality of British North American life. No longer did the onset of winter herald the "cessation of the active bustle which characterized the mercantile portion of our city."[24] Instead, commerce continued on a year-round basis. While the railway served to break down the physical isolation, industrialization destroyed the daily and seasonal rhythm, creating new concepts of time symbolized by the pervasive presence of the factory whistle. Organized mass sport was largely a creation of this process.

During the 1850's changes took place in the world of sport in Montreal. There were an increase in the number of clubs, especially those promoting team sport, a distinct shift in focus toward competition, the growth of specialized sporting facilities, and the beginning of the battle for supremacy between the strongly rooted British sports and indigenous Canadian sports promoted by the Canadian-born mercantile, professional, and commercial classes. Perhaps the most important change in terms of a distinctive Canadian sport culture was the emergence of lacrosse clubs. Lacrosse had been played on a demonstration basis in Montreal as early as 1834. This was followed by infrequent exhibitions, the most famous in 1844 when a team of whites for the first time took the field against an Indian team. However, it was not until 1856 that the first club, the Montreal Lacrosse Club, was formed. By 1860 there were at least six clubs in Montreal.

The importance of lacrosse lies in the group who promoted the game. Lacrosse was developed by young native-born Canadians of the highest social strata. These Canadians were strongly influenced by the British approach to sport but just as strongly opposed to the imposition of British sports on Canadian youth. The young lacrossists were typified by George Beers, the father of lacrosse, who was imbued with the British approach to sport in his education at Lower Canada College and played as goal-keeper in the famous exhibition for the Prince of Wales on the Montreal Cricket Grounds on August 27, 1860. More importantly, he published the first rules of lacrosse and was instrumental in the formation of the National Lacrosse Association in 1867. An avowed Canadian nationalist, Beers consistently promoted lacrosse as Canada's national game. The importance of Montreal and lacrosse to the growth of Canadian sport cannot be overemphasized, for it was the first evidence of an indigenous game, promoted by native-born Canadians, finding root in Canadian soil. That it was limited to Montreal until 1867 only substantiates the important and pioneering role played by Montreal sportsmen.

Other events in Montreal signified that sport was entering a new era. The first was the creation of indoor curling sheds for the Montreal Curling Club in 1838.[25] By 1862, in addition to the curling sheds, Montreal could boast one commercial and three private facilities devoted to sport: Montreal Cricket Grounds, McGill College Grounds, Montreal Lacrosse Grounds, and the semi-commercial Victoria Skating Rink, which opened in 1862. In snowshoeing, the predominant role of tramping was being challenged by some young showshoers who held that racing was the true test of a sportsman. This changing focus in snowshoeing was illustrated by the inauguration of yearly championship races in 1862, the development of a racing calendar for the month of February, and the formation of clubs whose prime concern was racing. At the same time, there emerged an increasing differentiation between club members and non-members. Separate races were instituted for Indians and NCOs from the regiments. Medals and trophies were awarded to the club members while money was given to the victorious Indians and NCOs. Sport was providing evidence of the emergence of a new value system, one in which winning became central. This was antithetical to the attitude to sport held by the proponents of the British amateur ideal and it led to the emergence of the problem that was to beset sport into the twentieth century, the amateur-professional question.

By the mid-1860's organized sport had become a recognized part of the social and sporting life of the anglophone Montreal elite. Cricket, curling, lacrosse, and showshoeing filled the calendars of a small but influential segment of society. These games were played within the context of British attitudes and values. At the same time, this consensus was threatened by the increasing emphasis placed on the outcome of the contest and by the aspirations of some young Canadians to distance themselves from British games. These concerns were to remain central to the growth of organized sport in the post-Confederation years and would provide a uniquely Canadian sport culture.

ORGANIZED SPORT ACROSS CANADA

It is impossible to encapsulate sport in British North America through the history of one city. Even though the trends were the same and Montreal's experience was repeated many times in the 1870's, local variations in the games played and the groups involved added to the richness and complexity of Canadian sport. What gave some coherence to sporting activity was the British influence; thus, cricket and curling were the most popular sports across English-speaking British North America, from Halifax and Saint John to Quebec City, Montreal, and Toronto. In addition, relatively permanent social sporting clubs emerged in the large towns.

More important to the growth of organized sport were events taking place in the vicinity of Hamilton, Upper Canada, in particular the spread of baseball among the pre-industrial working classes. Baseball-like games had been played in Upper Canada as early as 1838,[26] but in the early 1850's organized but short-lived clubs developed in Hamilton. The first inter-city game was held in 1859 between Hamilton and Toronto. During the next few years there was an explosion of interest in the American game in southwest Ontario, especially in towns such as Woodstock, Guelph, Ingersoll, Stratford, and London.[27] In 1864 a convention of baseball clubs was held and a short-lived Canadian Baseball Association formed.[28] By 1867 Hamilton boasted no fewer than seventeen baseball clubs. Baseball had taken root among the working class and was to remain, for the most part, outside the jurisdiction of amateur sport organizations dominated by the middle class that were to emerge later. Its importance lay in its continued popularity, its isolation from middle-class sport, and its close relationship with the United States. Baseball thus reflected the other major influence on Canadian sport – the United States. While organized sport was created by the anglophone upper and middle classes for their own leisure time, the working classes were actively involved in promoting activities for what little free time they had. Their efforts were characterized by lack of permanence, financial instability, but continued efforts. While few clubs persisted for prolonged periods, the games continued to exist. Any view of sport must take into account the organized activities of all segments of the community.

The basic similarities and regional differences of the sporting activities of British North Americans can be illustrated most clearly in a small town far removed from the more populated centres of Lower and Upper Canada: Victoria, Vancouver Island. The pervasiveness of sport among all segments of society, its embryonic development, and its basic characteristics were illustrated in the experience of Victoria in 1865.[29] Victoria had a population of only 3,270, yet even before 1865 it boasted various clubs. The sports that aspired to any formal structure and degree of regularity were cricket, rifle-shooting, and rowing. In all instances, club membership was drawn from the highest social levels – the officers of the fleet and the colonial government officials. The five cricket teams, two corps of Volunteers (riflemen), and one rowing club had considerable cross-membership. The status of the members can be gauged from the fact that the Chief Justice was a private in the 1st Volunteer Rifle Company while his superior officer in the Volunteers was the Attorney General, the Hon. T.L. Wood, who also served as secretary of the proposed rowing club. Highlights of the season in both cricket and rifle-shooting were the matches between HMS *Sutlej* and the local cricket and rifle clubs. Pride of place, however, went to the two matches with New Westminster. These were gala days in the social life of the community and concluded with lavish banquets attended by the Governor and all the high-ranking naval officers.

Still involving "society" were the horse races held at conveniently located Beacon Hill Park. In this instance, the base of support was somewhat larger. The two major meets organized by committees of leading citizens were those held to celebrate the Queen's and Prince of Wales's birthdays. Perhaps more popular and certainly more remunerative were the series of challenge matches held at Beacon Hill, the most important of which was the great challenge race for $1,000 between "Wake Up Jake" and the "Boston Colt," which attracted an "Immense concourse of spectators" to the best-two-out-of-three races. More interesting was the race held on May 22, 1865, as a result of a challenge from the Hon. H. Lascelles, Royal Navy, to Thomas Harris, Esq., Mayor of Victoria. Lascelles took a handicap of an extra jockey to offset the 208 pounds that the mayor weighed. Unfortunately for Lascelles, the mayor took an early lead, which caused the naval officer, from a well-known English family, to dump the extra jockey unceremoniously in a vain attempt to pluck victory from defeat. A rather sad day for British sportsmanship!

Cricket at Beacon Hill, Victoria, c. 1854. Courtesy Vancouver Public Library, photo no. 2417.

It is evident from the above that, for the most part, sport was the exclusive preserve of the social elite, and so it was for most Canadians. Sport was essentially pre-industrial, an infrequent break from work characterized by traditional games and pastimes. During the summer of 1865, various groups held picnics that included athletic events – climbing the greasy pole, and the highly popular dancing platforms. Such diverse groups as the Sunday schools of St. John and Christ Church, the Tiger Engine Company, the Caledonian Society, Ladies Collegiate Schools, and the Turn and Sing Verein Society held picnics at popular Cadboro Bay. For the most part, sport was a temporary break in a life of toil.

Providing rare spectacles for different segments of the population was a variety of challenge matches that took place in Victoria during 1865. At Buckley's Ball Court on Yates Street, several handball matches were held for stakes of up to $100. Later in the year, at the sporting venue the Royal Hotel Tap, Bob Ridley was to dance a jig against Tim Hayes for $100 a side. Unfortunately the contest was cancelled at the last moment because of the "indisposition of the fiddler." The same hotel hosted a sparring match between Ned Allan and Billy Williams. It was so successful that several other fights were promoted during the year. Finally, Hanley's Clover Point House was the location and sponsor for a number of quoit matches for stakes of $25 to $250. These first stirrings of commercial and professional sport were indicative of what was happening in many cities.

This brief view of Victoria in 1865 is probably more typical than what we have seen of Montreal. Organized sport on a regular, ongoing basis was available only to the elite of the community. On occasion their activities provided a spectacle for a more broadly based section of the community. For the majority, organized sport was limited to a few festive occasions such as the Queen's birthday and annual picnics. In these instances sport was part of a larger celebration and had not yet become the focal point of the day. At the same time there was evidence that commercial entrepreneurs, usually tavern-keepers, had already recognized the commercial potential of sporting activities. Thus, all the ingredients of the future were present. Organized sport prior to Confederation was limited to the elite of a small but growing number of towns and was foreign to the lives of farmers, habitants, lumbermen, and fur traders who typified the inhabitants of the country. At the same time it provided the foundation of the new society that emerged in the second half of the nineteenth century. The seeds sown in widely separated towns in the 1830's were to grow into the mass sport of the early twentieth century. The growth of the railway system in the 1850's began to break down the isolation that until then allowed only local sports activities. Thus the isolationist attributes of the various areas that are familiar to all students of Canadian history had their origins in the reality of life in nineteenth-century British North America. One factor, however, tended to provide a degree of commonality between various towns and across the colonies as a whole – this was the anglicization of British North America. The increasingly British character of the population provided a link between the isolated towns from the Maritimes to Vancouver Island. At the same time this served to further isolate and alienate one segment of the population – the French.

The British connection formed the *one* unifying experience. In nearly every respect the foundations of organized sport were unequivocally British. Certainly this was the case with respect to the sports that were pursued: cricket, racquets, curling, and fox hunting. This Britishness was accentuated during the early developmental stages by a massive influx of British immigrants in the 1820's and 1830's. Therefore, the foundations of sport were laid at that moment in time when the country was more British, as defined by birthplace of the population, than it was to be at any time in the future. In fact, the importance of this influence on the growth of sport was greater than the population figures suggest because of the predominant role the garrisons and the private schools, in particular Upper Canada College, played in the growth of sport and, in particular, in the value system and ideology attributed to sport. Sport was moulded in the image of the English aristocracy and was transmitted to young, native-born children in private schools that were unashamedly British in origin and focus. These young native-born "Canadians" were to play an important role in the organization of sport. While accepting the value system and ideology of Britain, these young men *were* Canadian and looked to North America, not to Britain, as home. They were not officers, nor were they members of a landed aristocracy; rather, they represented an emerging commercial middle class. While accepting the ideology of British sport, they rejected other aspects in favour of things identified with North America. This process of "Canadianization" was first observed in Montreal in the 1840's and 1850's in the battle between "British" and "Canadian" games, in particular between cricket and lacrosse. Young Montrealers, such as George Beers, consciously drew attention to the difference between "Canadian" and "British" games. Without doubt, there was a conscious recognition of being "Canadian" among some segments of the middle class. At the same time, this remained, in sport, a Montreal phenomenon, with the other towns remaining unequivocally British in nearly all respects.

The early 1860's witnessed events of great significance both to sport and to society. In Hamilton, Ontario, in the space of three years, baseball replaced cricket as the most popular summer sport. It was important because it was the first evidence of a significant intrusion of a sport originated and developed in the United States. In fact, baseball did not gain a foothold among the middle class but rather among the working class. This gives support to the view that not only were there significant cultural differences between the French and the English but also within the English-speaking community between the haves and have nots. The evidence gives some credence to the presence of a class division. In fact, the history of sport to 1914 affords concrete support to the contention that upper- and middle-class Canadians tended to turn to British models in both games and ideology while the working class turned to the United States.

The Canada that greeted Confederation in 1867 exhibited characteristics that were essential to the development of Canadian sport. In the first place there was a recognizable Canadian sport culture different, in some respects, from both Britain and the United States. At the same time Britain and the United States placed an indelible print on Canada with the British ideology and the increasing acceptance of American games and values among the working class. Finally, even as early as 1867, the French Canadians were completely isolated from their English-speaking compatriots. The die had been cast.

2

The Growth of Social Sporting Clubs in Canada, 1867-1914

Organized sport in pre-Confederation British North America was largely dominated by the more affluent members of society, in particular the British colonial officials, the garrison officers, and the commercial and mercantile middle class of the larger towns. These groups remained central to the development of amateur sport across Canada prior to the First World War. At the same time, the base of participants widened to incorporate Canadians from a variety of socio-economic backgrounds. On another level, however, the dominant social groups moved to create a network of social sporting clubs that were available only to the elite of society. These clubs were characterized by certain commonalities that gave meaning to the word "Canadian." By 1914 the clubs had permeated urban Canada except for French Quebec outside of Montreal and Quebec City. In each province the clubs first saw light of day in the largest urban centre before spreading to the smaller towns early in the twentieth century. Nearly without exception they involved the creation of facilities that allowed for extensive social interaction. In this instance there were definite levels of development that may be used as a rough gauge of their exclusiveness. At the lowest level were the curling sheds that allowed the game to be played inside and thus removed some of the limitations imposed by the weather. In golf some clubhouses were little more than changing rooms; at the other extreme, such as the Toronto and Montreal Golf Clubs, the facilities included dining rooms, reading rooms, and pro shops. These facilities promoted social activities that in many instances involved the ladies. Not only were the ladies involved in the social activities, but in golf, curling, and lawn tennis they also participated, albeit in a clearly defined and subservient role. Unlike the more popular team sports that demanded youth, these games did not impose an age barrier. Instead of being an activity of one's youth, a prelude to the more serious activities of life, these activities were lifetime sports and thus different.

Finally, and perhaps most important, were the entry requirements. Entrance was not given to any who applied. Often initiation fees, $750 at St. Charles Country Club in Winnipeg in 1912, automatically limited the source of potential members.[1] In other instances Anglican religion and attendance at private school were necessary requirements, as was the case in the Toronto Hunt Club, Ontario Jockey Club, and Toronto Golf Club.[2] A more obvious and popular method was the existence of clearly defined entrance procedures. A prospective member was nominated by one or two members. The application was then passed to a review committee who frequently had the right to reject without explanation. Finally the successful candidate's name was placed before the total membership, who then voted by secret ballot, and this frequently incorporated blacklisting,[3] a rather effective mechanism of ensuring that the membership reflected the most "desirable" social characteristics. What these characteristics were varied with the size and composition of the population. Thus the nature of club membership varied by size of town and by province. In the larger and more developed cities of Montreal, Toronto, and Ottawa a sophisticated hierarchical system developed and the membership of the clubs tended to be more homogeneous. The clubs that developed in smaller towns – Digby, Nova Scotia; Simcoe, Ontario; Minnedosa, Manitoba; Grenfell, Saskatchewan; High River, Alberta; Kamloops, British Columbia – tended to be more heterogeneous, including in their membership lawyers, doctors, ministers, teachers, and businessmen. At the same time, they did comprise the local elite.

THE HUNT AND TANDEM CLUBS

It was no accident that the most prestigious social sporting clubs were the hunt and tandem clubs. Few in number and limited to areas of strong British upper-class influence, these clubs attempted to duplicate the lifestyle of the British aristocracy. The earliest recorded club was the Montreal Hunt Club (1828), which owed its origin to officers of the British garrison. The garrisons continued to play a role in the promotion of hunting although there were no permanent clubs until late in the century. Ironically, it was after the removal of the British garrisons in 1872 that permanent clubs emerged in Montreal, Ottawa, Quebec City, and Toronto. The actual hunts and sleigh rides were the focal points of more extensive social activities. They were exemplified by the activities of the Montreal Hunt and Tandem Clubs. On September 27, 1884, the Montreal Hunt met at Verdun at "The beautiful country residence of Mr. J. Crawford, ex-Master of the Hunt. The gathering was large and fashionable, representing the elite and wealth of Montreal."[4] Sleighing and hunting were not just sporting occasions but part of the social life of the Montreal elite. Women were an integral part of both aspects of the hunt. The hunt breakfast and the Saturday afternoon sleigh rides around Dominion Square were moments of social display; the horses, sleighs, and women's furs were an impressive demonstration of the wealth and social status of the leading citizens of Montreal to the public and themselves. It requires little imagination to recognize the competition that would exist between various sleigh owners.

For the most part the hunt clubs remained limited to the aforementioned cities. However, there was some development, usually associated with a strong British upper-class influence. In 1889, a short-lived club was formed in Qu'Appelle, Saskatchewan. It was comprised of thirty-three members who purchased a pack of hounds from the Toronto Hunt Club.[5] A more solid foundation was laid in Victoria in the early twentieth century when the Victoria Hunt Club was formed. By 1915, Vancouver, too, had acquired its symbol of British aristocratic influence.[6] The importance of these clubs and their counterparts in the East lay not in their relation to the growth of organized sport but as an exemplification of the existence of a Canadian social elite. Members were drawn from the most powerful figures in commerce, industry, and government. The orientation was to England and thus reflected the aspirations of this segment of Canadian society. Although clubs emerged in urban areas, their whole focus was rural and and was rooted in pre-industrial forms of sport. They were indeed a vestigial remnant of an old social system.

THE YACHT CLUBS

More accessible, but still limited to the most wealthy, were the yachting and golf clubs that sprang up across Canada after 1870. Perhaps the most prestigious and certainly requiring the greatest financial resources were the yacht clubs. Considerable capital investment in the form of yachts ensured their exclusivity. The first clubs were formed in the 1850's in Toronto and Halifax. The Royal Canadian Yacht Club (RCYC) of Toronto, perhaps the most prestigious in Canada, dates back to 1852, and, in Halifax, a group of Bermudian merchants formed the Royal Halifax Yacht Club (RHYC).[7] However, it was not until the 1870's that significant growth took place in the three areas that were to become the focal points of future development: Halifax, Montreal, and Lake Ontario. In Halifax dissension with the RHYC led to the formation of a breakaway club, the Royal Nova Scotian Yacht Squadron. On the St. Lawrence River, around the island of Montreal, several clubs sprang up: Montreal Yacht Club (1877), Longueuil (1879), and Pointe Claire Boating Club (1880). Clubs were formed on the shores of Lake Ontario in Toronto, Hamilton, Cobourg, Port Hope, and the Bay of Quinte. The focus of the majority of these clubs was social rather than competitive. Pleasure cruising during the summer, moonlight cruises in the crisp fall evenings, and select balls at the clubhouses were the *raison d'être* of many of the clubs. In these affairs the ladies were an indispensable component of the activities. Only when competition moved to centre stage were the ladies relegated to the background.

With the advent of competitive sailing, yachting entered the world of competitive sport, and the racing emphasis threatened the unity of the clubs. At this juncture yachting confronted the problem that was to beset all sport: how to maintain the delicate balance between playing the game for the game's sake and the emphasis on winning. From its formation in 1877, the Montreal Yacht Club emphasized both the social and competitive aspects. Weekly and monthly races throughout the summer were inaugurated in the first year. The older RCYC was not free from the spectre of competitions, and the differences among the membership were so great that George Herrick Duggan was forced to lead a group of young yachtsmen to break away from the RCYC and form the Toronto Yacht Club (TYC) in 1880. The reason for the break lay in the negative attitude of the older members of the RCYC toward competitive racing. During the next four years the TYC lobbied other Lake Ontario clubs in the interest of competitive racing. This bore fruit in 1884 with the birth of the Lake Yacht Racing Association. From this time the majority of clubs emphasized both the social and competitive aspects of yachting. While competition remained within the confines of a small group it still experienced the problems that were to beset all organized sport, amateur and professional – an overemphasis on victory. Thus yachting entered the mainstream of sport history.

The 1890's witnessed an expansion in the number of clubs in the three areas plus the emergence of clubs in what was to become a stronghold of yachting, the West Coast. In the Maritimes, clubs developed in Saint John and Chatham, New Brunswick, and in Cape Breton. Early in the 1900's they were joined by clubs in smaller coastal towns such as Chester, Yarmouth, and Digby, Nova Scotia.[8] The summer was punctuated by a series of inter- and intra-club competitions. For example, in Halifax the yachting season commenced in June and continued with weekly races until October. The year was often highlighted by a Yachting Week, such as the one held in August, 1905, when yachts from Nova Scotia, New Brunswick, and Prince Edward Island competed with yachts from New York, Boston, and other East Coast U.S. cities.[9] The races formed the focal point of an array of social activities during which the wealthy from various regions engaged in a round of socializing. As such, yachting was a central feature of the summers of the wealthy. Such was the case on the West Coast after the formation of the Victoria Yacht Club in 1892.[10] The Victoria yachtsmen raced and socialized with their fellow sailors in Seattle, Tacoma, and Port Townsend in Washington. The Victoria Yacht Club was joined in 1903 by the newly formed Vancouver Yacht Club. By 1905, the Vancouver Yacht Club had expanded and moved into its new clubhouse in Stanley Park. They took with them boats worth $100,000.[11] Such was their power and status that they were able to locate their clubhouse in property that was set aside for public use.[12]

There is no doubt that the yachting clubs represented the pinnacle of the social sporting clubs. But even within the world of yachting there was a distinct hierarchy and it was no accident that the most prestigious clubs were located in the commercial and economic centres of Canada. On the St. Lawrence River and Lake Ontario, the Royal Saint Lawrence Yacht Club of Montreal and the Royal Hamilton Yacht Club joined the RCYC as the most prestigious in the country. Not far behind were the RNSYS of Halifax, the Royal Kennebecasis of Saint John, and the two West Coast clubs. These truly were the seats of social power and provided for social interaction between power brokers in different segments of Canadian society.

THE GOLF AND COUNTRY CLUBS

Certainly more varied and widespread were the golf clubs that developed in the last quarter of the century. Like so many sports in Canada, golf formally began in Montreal, in late 1873. The Montreal Golf Club was founded by Alexander Denistoun, a native Scotsman resident in Montreal. The Scottish connection with Canadian golf was to remain strong. The Quebec Golf Club followed closely on the inauguration of the MGC. By 1876 the two clubs were engaged in competition. The game spread to a limited number of towns in Ontario in the early 1880's – Toronto, Niagara Falls, Brantford, and Kingston. Its growth during the eighties was slow and limited to Ontario. As with so many other sports, the 1890's witnessed its spread from coast to coast. In this instance it was limited, except in Ontario, to the largest towns: Halifax, Fredericton, Saint John, Winnipeg, Calgary, Vancouver, and Victoria.[13] However, it was beginning to spread to the smaller towns of Ontario. During the pre-war years the game expanded both across the provinces and within the larger cities. By 1915, Montreal and Toronto could each boast at least eight clubs, while Vancouver and Calgary each had three. The major concentration of clubs was to be found in Ontario. It is important, however, not to overemphasize its development. By 1914, the Royal Canadian Golf Association (RCGA) could only boast a membership of forty-four.[14] Golf was still limited to a small segment of Canadian society.

Golf was always competitively oriented; the social aspects of the game developed later. Within a year of the formation of the Montreal and Quebec clubs they had entered into yearly competition that has continued to the present day. Early clubs soon developed a variety of intra-club competitions for a bewildering array of trophies, cups, and shields. The importance of competition was reflected clearly in the moves to organize that developed early in the 1890's. The first interprovincial match in 1893 was followed two years later by the formation of the Canadian Golf Association. This was followed by the first Canada-United States match in 1898. The development of these organizations and competitions revealed a basic fact about Canadian golf – the absolute domination of the large town clubs, in particular the clubs of Ontario. The RCGA and the national championships were dominated by individuals from Saint John, Ottawa, Montreal, Toronto, and Hamilton. Perhaps the pattern was most clearly illustrated in the composition of the first Canadian team – single representatives from Montreal, Quebec City, and Hamilton, and six from Toronto.[15] The competitive orientation was also illustrated by the ladies' involvement in the game. Women of the MGC were competing as early as 1881, but in the 1890's ladies' golf came into its own. In 1892 the ladies' section of the MGC was formed as a sub-group of the male club. Other ladies' sections emerged in Quebec City, Sherbrooke, and Victoria. The first Canadian Women's Championship was run by the RCGA on the Dixie course of the MGC in 1901. In 1904 the Maritimes Ladies Golf Association was formed. Perhaps the most important move was the formation of the Canadian Ladies Golf Union in 1913, which by the next year boasted thirty-seven clubs. Competition clearly lay at the heart of all golf.

In fact, the social aspect of golf did not develop until late in the century and even then its development was uneven, with some of the clubs remaining steadfastly male and competitive. It was at the highest social levels that the move to build ornate clubhouses with dining rooms and other facilities originated. The movement of the RMGC (by then the Royal Montreal Golf Club) to Dixie in 1896 signalled the building of more complete facilities. By 1901, Rosedale Golf Club in Toronto was housed in a "fine brick club house." The growing social base was indicated in a more concrete way in the changing of "golf clubs" into "golf and country clubs." Peterborough Golf Club changed its name in 1905. Similarly, in Simcoe, Ontario, in 1915 the Simcoe Golf Club became the Norfolk Golf and Country Club.[16] In Vancouver the three golf clubs had become golf and country clubs. In all these instances the change entailed an expansion of facilities, the most popular being the tennis courts. With the intrusion of the social element came the development of a hierarchy of clubs in the larger cities. In Winnipeg the prestigious St. Charles Golf and Country Club (1905) was significantly different from the older Winnipeg Golf Club. In 1912, the initiation fee to the St. Charles was $750, while the fee for the Winnipeg was only $400.[17] At the pinnacle of the social scale in Toronto were the Rosedale and Toronto clubs. There, money was not the sole distinguishing characteristic but rather Anglican religious affiliation, education at Upper Canada College or another of the prestigious private schools, and attendance at university – Toronto, of course![18] Thus the limited world of golf was not one homogeneous group but rather a complex system of social differentiation closely linked to the size of the urban population.

THE CURLING CLUBS

Hunting, yachting, and golf were limited to those who could afford the considerable costs involved. Lawn tennis and curling were potentially less costly and thus their claims to exclusivity lay on less certain grounds. However, by 1914 both were played by clearly defined segments of the community. Lawn tennis began as a game of the social elite in 1874. By 1914, its base of participants had expanded considerably but was still limited to the middle class. Curling, on the other hand, was glorified for its "democratic" nature and for providing an occasion when all classes could participate together in friendly competition. By 1914, curling had become, in some parts of the country, the exclusive preserve of the middle class.

Curlers in Canada were always conscious of their heritage. The game was associated with "Auld Scotia," with the frozen lochs of Scotland, and with the ideals of democratic participation uncontaminated by rank or station. These remained foundational to curling throughout the nineteenth century even when the reality was a far cry from the ideal. Throughout, curlers remained attached to Scotland and things Scottish. This provided curlers with a common heritage, whether they were in Truro, Nova Scotia, or Grenfell, Saskatchewan. From the outset, therefore, the Scots introduced the game to all parts of Canada. They were aided, after 1850, by the growth of the railway system, for the growth of curling throughout Canada in the second half of the century was closely linked to the tide of Scottish immigrants who were borne westward by the newly constructed railway.[19] The popularity of the sport first expanded in Ontario, which became the centre of the "roarin' game." By the 1890's there were over 100 clubs in the province.[20] In the 1870's it began to spread to its true Canadian home, the Prairies, where, prior to the invention of artificial ice, the climate allowed for a longer, uninterrupted season. The first permanent club on the Prairies was the Manitoba Curling Club of Winnipeg, formed in 1876.[21] This remained the sole club until 1881 when the Granite Club was established in the same city. By 1884, it had spread to Brandon, Emerson, Portage La Prairie, and other Manitoba towns. A year later Calgarians established their first clubs. This was followed, in 1888, by the

Table 1
Curling Clubs in Canada, 1895 and 1905

	1895	1905
Maritimes	23	
Nova Scotia (Royal Caledonian Curling Club)		14
Quebec	16	30*
Ontario	106	92
Manitoba and N.W. Territories	40	
Manitoba		80*
Saskatchewan		30*
Alberta		9*
TOTAL	185	255

*Approximate figures.

SOURCES: *Toronto Globe*, January 9, 1895; *Regina Leader Post*, December, 1905; *Halifax Herald*, March 13, 1905; *Toronto Globe*, October 21, 1905; *Winnipeg Free Press*, December, 1905; G. Redmond, "The Scots and Sport in Nineteenth Century Canada" (PH.D. dissertation, University of Alberta, 1972), p. 167.

founding of a club in Edmonton.[22] Curling reached the interior of British Columbia in the 1890's and the Kootenay Curling Association was formed in 1898.[23]

Table 1 illustrates the extent of curling in 1895 and its growth on the Prairies in the ensuing decade. While the eastern provinces remained relatively stable, there was considerable expansion in the number of clubs and organizations. Quebec and Nova Scotia had already established ties with Scotland. Ontario followed suit with the formation of the Ontario branch of the Royal Caledonian Curling Club in 1874. The Manitoba and North West Territories branch was founded in 1888. This was fragmented into three provincial organizations early in the twentieth century as the game took a firm foothold on the Prairies. In all cases the allegiance to the old country was clearly established. Only in Ontario was there any evidence of an independent spirit. This led to the breakaway of the Ontario branch on October 18, 1892, when the organization was renamed the Ontario Curling Association "to emphasize their achievement of complete autonomy."[24] Thus, curling had become entrenched across Canada except for French

Quebec and the West Coast, where climatic conditions prevented its development. At the same time, growth obviously was limited, with only 200-plus clubs in 1905. The growth in Ontario had been greatest in the 1870's and 1880's.[25] Only in the ideal climatic conditions of the Prairies did there appear to be substantial expansion. This limited growth suggests that the democratic nature of the game may not have been as real as its proponents claimed.

The game in the East was, for the most part, limited to the affluent middle class, although there may have been the odd token workingman. If there was any democratization it was in the smaller towns of Ontario, because in the larger cities of Montreal and Toronto the clubs were the preserve of the business and professional sections of the community.[26] The Montreal Curling Club was exclusive, as was the Queen City Curling Club (1896), Toronto, which in 1905 claimed as members "some of the most prominent business and professional men in the city."[27] Even in the smaller towns, curling was dominated by doctors, lawyers, bankers, and businessmen.[28] In Windsor, in 1895, the club contained a high percentage of middle-class members. The move toward middle-class membership was stimulated by the movement of the game from outdoor rinks to covered sheds and then to more ornate facilities that promoted the social aspects of the game. The move inside started in Montreal in 1838 and Toronto in 1859, though it was not until late in the century that the majority had converted to outdoor sheds. By 1895, there were reputed to be twenty-five covered sheds in the Maritimes, sixteen in Quebec, 100 in Ontario, and forty in Manitoba.[29] However, it was not just the move inside that promoted a middle-class membership but the building of more opulent facilities that promoted social intercourse. This also led to the addition of female members. Thus, different levels of involvement likely could be measured by the ornateness of the facilities.

Other factors also indicated the middle-class nature of the participants. Curling was closely related to the Presbyterian Church and in the most prestigious clubs the chaplain was a local minister. This was the case in Lindsay, Ontario, where the Rev. Robert Johnston was the club chaplain. On February 26, 1895, the Lindsay Curling Club attended Saint Andrews Church *en masse*. Rev. Johnston addressed his sermon to the curlers and eulogized the game. Curling exemplified the basic principles underlying an individual's life: it demanded diligence, faith, and obedience, which, according to Rev. Johnston, were the "Foundation principles of all true living."[30] These, of course, reflected

Red Cap Snow Shoe Club, Halifax, 1879.

Lorne Rowing Club, Halifax.

the cardinal values of middle-class Canada – hard work and obedience to the legally constituted authority. Curling, then, was the game of the middle class. It was justified because it promoted the values necessary for success and because it supported the system of unquestioned obedience.

On the Prairies there is evidence that the game was more broadly based: the development of rural clubs, the wholesale league in Winnipeg in 1905, and the hundreds of women curlers in Winnipeg at the outbreak of the war. However, this should not be overstated. Certainly some of the clubs in Winnipeg were open only to certain segments of society.[31] Even in the smaller towns, such as Grenfell, Saskatchewan, and Minnedosa, Manitoba, the doctors, dentists, barristers, bankers, and businessmen formed the backbone of the clubs.[32] At the same time, it would appear logical that in the smaller towns the curlers must have been drawn from a far wider segment of society, so that on the Prairies the reality of democratization *may* have been true.

LAWN TENNIS

Lawn tennis, with its emphasis on competition, would appear to fall within the bounds of highly competitive organized sport. This was not the case in the early years. The game that was first played in England in 1873 crossed the Atlantic to Toronto in 1874. It was adopted by the most exclusive social groups, the graduates of the British Public Schools and their counterparts in Canada, and soon spread to Ottawa (1876) and Montreal (1876). By 1885, it had found root in Halifax, Saint John, Winnipeg, Regina, and Victoria. However, its appeal was not limited to the larger towns and by 1889 such towns as Digby, Pictou, and Sydney, Nova Scotia, boasted clubs. On the Prairies, Plum Creek, Oak Lake, and Birtle in Manitoba also supported the game.

In the larger centres, lawn tennis soon became a vehicle for the display of the latest summer fashions. The games were the focal point of social gatherings with bands in attendance, tea on the grounds surrounding the courts, and a chance to mix with the social elite. From the outset ladies were always an integral part of the game both on and off the court so that, more than any other sport, tennis was a part of the social lives of "society." The play itself bore little resemblance to modern tennis. Ladies, for example, played in full-length skirts, which effectively restricted unladylike movements. While the game underwent significant changes by 1915, it remained a social game with strictly prescribed codes of behaviour. This was the great era of the game of the "respectable" middle class. Despite certain changes it was predominantly a game played within the confines of private clubs. This was true even in the smaller towns and was reflected in the role of the local elite. For example, the president of the Simcoe club in 1889 was the manager of the Bank of Commerce. In Grenfell, Saskatchewan, in 1895, the executive consisted of two doctors and a minister; in Digby, Nova Scotia, in 1905, two barristers and a dentist formed the executive. In 1915, Minnedosa was represented on the court by three doctors, a clergyman, the principal of the school, a barrister, and the owner of a real estate business. Lawn tennis was limited to members of the local elite. The summers were filled with intra-club competitions, local tournaments, and, for some, provincial and international competition.

The turn of the century witnessed changes in tennis. The number of private clubs increased, the involvement of the church increased greatly, and municipal government began to provide courts. The most significant change was the adoption of tennis by the churches. This was a result of a change in the churches' attitude to amusements and recreation.[33] From being opponents of physical recreation in the 1880's the churches gradually changed their position to one of support for morally uplifting recreation. One of the outgrowths of this was the ardent adoption of lawn tennis. In some areas this involved the entrance of church teams in the newly developing leagues. Such was the case in Winnipeg (1905), Regina (1915), and Peterborough (1915). In other areas the churches created their own leagues. By 1915, many of the largest cities – Winnipeg, Victoria, Vancouver, Montreal, and Toronto – boasted church leagues. These developments did not signify a major change in the groups playing tennis; tennis players, largely, were still from the respectable middle class. The final change, the provision of courts by municipalities, had the potential for altering considerably the availability of the game. By 1915, Montreal, Toronto, Hamilton, London, Winnipeg, and Vancouver all provided courts in city parks. This was related to the parks and playground movement that had its origins in the late 1900's. Even though the courts were built at public expense they remained available only to specific groups. This was reflected in the experience of Vancouver. In 1915 Vancouver had twenty-four public courts in seven parks.[34] These were not available to the general public but were allocated to the various private clubs by Norman De Graves, the park commissioner. Only 10 per cent were available for public play. Thus, in Vancouver, the public purse was used to provide for the leisure activities of the middle class.

By 1914, urban Canada was covered by a network of social sporting clubs that catered to the leisure time of the elites. This network was characterized by a variety of levels. At the pinnacle, in the large cities, the hunt, yachting, and golf clubs provided an intertwined system that allowed for members of the elite who moved across the country to gain immediate access to the highest level of social activity. Not only did the Royal Nova Scotia Yacht Squadron, Royal Montreal Golf Club, Toronto Hunt Club, St. Charles Golf and Country Club, and Victoria Yacht Club provide for the mobile elite but they also served to integrate the different elites. Members of the economic, commercial, political, and other elites met on common ground in the clubhouses of these exclusive clubs. It is not too much to expect that decisions affecting the course of Canadian history were discussed in these informal settings. Thus these clubs, at the highest level, served to integrate the Canadian elites. They were based on a belief in structured social inequality. The ideal of equality, so dear to many leading Canadians, was certainly not allowed to apply to their social lives.

It would be erroneous to overemphasize the homogeneity of these clubs and their development. Nearly without exception they developed first in the larger cities of each province before spreading out to the smaller towns. In the larger urban areas the clubs were more homogeneous and it was possible to differentiate between the various levels of elitism. In these instances, wealth was taken for granted and was not sufficient for entry. Entrance to the clubs was based on a combination of ethnic, religious, and educational criteria. For example, entrance to several of the exclusive Toronto clubs was enhanced if the applicant was an Anglican educated at Upper Canada College and the University of Toronto.[35] Similar systems with different criteria were to be found in Winnipeg and Montreal.[36] Thus in the large cities there was a distinctive hierarchy of clubs. In the smaller towns entrance was restricted to the elite, but wealth and social position alone were the criteria, so that the lawyers, doctors, bank managers, and businessmen joined together in one club. Though less homogeneous, these clubs, too, remained the preserve of the dominant figures in the community.

What, then, is the significance of these social/sport clubs to our understanding of the development of Canadian organized sport? Their importance lies in the fact that many of the key figures in the development of amateur sport were members of these clubs. In other words, the organization and the ideology of sport were created by a group of individuals with strong ties to the various elites of Canadian society. Amateur sport was not divorced from the mainstream of Canadian life but was an essential part of the control held by these elites. The ideology and structures of amateur sport were based in the values of the affluent middle and upper class, which were rooted in the ethic of Victorian England – hard work, structured inequality, and obedience to the legally constituted authority.

3

The Emergence of Organized Team Sport, 1867-1914

The objectives of this chapter are threefold. The first is to trace the emergence and spread of organized team sport across Canada, identifying where it started, who promoted it, and, as far as possible, who played it. Second, particular Canadian patterns of development will be identified by focusing on patterns of social and geographic domination. Finally, an attempt will be made to examine the degree to which sport was truly Canadian. The rise of a unique Canadian sporting culture was related to the ethnic origins of the men who created it and to the impact of certain dominant forces. With respect to sport, three dominant influences were reflected in the particular games that were played. The degree to which these games were common across the land is a rough measure of "Canadianness." Thus we will first examine the development of two uniquely Canadian games, ice hockey and Canadian football. The pervasiveness of English rugby, cricket, and soccer will be an indication of the influence of Britain on Canadian sport, and the spread of baseball a measure of American influence. Since none were completely independent and individuals played a combination of these games, the patterns of their development across Canada and the relationship between them provides a view of the complexity of the Canadian sporting culture and will allow us to draw some conclusions relative to the meaning of the word "Canadian."

URBANIZATION AND INDUSTRIALIZATION

While organized sport was created by men and thus was rooted in their own life experiences and cultural traditions, its particular form and characteristics were related to changes in the nature of Canadian society. Most important was the shifting pattern of population distribution, first from rural to urban and later from the dominant central provinces to the West. Increasing urbanization was a general process affecting the whole of Canada. The movement to the West created new tensions within the young Dominion that changed the nature of the country. Allied to and partially responsible for the process of urbanization was a change in the mode of production, the move to factory production or industrialization. These factors, in conjunction with related technological changes, created the necessary conditions for the development of organized sport. It is difficult to disentangle the concepts of urbanization and industrialization from each other and from the various technological changes either created by or a stimulus to the two processes. Despite these difficulties, it is necessary to attempt to unravel these complex relationships and examine each independently, while recognizing the symbiotic relationship between them. What is indisputable is that the end result was a new society with new patterns of behaviour, social structures, economic bases, and population distribution. Organized sport was directly related to these fundamental changes.

In a simplistic sense, urbanization entails both a process and a product. The product is an increase in the percentage of the population living in urban centres. As a process it results in patterns of living that are different from those of a rural society – a new way of life. This process resulted in major changes in both the form and function of sport. With respect to the form of the game, increased pressure on land use resulted in skyrocketing land prices that in turn affected sport by leading to restricted spatial boundaries and the development of specialized athletic facilities. This was illustrated in the development of ice hockey. Originally played on open bays, rivers, or any open space, ice hockey was a freewheeling, far-ranging game whose boundaries were determined by the availability of clear ice. Its movement into the city ice rinks changed the nature of the game by imposing defined spatial boundaries. Thus the game played on the city rinks was new, with restricted space, restricted team size, and new skills. A second change was related to the increase in the number of players and the expansion of inter-city and inter-provincial competition. This led to a standardization of rules in order to facilitate competition. By the turn of the century, the local rules in Kingston, Halifax, and Montreal gave way to a universally accepted code of rules, and this standardization led to the development of local, provincial, and national organizations to handle the problems of increased competition.

The relationship between urbanization and industrialization is so close that it is difficult, at times, to discern which was cause and which effect. Industrialization was also both a process and a product. The process entailed a change in the mode of production from small production units in which the end product was created by hand to mass production predicated on power-operated machinery located in a factory. The triad of power, machinery, and factories was basic to the changing society and sport. Central to sport was the changing concept of time.

Time lies at the heart of modern society and sport.[1] In a pre-industrial, predominantly rural society, time was flexible, lacking the clearly defined boundaries of modern society. The workday varied in length, being bounded by sunrise and sunset rather than by defined times. It centred on noon, with the two parts of the day being forenoon and afternoon. Work finished when the task was done and was task-oriented rather than time-defined. This was especially evident in rural areas where the intensity of work was dependent on the requirements of the seasons rather than the demands of a market. Thus, life was dominated by the rhythm of the seasons and the variable boundaries of sunrise and sunset. The tedium of life was relieved by infrequent feast days, agricultural festivals, and Sundays. Perhaps it can best be illustrated through pre-industrial sport.[2] Among the rural inhabitants of Canada, recreation was occasional, held at moments after the seasons of the year devoted to work. These infrequent occasions often lasted for two or three days – games and sports around the periphery of the Methodist circuit meetings, district dances held in some clearing, and the popular clearing or building bee that invariably concluded with contests of speed and strength. These activities bore no resemblance to organized sport, beginning when a task was completed and ending when the last man left. Central to all these gatherings was the idea that time was flexible.

The nineteenth century witnessed a change in this concept of time and its replacement by a system whereby the workday and week were measured in minutes and hours. The day was divided into employer's time and other time. This change, which eventually became a worldwide phenomenon, developed first in England during the 1830's and 1840's in the battles for the Ten Hours Bill. It was an ongoing battle in Parliament and the press to define the workday in terms of hours to be worked and the system of measurement for payment. There were successive definitions of work and the workday, first by the task, then by the week, and finally by the day and hour. A logical outgrowth of this move to delineate and define the workday was the idea of time bought and sold. Time itself had a quantifiable value. Allied to this was the division of the day into time belonging to the employer and that belonging to the employee. For many workers, this was the first time they "owned" time that was free from constraints placed on its use by their employer. From this emerged the idea of free time. Regular free time for a large segment of the community is a necessary condition for mass sport and during the second half of the nineteenth century, with the ongoing battles to reduce the work week, significant numbers of Canadians gained the time to participate in things other than survival. As the workday decreased and the Saturday half-holiday was gained by different segments of the work force, a large enough reservoir of people with free time was created to provide the basic conditions for the beginning of modern sport. However, mere free time was not as important as regular free time. This was first gained in the large industrial towns of Canada.

The impact of this changing concept of time and its unrecognized side effects were illustrated in the changes in sport that occurred during the second half of the nineteenth century. First, the form of the game was changed. Many of the pre-industrial games – baseball, curling, cricket – contained within them the potential for an endless contest. Their time boundaries were never laid down as they were in football but were restricted by a number of innings or ends – the potentiality for an endless contest is obvious. The history of lacrosse illustrates the gradual change from a pre-industrial to an industrial form. In the 1860's and 1870's, lacrosse matches were decided by the best three out of five games (goals), which produced differences in the length of a particular contest varying from two to three minutes to a contest of four or five hours that was only terminated by darkness, a most unsatisfactory state of affairs. During the 1880's, several attempts were made to change to a defined time period of two hours. The change was resisted, as most changes are, and it was not until 1889 that the two-hour limit was adopted. A second consequence of the changing concept of time was the acquisition of free time. The development of leagues was based on team members being available every week at a specific time. This condition emerged in the 1870's and 1880's when increasing numbers of factory workers acquired a regular work schedule. It was no accident, therefore, that the late 1870's and 1880's witnessed an increased frequency and regularity of games in soccer, baseball, and lacrosse. In addition, mass spectator sport required people with regular free time, and once again, the first professional teams in Canada were in baseball in Ontario in the early 1880's. Finally, the changing concept of time was reflected in an increased emphasis on quantification. It was not until the second half of the century that concern was expressed over the time of a race rather than the race itself. Thus began a shift in focus from the process, the contest itself, to the product, the record.

Integrally related to industrialization were several technological changes that, in part, resulted from the demands of industry and, in part, themselves precipitated industrial change. Certain of these technological inventions were necessary for the creation of organized sport in Canada, namely changes in transportation and communications. The invention of the steam-powered engine was important to Canada in that the railway became the real and symbolic link that tied Canada together. Easy, fast inter-city transportation systems were necessary before sport could develop. The 1840's witnessed the building of the first railway lines. By 1867 the new Dominion was covered by 2,278 miles of track, mainly in Ontario and Quebec. The year 1885 witnessed the opening of the first transcontinental railway. By the outbreak of the First World War there were 30,795 miles of track. Populated Canada was covered by a network of railways that facilitated inter-city travel. From the 1850's railway companies actively solicited the patronage of sporting teams.[3] Another aspect of transportation that grew to be increasingly important in the large urban centres in the early twentieth century was the growth of intra-city transportation services. Although there was a horse-drawn omnibus in Toronto in 1849, the first street railway was not opened until 1861.[4] More important, in terms of speed of movement, was the electrification of the street railways that had progressed to such a degree that by 1900 Canadian cities contained 700 miles of electrified track.

While the progress of urbanization and industrialization and the development of the transportation system created the conditions necessary for the growth of organized sport, one further ingredient was needed to link the different parts of Canada together and give some meaning to the word "Canadian." This was the development of a communications system to allow for the rapid dissemination of information across the length and breadth of the country. The foundations of this were laid with the invention and development of the telegraph system, which ensured nearly instantaneous knowledge of results across Canada. Increasingly associated with the telegraph, yet independent of it, was the emergence of the mass press.[5] Until late in the nineteenth century, the reading audience was restricted to a small segment of the population. During the latter quarter of the century, the newspaper made significant moves toward becoming the popular press of today. In 1874, there were 500 periodicals published across Canada; by 1900 this number had increased to 1,200. More important to sport were the sports page and sports editor. In the 1870's and 1880's, in both Montreal and Toronto, a sports page emerged and sports editors were appointed. This was the beginning of popular sports reporting in Canada. The development of the media provided the catalyst since it allowed knowledge of sport to spread beyond its immediate locale and become a truly national concern. And thus it was that Canadians from Halifax to Victoria learned of the exploits of Canada's first sport hero, Ned Hanlan.

The change from a predominantly rural, frontier society to one increasingly reflective of urban-industrial society occurred in Canada at a critical juncture in its history when four separate provinces in the eastern part of the continent decided to form a Confederation. During the ensuing forty years the physical boundaries of Canada expanded from the limits of Ontario to nearly its present size. At the same time, Canadians were attempting to define their own specific identity and character. The imposition of a new society upon this young country at this particular time had a profound effect on the development of an identity, an awareness of self. While industrialization began in Montreal in the 1850's, it was not until the 1870's that it began to create significant changes in the structure of society. By the First World War, Canada was well on the way to becoming an urban-industrial society. Thus, the period 1867-1914 was critical to the foundations of modern Canada and Canadian sport. Within the context of rapidly changing population distribution and concentration organized sport emerged. Many of the important developments occurred in Montreal, Toronto, and elsewhere in Ontario. By the time settlers from Britain and Ontario moved to the Prairies, sport had already become part of their cultural baggage, so that sport on the Prairies, while greatly influenced by the physical environment, was also subject to strong ethnic and cultural influences. Sport in the West reflected a uniqueness born of the region's own particular conditions of population distribution, ethnic background, and an awareness of its own relationship to central Canada. It is possible to identify similar differences in the Maritimes, Quebec, and British Columbia. Hence, the emergence of organized sport in different parts of the country was always subject to particular local conditions. While there were general Canadian patterns related to the development of urban centres across the country, the Canadian mosaic was different, born of unique local conditions. In this respect, there were certain distinctly Canadian characteristics.[6]

The innovations and development of organized sport were inextricably related to the large urban areas of over 100,000. Until the first decade of the twentieth century these were limited to Montreal and Toronto, which dominated sporting development as they did the industrial and commercial development of the country. They were joined in the twentieth century by Winnipeg and Vancouver. Providing a uniquely Canadian pattern were the other urban areas of over 20,000. Outside Ontario and Quebec, these cities tended to be limited to one per province; thus, these centres became the nodal points of sporting development in the individual provinces. The picture, then, is of a dominant Montreal-Toronto axis imposed on a series of isolated provincial centres that in turn dominated their own hinterlands. By the turn of the century the absolute domination of Ontario and Quebec was being eroded as the population spread out across Canada. At the same time, the domination of urban sport must not be overemphasized, for rural traditions, games, and ways maintained a presence well into the twentieth century, especially in certain provinces and sports. The emergence of organized sport, therefore, must not be seen as an inexorable process but rather as one in which the residual elements maintained a strong presence.

It is within the context of Canada's unique patterns of urban development, increasing free time for different segments of the population, and the impact of technological changes that the growth and development of organized sport must be viewed. However, it was people who created and played sport and it was a mixture of distinctive ethnic influences that created a uniquely Canadian sport culture.

CANADIAN SPORTS

By 1914, if newspaper coverage is an accurate measure, three Canadian-born sports loomed large in the sporting life of the country. Ice hockey, Canadian football, and lacrosse were recognized as Canadian and propagated as being the sports Canadians should play.[7] However, a more impartial analysis leads to the realization that their degree of "Canadianness" depended to a large extent on the definitions used, and in many respects the claims were based on biased analysis. Thus we must turn to an analysis of ice hockey and football.

Canadian Football

The origins of football are to be found in pre-industrial England, where various distinctly different football games were played on various traditional holidays. These local games were transported across the Atlantic and played by soldiers and immigrants. There is evidence of informal football games being played in Upper and Lower Canada prior to Confederation. However, it was not until the late 1860's that evidence of formal organization appeared. Appropriately it was in Montreal, in 1868, that the first two clubs were formed, the Montreal and Britannia football clubs. They played infrequent games against each other and the garrison teams. This interest in football paralleled developments in England and the United States. In all three countries various groups struggled to establish sets of rules. This did not ease the task of the groups in widely separated towns. The result was a decade of chaos.

The 1870's were characterized by the emergence of several different forms of football and the development of strong local attachments to a particular brand of the game. Thus, different forms emerged in Montreal, Toronto, Quebec City, Ottawa, and Halifax. In each instance they adopted some form of the English games as the basis of their own. Since the English were themselves struggling toward a uniform code, it did not bode well for the Canadians. In any event, it became increasingly difficult to arrange games with teams from other towns. The history of the Quebec City-Montreal rivalry illustrates this point. On October 25, 1872, Quebec City and Montreal had great difficulty reaching agreement over the rules to be used. Agreement was finally reached and the game was played. It was followed in 1875 by a game watched by 4,000 spectators. However, by 1877 the differences between the two had reached such a point that the pre-game discussion could not effect an adequate compromise. The game was played only because the visiting Montrealers agreed to play soccer rules on the cobblestones of the Esplanade. This was the last of the Quebec-Montreal series.

A uniquely Canadian football game saw light of day in two separate cities, Montreal and Toronto. For a variety of reasons they independently arrived at a form of the game similar enough to allow inter-city competitions. The real origins, however, lay in Montreal. Between 1868 and 1872 the Montreal teams, strongly influenced by the British garrison, were moving toward adopting the English rugby version of the game. The rules of rugby had not yet been codified in England, so the removal of the garrison in 1872 left these young Canadians to their own devices. The three Montreal clubs developed a game based on their own interpretations of rugby and looked elsewhere for inspiration and competition. In 1874, McGill University started a decade-long interaction between Quebec and Ontario teams and their southern neighbours. McGill's historic visit to Harvard in 1874 influenced the course of American football when the Harvard team adopted the Canadian form of the game.[8] At the same time, the Canadians were influenced by the Americans and thus moved the Canadian game to an intermediate position between the British and American games. During the next few years, the Montreal game spread to eastern Ontario with games in Ottawa (1877) and Kingston (1879). In the other bastion of football, Toronto, the battle was between English rugby and soccer. While the University of Toronto was to remain a powerful force in soccer, the major decision was made in 1877 when they decided to adopt rugby rules. Thus they were in a similar position to Montreal in 1872. The visit of Varsity to Detroit to play the University of Michigan in 1879 switched Toronto onto the same track as Montreal. Impressed by the American game, Varsity decided to incorporate many of its features into their game. By the early 1880's, both the Montreal and Toronto teams were playing a game that owed something to England and something to the United States yet was different from either.

By the early 1880's, there had developed two Canadian games similar enough to allow competition between McGill and Varsity (1881) yet different enough from the American game to bring to a conclusion, in 1883, the games between Canadian and American teams. At the same time, the clubs in Ontario and Quebec moved to institutionalize the differences by establishing two separate provincial organizations, the Ontario Rugby Football Union (ORFU) in 1882-83 and the Quebec Rugby Football Union (QRFU) in 1883. The differences between the two lay in a problem that was to plague football until the 1920's – a unified code of rules. Failure to reach agreement on rules was to split football into four groups by the early twentieth century. At the same time, footballers were aware of the problem and tried to solve it by the creation of a national organization. In fact, the first advances were made by the Montreal Football Club on December 9, 1872, when they proposed a meeting of footballers; the result was the creation of the Canadian Football Association in 1873. This organization was plagued by the rules problem that was to face all other national organizations. By 1880, the CFA was defunct. On February 8, 1884, the Canadian Rugby Union (CRU) was formed: "Its object being the furtherance of Rugby Football and the enforcement of a uniform code of laws for the game throughout the Dominion, Ontario and Quebec."[9] The CRU failed. It was not until 1891 and a reorganized CRU that it even had a voice in football affairs.

By the mid-1880's Canadian football had acquired the characteristics that were to remain central to its development until 1914. Football was a creation of anglophone Canadians in the large towns and cities of Canada. It never gained a foothold in the smaller towns, villages, and rural areas of the country. Montreal, Toronto, and the larger towns of Ontario were to remain the heartland of football. In the West football took root in Winnipeg and the towns of Manitoba.[10] They remained isolated from the game in the East and tended to look south to Minnesota and North Dakota for competition. Not until the 1920's would they begin to have an impact on the national scene. Even more important was the domination of educational institutions. It is not too much to say that in the 1880's football was played exclusively by the elite of Canadian society. Children were introduced to the game at the prestigious private schools epitomized by Upper Canada College or at the high schools and collegiate institutes. From there they moved to the universities, which soon came to dominate the game. The university dominance was evidenced in the ORFU championship games between 1883 and 1896, only six of the twenty-two championships being won by town teams. Thus, football in the 1880's was very much a game for the anglophone elite of the large towns.

The 1890's witnessed developments in the world of football that foreshadowed the events of the first decade of the new century. These changes precipitated the game into the world of commercial and professional sport. In particular, the nineties saw the slow spread of the game and changes in its structure that threatened the delicate balance between "sport" and "athletics."[11] Football began to expand beyond its narrow geographical confines to the towns of Ontario, such as Peterborough, London, Petrolia, and Brockville. On the Prairies it crept west with the tide of settlement and became established in a small way in Regina, Edmonton, and Calgary by 1895. In these instances, the North West Mounted Police played an important role in its development.[12] While these changes presaged the growth of the early 1900's, the game was still rooted in the large towns as the membership of the ORFU in 1895 testified. Of the twenty-one teams that comprised the union, ten were from Toronto, five from Kingston, and three from Hamilton. These towns, in addition to Montreal and Ottawa, were the football centres of Canada.

A number of changes made victory more important. From its inception in 1882 the ORFU had at its pinnacle the senior championship. In 1890 they expanded the championship series to include a junior series and in 1893 introduced an intermediate series. In addition, the development of a so-called Canadian championship between the ORFU and the QRFU gave a higher profile to these games. The impact of these changes was recognized in 1895 by George Lyman, secretary of the Montreal Football Club, when he explained the increase in "pugilism" by saying that the cause was "The prize which is now at stake, the championship of the Dominion. There is no doubt that the thought we must win at all costs is too often harboured."[13] Placing a higher premium on winning was also implicit in the development of leagues in the place of the old challenge system. In 1892, after several years of vacillation between challenge and series, the QRFU finally adopted the series system – a league.[14] The impact was soon evidenced on the playing field with increased complaints over rough play and in a more concrete sense in the ever-increasing injury list. Concern over "brutality" and "roughness" was voiced with increasing frequency. The explanation for these disturbing changes was not the structural shift and the nearly inevitable emphasis on winning but professionalism, or, more specifically, the intrusion of undesirable elements on the playing field. Who these newcomers were was vividly illustrated in Varsity's excuse for a loss at Queen's in October, 1893. "Owing to strikes among the stone masons as well as the employees of the Kingston Street Car Company, Queen's was enabled to place their strongest team in the field."[15] Thus, the changes in the game were due not to the university students but to the intrusion of outside elements, and this led to the denouement of 1897.

The year 1897 was a watershed for football. Attempts were made to turn the clock back and return to idealized versions of the game. In fact, the actions taken by the universities did little more than retard the inevitable consequence of growth. The action was precipitated by an increasing dissatisfaction with the dichotomy between "town" and "gown" teams, concern over the purity of football, and the intrusion of undesirable elements. The denouement was precipitated by the action of the senate of Queen's University on October 13, 1897, when it ruled that only *bona fide* students would be allowed to play for Queen's. With a single action the success of the Queen's football team was threatened. This brought the underlying dissatisfaction with affairs in university football to a head and led to the formation of the Canadian Intercollegiate Rugby Football Union (CIRFU) on November 25, 1897.[16] The reasons given for its formation were that the universities were against professionalism and against mixing with other groups. This meant that there were now three separate unions, each with different interpretations of the rules. Perhaps more important was the fact that it was a last-ditch attempt to maintain the exclusivity of university sport. There was no pretence that "town" equalled "gown"; football was a game for the elite.

The twentieth century ushered in real changes in the world of sport. In football these were evidenced both within the game and in its position in society. The base expanded both socially and geographically. Football began to take root in the Prairies with the establishment of the Western Canada Football Union in 1911 and, later, the Alberta Football Union. However, as with its development in the East, football was limited to the larger urban centres. More important was its expansion within the larger cities, in particular, Toronto, Winnipeg, Montreal, Ottawa, and Hamilton. The period after 1905 witnessed the creation of intra-city leagues in these cities. There were, however, differences in the patterns of development. Each of the cities saw the inauguration of city leagues that brought a variety of teams together. In Toronto,

Montreal, and Hamilton other developments also occurred. In Hamilton, the churches promoted the game while in Montreal and Toronto interscholastic leagues flourished. In Toronto, the Boys Union and the playgrounds got involved in promoting football. In these cases the sponsoring groups were closely aligned with amateurism and the educational system. Thus, while the base was expanding, it still lay within the ideological framework of the middle class.

During the early 1900's football faced the central problem of all sport – professionalism.[17] Since the CIRFU maintained a rigid policy on player eligibility, it was in the two provincial unions that the problem became acute. In 1907, the Canadian Amateur Athletic Union, in its war against pseudo-amateurs, expelled the Toronto Argonauts and the Montreal Winged Wheelers for professionalism. This action, in conjunction with increasing dissatisfaction over the calibre of opponents, led to the withdrawal of the four top teams in the ORFU and the QRFU. They joined together and formed the Interprovincial Union. The names of the teams are familiar to all Canadians: Toronto Argonauts, Hamilton Tigers, Ottawa Rough Riders, and Montreal. Thus football was fragmented into four separate unions held together loosely by the CRFU. In fact, at the highest level the CIRFU and the Interprovincial Union vied for pre-eminence. Their annual clash for the championship of Canada was given a higher profile by the inauguration of the Grey Cup in 1909.

One of the major changes in the 1900's was the emergence of football as a spectator sport. This shift reflected a break with a central tenet of the amateur ideal, and, significantly, the university teams were at the forefront of the changes. The universities had started down the road late in the 1890's when they began to charge admission. The first real gate was taken on October 31, 1896, in a game between Varsity and Queen's.[18] With the increasing importance of the Canadian championship the attractiveness of the spectacle increased. In 1904, 3,000 spectators attended the game; by 1905 the Varsity-Rough Riders final attracted 6,000 spectators; and by 1910 the Varsity-Hamilton Tigers Grey Cup attracted 12,000. Perhaps more significant were the presence of over thirty telegraphists representing papers from across the country and the filming of the game. It had become a truly Canadian event. But the most telling evidence of all was the decision taken by the board of governors of the University of Toronto in 1911 to build a 12,000-seat stadium, a concrete recognition of the arrival of football as a money-making proposition.

These changes in the sport were reflected by changes aimed at improving the game as a spectacle. In a general sense they were related to the adoption of American practices and ideals. At the cognitive level these were resisted most strenuously by the universities, but in practice they were adopted when it helped them to win.[19] The most important changes were in the rules. In 1898, J.T.M. "Thrift" Burnside, captain of Varsity, proposed a comprehensive set of rules that incorporated the best of the Canadian and American games. The CIRFU rejected them. During the next twenty-three years the CIRFU gradually instituted the rules until finally in 1921 the Burnside rules were accepted *in toto*. This reflected the inherent conservatism of the universities and the politicization of the game. The more pragmatic ORFU adopted the rules on December 15, 1902.

While football cautiously adopted American rules, it also took up American practices. The first signals were used in 1898. More important was the hiring of American coaches. In 1902, Ottawa College hired Tom "King" Clancy, the first American collegiate coach in Canada. This was the beginning of the professional-coach question that was waged with varying intensity until Varsity hired Warren Stevens in 1932. McGill was the first of the major universities to toy with the idea when it hired "Pud" Hamilton in 1907. The experiment was not a success and he was fired in 1909. However, the failure of the McGill teams in the ensuing years led to the hiring of the highly successful "Shag" Shaugnessey in 1912. Football was on the road to becoming a professionalized, commercial enterprise; although it did not reach this stage prior to 1914, some of the consequences were becoming visible even in university sport. In October, 1912, at the conclusion of the Ottawa College-Queen's game, "The Match wound up with a free fight in which the players and spectators took a hand," a vivid example of problems that faced all sport as it became an increasingly visible and important aspect of society.

What, then, can be said about football in 1915? Perhaps the clearest picture can be gained from the newspaper coverage accorded the game. Table 2 illustrates its origins, spread, and popularity. By 1915, it was solidly entrenched in the East and in Winnipeg; however, its presence was just beginning to be felt on the Prairies and in Vancouver, and it was not a part of the

Table 2
Football as a Percentage of the Sports Coverage in October and November in Selected Newspapers: 1875-1915

	1875	1890	1905	1915
Montreal	23	48	33	11
Toronto		11	42	57
Winnipeg		18	23	13
Edmonton				2
Vancouver			1	2
Victoria				0
Halifax				0

SOURCES: *Montreal Star*; *Toronto Globe*; *Winnipeg Free Press*; *Edmonton Bulletin*; *Vancouver Sun*; *Victoria Daily Times*; *Halifax Herald*.

lives of Canadians in the Maritimes, Vancouver Island, and French Quebec. Thus it could not claim to be a truly Canadian game. The strongholds were in the larger towns of Ontario and Manitoba. For the most part the players were English-speaking, although Montreal could boast at least one French team. On the Prairies the game was in its infancy – the great days of western football were yet to come. In Windsor, Sault Ste. Marie, and Manitoba the American game was played. It certainly could not be called a mass sport. The base of support was still small, the majority of players being drawn from those that could afford to go to university. However, the winds of change were evident in the universities' battle against commercialization. While retaining their pre-eminence prior to World War I they were unwilling to accept the consequences of commercialization and lost their position soon after the war. What can be said is that football remained Canadian, different in subtle ways from the game played south of the border, and thus it served as a visible symbol of something uniquely Canadian.

Ice Hockey

Ice hockey, like Canadian football and lacrosse, was created by anglophone Montrealers. Although there is evidence of games played on ice with sticks in Holland, England, Halifax, and Kingston, the earliest historic record of the modern game places its origin in the Victoria Rink, Montreal, on March 3, 1875. What differentiated this game from others was the limited spatial

Pincher Creek, Alberta, Bartenders hockey team vs. Wanderers, 1906. Courtesy Provincial Archives of Alberta, photo no. A11692.

boundaries with the concomitant emphasis on skill. Two nine-man teams from the Montreal Football Club looking for some winter training played the first game.[20] During the next few years teams drawn from the elite of Montreal society played infrequent games at the Victoria Rink. Students from McGill University introduced formal rules based on those of English field hockey.[21] By 1879 the number of players per side had been reduced from nine to seven and a standardized set of rules had been adopted. These rules were the foundation of all future rules.

Until the early 1880's hockey remained a Montreal game. The year 1882 witnessed the formation of the first relatively permanent club, the Victoria Hockey Club of Montreal.[22] The Victorias were participants in the hockey tournament held at the first Montreal Winter Carnival in 1883.[23] This carnival served to provide exposure for the game and it began to spread to other towns. Clubs developed in Ottawa, Quebec City, Kingston, and Halifax.[24] In December, 1886, representatives from Montreal, Quebec City, and Ottawa met to form the Amateur Hockey Association of Canada. While this was a grandiose title for what was essentially a local organization, it did represent the beginning of a tripartite relationship that was at the centre of the highest calibre of hockey in Canada until the 1920's. Teams from these three cities dominated the Stanley Cup from 1893 until 1914, winning nineteen of the twenty-three competitions. This was also the real beginning of inter-city competition.

The late 1880's witnessed the expansion of ice hockey beyond the boundaries of western Quebec and eastern Ontario and the commencement of extensive inter- and intra-city competition. Teams were formed in Toronto, Winnipeg, and Halifax. This was followed by the development of inter-city and intra-city leagues. The AHAC, after vacillating between the old challenge system and the series system, finally adopted the series (a league) in 1892.[25] By the mid-1890's inter-town leagues were springing up throughout Ontario and Manitoba. The Ontario Hockey Association (OHA) included towns in eastern Ontario in its championship series. To the west of Toronto the SOHA linked eight towns around Brantford, Hamilton, and Niagara Falls into two leagues.[26] In Manitoba, Portage, Selkirk, Brandon, and Winnipeg played in a series. At the same time, the larger towns witnessed the development of intra-town leagues. By 1895, Montreal, Toronto, Winnipeg, Halifax, Saint John, Quebec City, Peterborough, and Ottawa all boasted intra-city leagues. These leagues demonstrated a common characteristic – the sponsors were invariably middle-class groups: amateur athletic associations, universities, garrisons, banks, collegiate institutes, and, in Winnipeg, several mercantile firms. Thus, organized ice hockey was still restricted to the privileged segments of the community. However, leagues only encompassed a small percentage of the teams playing hockey. Challenge matches between a variety of impermanent teams were common. In Peterborough, in 1895, the six league teams were outnumbered by eleven others that played challenge matches. In all probability this pattern would be found in other areas, and certainly this was the case in the other larger towns and even as far away as Regina, Calgary, and Edmonton. For the most part, these teams were drawn from schools, colleges, banks, newspapers, and government offices, although there is some evidence of other groups becoming involved: a plumbers' helpers' team in Ottawa, two teams of workers from the brass department of Canadian General Electric in Peterborough, the Fire Brigade in Calgary, and French Canadians in Montreal. Obviously, ice hockey was being adopted by a variety of groups. Perhaps the most interesting of all occurred in Halifax, in February, 1895, when the Young Jubilees of Dartmouth played the Eurekas of Halifax for the "Coloured Championship of Halifax and Dartmouth."[27]

In 1895, ice hockey was still limited primarily to select social groups in specific locations. By 1905 it had invaded all corners of Canada. Nearly every community contained a commercially operated ice arena where games were played from January until early March. The North End Rink at Digby, Nova Scotia (population: 1,247), the Shediac Rink at Shediac, New Brunswick, the Palace Rink in Waterford, Ontario, and the Victoria Rink in High River, Alberta (population: 1,182), attest to the pervasiveness of the game. Except for British Columbia and Alberta, relatively permanent inter-town hockey leagues had taken root throughout rural Canada. The majority of these linked small towns and villages located on a railway. For example, the Saskatchewan league of Oxbow, Estevan, Almeda, Glen Ewan, Gainsboro, and Carvale provided competition for these villages and towns located in southeast Saskatchewan.[28] This example could be duplicated for any rural area of Canada. Some were short-lived, and the numbers and composition varied from season to season, but, by 1905, they had become a permanent part of the Canadian winters.

In the larger towns the number of intra-city leagues increased. Without exception these leagues were sponsored by middle-class groups who adhered strictly to the tenets of amateurism. By 1905, there were bank leagues in Saint John, Winnipeg, Ottawa, and Toronto, and leagues involving manufacturing, mercantile, and hardware companies in Ottawa, Winnipeg, Toronto, and Montreal. More important to the future development of the game was the emergence of inter-school leagues. These were important because it meant that hockey was now recognized as important in the education of Canadian boys. School leagues were to be found only in the larger cities, such as Winnipeg, Ottawa, and Montreal; however, schools across the country were beginning to play ice hockey in a variety of exhibition and challenge matches. The other institution that was to play an important role in the development of hockey was the church. By 1905, churches were participating in city leagues in many of the larger towns. Only in Peterborough, however, had a separate church league been formed.[29] Perhaps the most important change of all was the inauguration of the Toronto Lacrosse Hockey League, which by 1905 consisted of thirty-three teams. The establishment of a juvenile series for youths under the age of seventeen implied that hockey was being recognized as important in and for itself and not as a means to some other end, as was the case in schools, churches, and the YMCA.

Despite the significant expansion of leagues, hockey had not moved outside the boundaries of the middle classes, whose control of league hockey was complete. In a limited number of towns, though, there was evidence of teams comprised of different social groups. These teams were not formally constituted and rarely existed for a prolonged period of time. In Quebec the game was gaining some support within the Roman Catholic Church – teams from various seminaries played infrequent exhibition games.[30] More pervasive, but still limited, were some working-class teams. In Peterborough, teams in various factories played inter-departmental contests, and in Ottawa and Winnipeg teams of barbers took to the ice. The working class was peripheral to the development of organized ice hockey. If they were involved it was as members of teams sponsored by middle-class-dominated institutions. Hence, amateur ice hockey, across the country, was created in the image of the middle class.

Ladies playing ice hockey at Banff, c. 1911. Courtesy Glenbow Archives, Calgary / NA-3890-14.

Ice hockey had also gained a foothold in French Canada. The game was first played in Quebec City and Montreal in the mid-1890's. During the ensuing decade the expansion among the French was phenomenal. So quickly did they take to the game that French Canadians were among the first professional players. By 1905, ice hockey had spread throughout Quebec to Nicolet, Ormstown, Chicoutimi, Trois-Rivières, Grand Mère, and other towns. Although many teams were involved in league competition the majority played in exhibition and challenge games.

One other group began to grace the ice rinks – women. For the most part their participation was limited to exhibition games. At the same time, their presence does lead to the conclusion that the game was fairly widespread. In each of the larger towns of Saint John, Montreal, and Toronto, there were three or four women's teams. In the case of Saint John, one of the women's teams became involved in a series of competitions with Fredericton, Woodstock, and Mount Allison University. Ottawa and Edmonton also boasted teams that played infrequently. Perhaps more interesting was the evidence of women's teams in some of the smaller towns and villages across the country – Millbrook, Tweed, and Marmora in the Trent Valley region of Ontario, Bruce Mines and Richards Landing in northern Ontario, and the area around Simcoe, Ontario.[31]

By 1905, the basic structure of hockey was in place and did not change substantially prior to World War I. What did change were the number of teams and the depth of the game's intrusion into Canadian life. The most significant change, which was to revolutionize hockey in the 1920's, occurred in 1911-12 in Vancouver and Victoria – the construction of the first artificial ice rinks in Canada. Thus, ice hockey spread to the West Coast into an area where the climate was not conducive to the game. Toronto (1912) quickly followed suit, and this provided the conditions that allowed it to compete on an equal footing with teams from Quebec and Manitoba, where the climate allowed for a longer and more continuous season. Therefore, by 1914, inter- and intra-town leagues were in evidence from Halifax to Victoria. The nature and structure of the leagues depended to a large extent on the size and nature of the towns. In the majority of towns and cities, ice hockey was still promoted by the middle class. Only in the rural areas was the base of participants wider. But significant changes took place in the larger towns with respect to the groups having access to organized hockey.

Table 3
Sponsorship of Ice Hockey Leagues in Seven Urban areas in Canada, 1915

	Montreal	Toronto	Ottawa	Winnipeg	Regina	Calgary	Vancouver
Schools							
High Schools	•	•		•		•	
Public			•		•	•	•
Church	•	•	•				
Spalding*	•						
Playground		•	•	•			

*Spalding leagues were promoted by the Spalding Sporting Goods Company, a major U.S. sporting goods firm.

SOURCES: *La Presse*; *Toronto Globe*; *Ottawa Citizen*; *Winnipeg Free Press*; *Regina Leader-Post*; *Calgary Herald*; *Vancouver Province*.

The most important change in the years leading to the war was the promotion of ice hockey among the youth of Canada. Ice hockey became recognized as important in the educational experiences that Canadians gave to their male youth. In this instance ice hockey was adopted by various middle-class institutions: schools, churches, and government (Table 3). In several of the larger towns and cities these institutions actively sponsored ice hockey. In the seven urban centres listed in Table 3 either high schools or public schools (or, in Calgary, both) promoted ice hockey. Thus the game was brought within the purview of the educational system across Canada. Perhaps more important to the development of hockey was its adoption by the churches. Leagues were limited to Montreal, Toronto, and Ottawa, but in Toronto the church leagues became a dominant force in the growth of the game and thus ensured development along particular lines. Finally, in Toronto, Ottawa, and Winnipeg municipal government, through Departments of Parks and Recreation, had begun to provide recreational opportunities for the youth of the burgeoning cities. Ice hockey had gained a firm foothold in the larger urban centres of Canada, and from these centres the new ways of the sport emerged.

As ice hockey spread beyond the narrow social and geographical boundaries of its origins, problems emerged that have plagued it to the present day. The rise of these problems parallelled the expansion in the number of teams, the development of leagues, and the awarding of championships such as the Stanley Cup in 1893 and the Allan Cup in 1908. While these problems manifested themselves wherever ice hockey was played, the particular configuration differed across the country. In some places the problem was unnecessary violence, in another spectator behaviour, and in yet another poor officiating. What can be stated is that they were common across the country and have not been completely eliminated even today.

Soon after its invention, ice hockey was recognized as an ideal vehicle for the demonstration of "manly" qualities.[32] In fact, this quality provided the justification for its acceptance in society. Manly qualities included "The kind of courage and toughness that indicated, not sheer strength and recklessness, but determination and discipline."[33] In other words, "manliness" was a concept that defied simplistic definition – one man's manly behaviour became another man's "roughness" and "brutality." The line between acceptable and unacceptable behaviour was thin indeed, depending on the social and educational background of the individuals, local conditions, and the importance of a particular contest. Thus it was extremely difficult to determine when actions on the ice actually constituted "brutal" as opposed to "manly" behaviour. Accusations of unacceptable behaviour first surfaced to a significant degree in the early 1890's. There were various levels of undesirable conduct as reported by the newspapers. Hacking, tripping, and roughness were frowned upon but not unilaterally condemned. Brutality, donnybrooks, and fighting raised the ire of the reporters and led to a demand for action. Some instances lay totally outside the acceptable boundaries and led to action being taken. This was illustrated in the escalating violence in the OHA around the turn of the century that culminated in four deaths on the ice in 1904.[34] The solutions adopted by the OHA emphasized a rigid distinction between amateurs and professionals and revealed some important insights into ice hockey and sport.

With the increasing popularity of hockey as a spectator sport, the interaction between players and spectators became a concern. Complaints over spectator behaviour did not become visible until the turn of the century. The OHA annual meetings heard an increasing number of complaints over the behaviour of the spectators. In 1904, President James Ross Robertson drew attention to the coal-throwing proclivities of Lindsay fans, the bottle-tossing in Peterborough, and the inadequacy of police protection in the smaller towns.[35] This behaviour was not limited to Ontario. In 1905, at a game in Saint John, the crowd invaded the ice after a disputed goal.[36] Ten years later in Kentville, Nova Scotia, the fans attacked the visiting team.[37] Examples such as these could be given from all over the country, but it is important to emphasize that for every bad report there were 100 reports of the friendly relations between the two teams. At the same time, the reports of unruly fans gained the headlines and gave the opponents of hockey a chance to condemn it out of hand.

During the 1890's Winnipeg was remarkably free from complaints of roughness or brutality. In Manitoba the complaints centred on the perpetual squabbling between the players and the referees.[38] This was not limited to Manitoba. In Ontario and Quebec there were continual references to the difficulty of getting referees. Even more than roughness and spectator behaviour, the problem of officiating was a national concern surfacing in Peterborough (1895), Saint John and Halifax (1905), and Grenfell, Saskatchewan (1905). The referee problem had two facets. On the one hand, it reflected a basic philosophic view as to the nature and meaning of the game, and, on the other, the increasing importance of a referee in a situation where the emphasis on victory was increasing. The first, the philosophic, was related to the fundamental ideals of amateurism where the referee was there only to arbitrate disagreements between two captains who, by definition, were gentlemen. The second was never seriously addressed, although it was recognized. As will be seen, the answer of amateur administrators to this question lay elsewhere.

The final problem was in the end the most important and was used as the explanatory factor for all the others – the emergence of professionals. The problem surfaced early in the 1890's with the increasing number of claims that teams were using "ringers." In 1895, Port Hope was accused of using ringers in a game against Belleville.[39] Perhaps even more revealing was the use by the Toronto bank team of two non-bank employees in a game against the Peterborough banks. The more important victory was perceived to be the more individuals, teams, and communities sacrificed in order to win. The next step was logical – the payment of players. This question surfaced in the OHA in 1897 when James A. MacFadden, the OHA president, accused someone (unnamed) of offering two Stratford players $7 and $5, respectively. Thus the question that was to consume the energies of amateur hockey for many years to come moved to centre stage. Professionalism was seen to be the root cause of all the other problems. Rough play, the use of ringers, fan conduct, and any other evils all coalesced into one ailment – professionalism. The moguls of ice hockey entered into the battle to protect amateurism, a battle that was to have far-reaching consequences for both hockey and amateur sport.

Professionalism was addressed by the organizations that had developed to organize the game, in particular the OHA. The position taken by the OHA was, in essence, adopted by all the other hockey organizations. It became, prior to the First World War, the most prestigious hockey organization – the prototype of all others. As the secretary reported in 1912:

> The constitution of the OHA has been adopted by new leagues and associations in Canada, from the Atlantic to the Pacific as well as in the new hockey organizations across the border.[40]

On November 20, 1890, thirteen Members of Parliament, Queen's Counsels, university professors, and military officers met at the Queen's Hotel, Toronto, and formed the Ontario Hockey Association. Within the next twenty years it became recognized as the pre-eminent amateur sport organization in Canada and was recognized as a staunch defender of "true" amateurism. This was not undeserved and it was derived from the actions taken during a critical period in the history of sport in Canada, 1897-1905. During this period sport faced the problem of professionalism and developed its basic approach to the way in which amateur sport would relate to professional sport. The position taken by the OHA became the cornerstone of the AAUC when it was founded in 1909.[41] The problem was first faced at the annual meeting of the OHA in 1897 and finally resolved in 1904. The intervening years were among the most turbulent in the history of sport in Canada. The world of sport was in an uproar over professionalism in lacrosse, baseball, soccer, and ice hockey. At the helm of the OHA for much of this period was John Ross Robertson, MP, owner of the *Toronto Telegram* and president of the OHA from 1899 to 1905. He was an ardent proponent of pure amateurism and an unswerving enemy of professionalism, semi-professionalism, and pseudo-amateurism. During his presidency he fought to keep hockey free from the taint of professionalism. In 1904, at the decisive meeting, he made an impassioned plea in which he stated the basic principles:

Is the OHA to fling away the sword of amateur principles and wield the whitewash brush of vote hunting policy? Is the OHA to be what it has been – a power in the land to drive wolves out of the sheep fold or is the OHA to degenerate into a CAAU ready to kalomine every tarnished professional with brand new suits of whitewash.[42]

The meeting adopted Robertson's position by a 43-27 vote. Thus, they adopted as the basic foundation of amateur sport a most conservative position, "Once a professional always a professional." This basic tenet, which excluded any reinstatement of professionals or anyone accused of being a professional, was to remain central to the OHA until March, 1936. Perhaps even more important was the continued adherence to a principle first enunciated and adopted in 1897: "When the status of any individual is questioned the burden of proving his innocence shall rest with the accused."[43] Thus the die was cast – there would be no contact with anyone accused of taking money, no matter how little. If the OHA could impose its will, amateur hockey would be the exclusive preserve of those who could afford to play. The position taken by the OHA became the position taken by the majority of amateur sport organizations that became affiliates of the AAUC after its formation in 1909. However, even at this early date the western provinces were not as enthusiastic in their support for a rigid definition, and the East-West rivalry that was to escalate in the 1920's had already begun to take shape.

In the ensuing years, as hockey spread rapidly across the Prairies, new provincial organizations developed in Saskatchewan and Alberta. At the same time, professional hockey expanded significantly after 1908,[44] and all amateur organizations consequently faced the threat of professionalism. This stimulated the western provinces, in particular Manitoba, to lobby for the creation of a national ice hockey organization. Their lobby bore fruit in 1914 when the Canadian Amateur Hockey Association (CAHA) was formed as an affiliate of the AAUC. At the outbreak of World War I, then, hockey faced the threat of professionalism with a united front. By this time, though, hockey had expanded to such a degree that the CAHA had jurisdiction over only a small portion of the teams and leagues playing the game, so that hence a view of monolithic control would do an injustice to the reality of hockey. It had expanded far beyond the boundaries established by a social elite to become Canada's national game.

The distinctly Canadian games of football and hockey provide concrete evidence of the central role played by Montrealers and Torontonians in codifying rules, developing organizations, and promoting games. They remained dominant forces in all levels of both sports. While both ice hockey and football developed separately in other parts of the country, the central Canadian form of the games came to dominate. In addition, both games in origin were rooted in the middle-class institutions, particularly the universities. Football remained closely tied with institutions of higher education and thus limited in development. Hockey, on the other hand, pervaded the whole country. This led to a far stronger regional development and a greater resistance to the hegemony of central Canada. At the same time, partially because of the expense of the game, it remained tied to middle-class-dominated institutions. Both football and hockey remained tied to the middle classes of Canadian society, and this allowed for a degree of control over who would play and how the games should be played. Such was the popularity of hockey that clubs and leagues developed outside the jurisdiction of the amateur organizations, yet, organized *amateur* hockey and football were created and run by a small segment of society.

BRITISH SPORT

The central role of the British in Canadian history takes on an a priori existence. The British influence was transmitted through people, ideas, and the games played. Perhaps the simplest and most accurate measure of the British influence lay in the degree to which certain games were played across the country. English rugby, soccer, and cricket provide different views of the British influence on Canadian sport.

English Rugby

Like Canadian football and soccer, English rugby emerged out of the chaotic 1870's when footballers were attempting to establish unified codes of rules. In Ontario and Montreal, English rugby lost out to the distinctly different Canadian form of the game. Rugby gained root in only two areas of the country, the Maritimes and British Columbia. This was to remain the case until after the First World War, although some interest was expressed in Toronto in the mid-1870's and in Winnipeg after 1908.[45] Rugby developed in the 1880's in settings with a strong British presence –

in this case, naval garrisons. The ongoing presence of the garrisons provided the stimulus to the development of civilian clubs.[46] During the formative years the naval teams were in the majority in both Halifax and Victoria.[47] However, the experiences of the two regions were different. In the Maritimes the game was adopted by the universities as the fall game. Dalhousie, King's College, the University of New Brunswick, and Acadia all adopted the game. The annual rivalry between Acadia and Dalhousie commenced in 1884.[48] By the 1890's rugby had been incorporated into the high schools and town teams had emerged. It had permeated middle-class Maritime society and by 1905 had spread to all English-speaking areas of the Maritimes. In British Columbia the game was limited to Vancouver and Vancouver Island. The garrisons played a more central and ongoing role in its development although it was adopted by the schools. There was one significant difference on the West Coast: the importance of immigrants to the game. By 1905, most players in Vancouver were from England, Ireland, Scotland, New Zealand, and Australia.[49] Thus, in the Maritimes the game became more Canadian while in B.C. it remained closely tied to Britain and things British.

Rugby never permeated deeply into Canadian society even in the areas where it became the most popular form of football. It remained the game of the middle class, those who were able to afford to go to secondary school and university, although in places like Cape Breton its roots likely spread much broader. At the same time it was not a mirror image of the game played in the old country. In Britain, rugby union was rarely played in leagues but in both the Maritimes and British Columbia leagues flourished by 1895.

Soccer

Of all the forms of football, only one could claim to have acquired the characteristics of mass sport by 1914. Soccer was played in inter- and intra-town leagues, had developed local, provincial, and national organizations, and had teams competing for national championships. With the notable exceptions of French Quebec and the Maritimes, soccer was played in villages, towns, and cities across the country. It was, however, recognized as a British game, in some ways an alien intruder on Canadian soil. Prior to the 1890's it is extremely difficult to provide an accurate account of its growth since the term "football" was used to denote all forms of football, but it is possible to identify, quite clearly, some

Edmonton Eskimos vs. Tigers, Edmonton, Alberta, 1911. Courtesy City of Edmonton Archives / EA 246-33.

important elements of the growth of soccer. There were references to "football" being played from coast to coast: in 1876 soldiers at Osborne Barracks, Winnipeg, were playing games of football;[50] it was introduced to Minnedosa, Manitoba, as early as 1879;[51] the British garrison in Victoria played games in the 1870's.[52] But the most important events, in terms of its future development, were taking place around Berlin, Ontario, in the mid-1870's.

Evidence of football in Ontario preceded Confederation but until the mid-1870's it is not possible to differentiate between the different forms of the game. Perhaps the first club was the Carlton Club of Toronto formed by some bankers from Glasgow. The first evidence of formal organization and continuity appears in 1876 in a small group of high schools and collegiate institutes located around Berlin (renamed Kitchener during World War I) and Galt, Ontario. Interestingly, the stimulus to this development came not from immigrants but from native Canadians.[53] One of the main figures behind the development of soccer was David Forsyth, a native of Scotland who came to Canada when only one year old. Forsyth was educated at the University of Toronto and from there went to Berlin High School where he was to remain for over thirty years. In conjunction with a group of teachers in neighbouring schools, he promoted soccer. In 1879-80 he was instrumental in forming the Western Football Association (WFA), which expanded into an organization of over 100 teams spread from Detroit in the west to Norwood in the east. David Forsyth remained an active member of the WFA for fifty years before retiring to Beamsville, Ontario.

The formation of the WFA ushered in what Forsyth later referred to as the greatest era of Canadian soccer,[54] when graduates from Berlin, Galt, and other schools moved to the University of Toronto or to the Berlin Rangers.[55] In 1884 a representative team was sent to St. Louis, Missouri. This was followed, in 1885, with the first international match with the United States.[56] Perhaps the high point of the era was the WFA tour of Britain in 1888, when the Canadians played the top professional teams. The composition of the team reflected the strength of various areas: Berlin (7), Toronto (4), Galt (3), Dundas, and Norwood.

Prior to the 1890's, except in Ontario, Canadian soccer reflected its pre-industrial origins. There were no formally constituted clubs, no leagues, and no organizations. This changed dramatically during the 1890's. By 1895, there were intra-city leagues in those urban centres that became dominant forces in soccer. The Toronto

Football League, formed in 1889, was the forerunner of leagues in Montreal, Winnipeg, Brandon, and Victoria.[57] These became the focal point of local development and provided the leadership for the formation of provincial organizations in the two hotbeds of pre-war soccer: the Manitoba Football Association (MFA), founded in 1896, and the Ontario Football Association (OFA), begun in 1901.[58] Soccer also took root in the rural areas, especially in Ontario, Manitoba, and Saskatchewan. In 1895, for example, there were twenty-three teams within forty miles of Exeter, Ontario.[59] In 1894, at least twelve teams were within a dozen miles of Hartney, Manitoba, and in eastern Saskatchewan between Grenfell and Qu'Appelle, a distance of under forty miles, fourteen teams were active.[60] It is difficult to generalize from these local examples; perhaps it would be more appropriate to state that soccer gained a firm foothold in specific rural areas across Canada dependent to a large extent on the ethnic composition of the population. Rural soccer during the 1890's was significantly different from its urban counterpart. It was characterized by a lack of stability, few leagues, and no organizations. Villages would have teams one year and not the next. Teams would play one match a year, or more, depending on the interest of the participants. There were no leagues, although they were beginning to develop along the railways by the turn of the century. Soccer was more of a community event than in the larger towns. Teams were developed to represent the community in the tournaments and picnics, particularly on May 24 and July 1. At these times the communities celebrated their British heritage and communal spirit. This was the case at the Dominion Day tournament at Indian Head, Saskatchewan. In 1905 there were several tournaments in the area between Sudbury and Sault Ste. Marie,[61] and in 1915 the soccer players of High River, Alberta, played in various picnics.[62] The rural experience was different.

During the early years of the twentieth century league competition spread to the rural areas across the country. In 1905, the Soo Line League in southeastern Saskatchewan included teams from Milestone, Weyburn, Yellow Grass, and Rouleau. Farther east, in the area around Peterborough, Ontario, the Midland League (1903) had expanded from four to eight teams by 1905.[63] In addition, town and city leagues had spread to Quebec City, Ottawa, Calgary, and Vancouver. With the expansion of the game, local and provincial organizations emerged to co-ordinate and control soccer. Toronto, Victoria, Vancouver, Montreal, and Winnipeg witnessed the formation of local associations. Saskatchewan (1905) and Alberta (1909) joined Ontario and Manitoba with provincial associations. Finally, in 1912, the separate groups across the country were, for a short period, able to submerge their differences and form the Dominion Football Association (DFA). Soccer had now acquired all the characteristics of organized sport.

Soccer had become an important part of the sporting culture of Canada, attracting as participants and spectators larger numbers than any games except baseball and ice hockey. At the same time it remained a British game and was never accepted as Canadian. This was reflected most graphically in the newspaper coverage devoted to it and its Canadian football counterpart. Despite the fact that soccer was played more widely, attracted more players, and had gained greater international success for Canada, the coverage in three strongholds of the sport indicate some important differences. Toronto gave 4.4 per cent of sport coverage to soccer and 6.7 per cent to Canadian football; Montreal 0.5 per cent and 10.5 per cent; and Winnipeg 1.8 per cent and 8.6 per cent. In fact, the disparity was even greater since the Canadian game was only reported for four or five months while soccer was covered for ten or eleven. Canadian football was recognized and promoted as being Canadian; soccer was always alien. In fact, after its initial development in the 1870's, it became heavily dependent on recently arrived immigrants as a source of replenishment.[64] This was demonstrated in the larger urban centres with the emergence of identifiable ethnic teams. Across the country around the turn of the century many teams emerged with ethnic names, especially those denoting Scottish ancestry.[65] Thistles, Scots, Sons of Scotland, and Caledonia were to be found in Montreal, Toronto, Ottawa, and Calgary. They were joined by Shamrocks, Celtics, Sons of England, and several others. Perhaps the relationship with the old country was illustrated most clearly in Toronto: in 1915, eighteen of the forty-eight teams in the Toronto and District League had such names such as Sunderland, Manchester United, Ulster United, and Corinthians. The strength of soccer was a measure of the immigrants' ties to the old country. It allowed them to perpetuate cultural practices they had learned when young. At the same time it retarded their assimilation into Canadian society.

The alien nature of soccer was demonstrated most clearly in the failure of the universities, schools, and churches to promote the game. This was critical, for if any practice was to be institutionalized and transmitted to the new generations it must be propagated by the major socializing institutions. A brief perusal of the universities illustrates the basic approach. At Dalhousie, soccer was never a major sport and rugby always had pride of place. McGill University never seriously participated in the game. Although it was solidly entrenched at the University of Toronto it gradually lost out to Canadian football in the first decade of the new century when the crowds flocked to the Canadian football games. The only exception was to be found in Winnipeg, where soccer played a dominant role. On the West Coast, as at Dalhousie, English rugby was most important although Victoria College did participate in soccer. Thus, soccer was not the preferred sport in the majority of the universities in Canada. It is no surprise, then, that the high schools and collegiate institutes did not promote the game. Only in Winnipeg, Victoria, and Vancouver were there strong soccer programs. From 1901, Winnipeg public and high schools promoted soccer. They were followed by Victoria schools around 1905 and Vancouver by 1915. In the other areas of the country, school involvement in soccer was uneven and lacked continuity. Perhaps part of the reason for this was because soccer in Britain was regarded as a working-class game and was not promoted by the middle classes.

The consequences of this were manifested in the amateur-professional conflict waged so fiercely in the early years of the new century. Because of the strong working-class roots in England, soccer enthusiasts in Canada found themselves in an untenable position with respect to the pure amateurs. If they accepted the definition that embraced the idea of "Once a professional, always a professional," it meant that soccer, as played in Canada, would cease to exist since many of the players were former British professionals or had played against professionals. Thus, the soccer organizers were opposed to the rigid definition adopted by the AAUC on its formation in 1909. Soccer could not become part of the amateur movement without destroying itself. Of course, this also served to split soccer into opposing camps and prevented the organizers from creating a strong central organization. This was illustrated at the formation of the DFA, in 1912, when British Columbia failed to attend because there were two separate organizations, one pure amateur and the other more pragmatic. However, soccer demonstrated great resiliency. Like its summer counterpart, cricket, it was invariably perceived to be in trouble but always managed to maintain a strong presence throughout the regions where the British presence was strongest. Still, it was always regarded by Canadians as an alien game. It was never adopted with great fervour by those central institutions, the media, schools, and churches. Soccer was tainted by its origins and popularity among the British working class. A continual flirtation with professionalism placed it beyond the pale for the moguls of amateur sport and their middle-class supporters. For all these reasons, it failed to get strong support from those groups central to the development of amateur sport and therefore remained isolated from the mainstream of Canadian amateur sport.

Cricket

If any game is identified with England it is cricket. Its history reaches back into pre-industrial England and the game reflects a different society and different patterns of social organization. In Canada, cricket had been played since the early 1830's and by the 1850's was being played wherever the English settled. In fact, Wise and Fisher claim that the 1850's were the halcyon days of the game in Canada.[66] There is no doubt that, by 1867, it was played widely across the country. During the next twenty years, it spread wherever the English went as immigrants, traders, or soldiers and through the private schools that provided English education for the children of the social elite. Cricket was popular in Victoria, Montreal, the Eastern Townships, Quebec City, Toronto, and the towns and villages of Ontario. New Westminster formed a club about 1872 while the new settlement of Winnipeg boasted the Manitoba Cricket Club in 1876. The Maritimes were not exempt from the tide of cricket clubs, with Halifax, Truro, Antigonish, Sydney, Saint John, and Fredericton all playing regularly in the early 1880's. Possibly the most vivid illustration of the popularity of the game lay in southwestern Ontario in 1880, where the small town of Leamington and the hamlets of Ruthven and Blytheswood were each able to field teams. Cricket was played throughout English-speaking Canada.

Despite the pervasiveness of cricket there was no evidence of substantial growth in the larger towns. In Montreal there were six clubs in 1871, three in 1881, and eight in 1887; Victoria had three relatively permanent clubs throughout the period; and Toronto remained stable at five or six. Cricket was established with a core of permanent clubs supported by an ever-changing group of short-lived teams, a logical pattern when one considers the game's dependency on English immigrants and products of certain institutions. A further similarity is to be found in the distribution of the sport across the country. The larger urban areas, such as Montreal, Toronto, and Halifax, contained several teams while the smaller towns only supported one club – towns such as Chatham, Stratford, Port Hope, Grafton, Cobourg, and Collingwood in Ontario all had cricket clubs in the early 1870's. Nearly without exception these areas were settlements containing English immigrants or institutions.

The development of clubs across the country was not a standardized process; rather, it reflected a particular set of circumstances related to the nature of the area. In the first place, there was a difference between urban and rural, the permanent town teams being drawn from the social elite while in rural Canada the members were drawn from a far wider social spectrum. Even within the large urban areas, the stimulus lay with different groups. Toronto had a strongly educational orientation, four of the five teams being Trinity College Cricket Club, Upper Canada College, Toronto Cricket Club (comprised mainly of graduates of UCC), and the Bankers team. In Halifax and Victoria the influence of the naval garrisons was predominant, for they supplied teams and opposition for the civilian clubs. Montreal, on the other hand, exhibited no strong institutional orientation except that participants were drawn from the upper levels of society. Even though the game was popular across Canada, there were subtle differences arising, for the most part, from the extent and nature of the English influence in the particular locale.

The lack of growth in cricket was also evident in the stagnation in competitive opportunities. All the games were exhibitions or challenges; no leagues or even championships were played until the 1880's, and then only to a limited extent. Added to this was the irregularity of the schedules, which depended on the availability of suitable opposition. In general, except for the most important clubs, competition was restricted to the local area, usually with teams within easy rail access. This was the case in Nova Scotia, in 1885, where the competition was limited to irregular games between teams, all of which were linked by railway. In Ontario, Trinity College Cricket Club played seven games in 1882, all with local teams, all between May 19 and June 3. One of the most active teams in the country was the Montreal Cricket Club, which in 1874 played thirteen games, eight with opposition from within Montreal, two against Belleville and Ottawa, and three on a short tour of the United States.

While local competition was the lifeblood of cricket, it was also played at a higher level by representatives from a small group of clubs in the inter-provincial and international competitions. Infrequent contests between Ontario and Quebec illustrate the role of cricket in the two provinces – ten of the Quebec players were drawn from the Montreal Cricket Club while Ontario was represented by players from eight different towns. In the international arena, Canada was visited by several touring teams from England and Australia: in 1872, a Gentlemen of England eleven with Dr. W.G. Grace; an Australian eleven in 1878; and Dafts team from England in 1879. In each instance, the majority of matches were played against teams composed of twenty-two Canadians – a comment on the level of Canadian cricket, since normally a team would field only eleven players. For the cricketers of Ontario, the high point of the era was the game played against the United States at Philadelphia or Toronto, first in 1875 and annually from 1879 to 1885. It is apparent that cricket parallelled the developments in England, remaining pre-industrial.

By the 1890's, distinct patterns became clear. In the larger towns it maintained a strong presence and experienced modest growth. For example, Toronto in 1895 could boast twenty-eight teams, Halifax, thirteen, and Victoria, fifteen. On the other hand, its presence in the rural areas was less certain – teams came and went, flourishing one year, disappearing the next, and reappearing again a few years later.[67] At the same time, it was rare for districts with English settlers not to have a team somewhere in the vicinity. This pattern of urban stability and modest growth and rural uncertainty and perhaps decline was reflected more clearly in the following twenty years. The game had taken a solid root in the larger urban centres while it disappeared in many of the rural areas. However, it would be erroneous to suggest that it had disappeared totally, for cricket was declared dead many times only to reappear.

It is important to emphasize the difference between the urban and rural game. In the urban centres it maintained a solid though limited base, but in the rural areas it lost pride of place to baseball. The newspapers were replete with comments about past teams, lack of interest, and the scarcity of competition. A writer in Weymouth, Nova Scotia, in 1889, commented on the cricket team that used to be.[68] In Simcoe, Ontario, in the same year the team was so disorganized that it was unable to compete.[69] Not far away, in Exeter, the editor commented on the scarcity of teams in the area.[70] In nearby Bayfield, in 1895, the first game of the season was not played until August 15, when the baseball players took on the businessmen.[71] Examples such as these could be given from all over the country. The villages were dependent on a continuing supply of immigrants, and when the supply dried up cricket disappeared. It would appear likely that the game in the small towns would be more broadly based than in the cities, yet fragmentary evidence suggests that many of the players and organizers were drawn from the business community of the towns. In Edmonton, in 1905, there were enough bankers and ex-bankers on the team for an intra-club game.[72] In 1889, three leading Peterborough players were barristers.[73] Clubs in Grenfell and Qu'Appelle boasted MPs, doctors, barristers, auctioneers, and solicitors.[74]

Within the larger towns and cities cricket was the game of society. It was part of the social life of the elite. On nearly any afternoon during the summer the private cricket grounds were the scene of much social play and display. On these select grounds amateurs and professionals competed together without fuss or fanfare. One of the most ardent supporters of the game in Toronto was John Ross Robertson, the arch-enemy of professionalism who labelled as professional those who had innocently competed against professionals. Cricket was the game of the English landed aristocracy transmitted to the "colonial" elite in Halifax, Saint John, Quebec City, Ottawa, Montreal, Toronto, Hamilton, Winnipeg, Edmonton, Vancouver, and Victoria. The most prestigious clubs in these cities were characterized by certain attributes. At the very highest level they were as much social as sporting clubs. For example, in 1895, the Toronto Cricket Club with its private grounds, clubhouse, and tennis courts boasted a membership of 243. In Toronto, the Cricketers Ball was one of the highlights of the social season and was attended by the Lieutenant Governor.[75]

Many of the clubs had a long and honourable history, some having been formed prior to Confederation – the Toronto, Ottawa, and Victoria Cricket Clubs. As to the game itself, the fixture list of up to thirty-six games was arranged by the club secretary and usually included the other prestigious clubs in the province. Many of the clubs hired professionals from England to act as groundsmen, coach the players, and play on the teams. Such was the case with the Wanderers of Halifax (1889), Saint John Cricket and Athletic Club (1889), Ottawa (1889, 1895), Toronto and Rosedale (1890, 1901), and Winnipeg (1900). For many of the clubs the high point of the season was the annual summer tour. In 1885, the Wanderers of Halifax toured Stellarton, Pictou, Charlottetown, and Saint John.[76] The Toronto Cricket Club toured the Maritimes in 1889. Ottawa undertook its annual tour to Toronto and western Ontario in 1895. And in 1905 the Saint John Cricket Club played eight games during a tour of Nova Scotia.

Cricket was indeed an important element in the social lives of the Canadian elite. They were introduced to the game at the private schools of Canada. These young Canadians were educated to be "English" gentlemen at St. Andrews College, Halifax; Rothesay School, Saint John; in Ontario, Upper Canada College, Lakefield School, Trinity College School, Ridley College, Ashbury College; Lower Canada College, Montreal; and University School, Victoria. These private schools stocked by English masters promoted cricket above all other games and provided the Toronto Cricket Club, Victoria Cricket Club, and others with a continual supply of recruits.

Other cricket teams existed besides those already mentioned, and it was among these teams that changes were introduced. In England, cricket was never played in leagues, but by 1892, in Manitoba, cricket was being played in a league.[77] For once Toronto did not lead the way in terms of sporting innovations. The league system soon spread to Ontario with the formation in Hamilton of the Wentworth Junior Cricket League in 1895.[78] The Bankers League of Toronto soon followed the Hamilton lead.[79] By 1905, cricket leagues had been formed in Montreal, Winnipeg, and Toronto. In 1911 there were leagues in only seven of the larger cities.[80] Cricket thus moved outside the English model, as had been the case with rugby, and adopted the practices common to other sports in Canada.

By 1915, cricket had lost its place as a premier sport but at the same time it demonstrated great resiliency because of its adoption by the private schools and its privileged place in the lives of the Canadian social elite. The game had all but died in the smaller towns of Canada and became a remnant of the dominant English influence. Thus, it symbolized the yearnings and aspirations of the Canadian social elite not to be Canadian but to be like the English landed aristocracy. Its place in Canadian sport is most accurately reflected by its changing position within the sports pages of the *Toronto Globe*. In 1885, cricket was the third most popular sport with 12 per cent of the sports coverage.

By 1915, it had declined to seventeenth and 0.3 per cent, surely a telling reflection of its decreasing importance.

British sport maintained a continuing presence from coast to coast. However, the histories of the three sports reflect variability rather than sustained growth, the popularity of all games being related to either the influx of British immigrants or their adoption by British-dominated institutions. Soccer was very much dependent on a continuing supply of immigrants. Cricket and rugby were different. Although immigrants did provide some of the sustaining membership, their continuing presence was due to their adoption by the Canadian private schools, the universities on both coasts, and, to a limited degree, the Anglican Church. All three, then, were related to the strength of the British presence.

None of the sports was central to the growth of Canadian amateur sport. Only soccer played any role in the establishment of the AAUC (1909) and even then its affiliation was of a temporary nature. Soccer was rooted in a different segment of society – the British working class – and its relationship with amateur sport was already a troubled one. Also, none of the sports managed to establish strong national organizations, so that they had greater difficulty than most in establishing a national presence. These games were always recognized as being British and therefore were rejected as such by the Canadian leaders of amateur sport and by the Canadian media. Yet, it must be recognized that for a large segment of young males soccer was the game. A large, if indeterminate, segment of Canadian society identified with games that were, by definition, non-Canadian.

AMERICAN SPORT: BASEBALL

If any one game was played in the hamlets, villages, towns, and cities across the length and breadth of Canada, it was the American game of baseball. Certainly it was played and watched by more people than any other sport. Its dominant position is reflected in its position on the sports pages of the country's major newspapers in 1915. In Halifax, baseball placed first with 37.6 per cent of the sports coverage. Similarly, it was the most reported sport in Montreal (18.6 per cent), Winnipeg (21.2 per cent), and Edmonton (32 per cent). In Toronto, it represented 23.5 per cent and was second.[81] In the period following Confederation baseball moved to the Prairies with the first settlers. Thus, the history of baseball was different from the other sports. On only two counts was it the same: the development of inter- and intra-city leagues and the difference between urban and rural areas. Its history was different on several important accounts: the American influence; the intrusion of the professional element; the lack of local, provincial, and national organizations; and the groups who played baseball.

Games resembling baseball involving organized teams can be traced back to 1838.[82] During the 1850's various teams, playing local rules, emerged in the area to the west of Toronto, in particular in Hamilton and Woodstock. The first inter-city game was played between a Toronto team and one from Hamilton in 1859. From this date the move to standardize rules can be dated. In the 1860's the game gained popularity among the working class of Hamilton and in towns such as Ingersoll and Dundas. By the early 1870's, baseball clubs had been formed throughout Ontario.[83] By 1876, the Ontario clubs finally adopted the New York rules and thus the stage was set for the real development of competitive baseball.[84] During the 1870's, too, clubs emerged in other parts of Canada. In 1872, the first French-Canadian club in Montreal, appropriately named the Jacques Cartier, was formed.[85] Clubs were in existence in Victoria and Winnipeg by 1875.[86] In the Maritimes, Saint John and Halifax boasted teams by the late 1870's. By the 1880's, the game had spread to rural areas of Canada. Villages like Ruthven and Woodslee in Essex County, Ontario, had teams.[87] In Manitoba, baseball clubs were formed soon after the first settlers moved into an area.[88] The larger urban areas witnessed the development of intra-town leagues; Halifax, Saint John, Toronto, Winnipeg, and Victoria all had leagues by 1889.[89] During the 1890's, a variety of leagues involving small towns linked by railway began to emerge in the Maritimes and Ontario. For instance, in 1895 four new leagues were formed in Ontario: the Niagara District League, the Georgian Bay Baseball League, the Halton County League, and the Waterloo County Baseball League.

These leagues, like those in the cities, were characterized by baseball's basic malady – instability. Few of the leagues in rural or urban areas lasted for more than a few years. Baseball was plagued by a lack of stability in clubs, leagues, and organizations, but this did not appear to retard the development of the game in the twentieth century. The early 1900's witnessed the massive expansion of clubs, intra-city and inter-city leagues, and the involvement of various institutions in the promotion of the game. It had developed to such an extent that intra-town leagues were to be found in Oxbow, Saskatchewan, and Kamloops, British Columbia.[90] At a less organized level it had reached Normandin, Quebec, Shediac, New Brunswick, Grenfell, Saskatchewan, and High River, Alberta.[91] If "Canadian" is to be measured by number of teams and presence throughout Canada, then baseball must truly be called the Canadian game.

There was a significant difference between baseball played in the urban areas and that played in the rural areas, in particular in rural Ontario and the Prairies. The rural game remained tied to a different form of competition more in line with the origins of the game and the realities of rural life. The demands of farming, its seasonal nature, and the lack of regularly scheduled free time militated against the development of regularly scheduled competitions. Thus, baseball tended to be associated with particular communal events such as May 24, Dominion Day, and Labour Day. Baseball became part of the communal celebrations and a vehicle for the demonstration of community spirit.[92] As a result, until the war baseball retained the traditional forms of competition in rural areas, with challenges and exhibitions remaining the popular forms. As part of community life, it played a central role at the village celebrations of national holidays and at the annual village picnics, yet it also developed as a competitive sport. In this, it continued the practices of the 1850's and 1860's in adopting the tournament as a major form of competition. In nearly every instance, tournaments were played for a money prize, and this was to separate baseball from the mainstream of amateur sport. There were various levels of tournaments depending on the money prizes offered, from the $15 at a tournament in Huron County, Ontario, to $500 at the Calgary tournament in 1905.[93] Tournaments, although present in all parts of the country, were most popular in Ontario, the Prairies, and the interior of British Columbia. For example, in Norfolk County, Ontario, they were popular throughout the period 1889-1915. Village rivalries developed and could on occasion become violent. As late as 1915, twelve village teams competed in eight different tournaments between May 27 and August 19.[94]

Baseball, in the areas outside the urban centres, played an important role in the lives of the communities. It provided a vehicle for the demonstration of community pride and spirit. Nowhere was this more clearly demonstrated than in the rivalry between three small settlements on the North Thompson River, thirty miles north of Kamloops. In the summer of 1915, teams from Mt. Olie, Chu-Chua, and Barriere took to the baseball diamond to defend their honour at the Mt. Olie Dominion Day celebration, the Barriere Fair, and on two other occasions.[95] Examples of similar local rivalries could be found in nearly any rural area of Canada at the end of the nineteenth century. Only in rural Quebec and the Maritimes do such rivalries seem to have been missing.

The system of exhibition and challenge matches was not restricted to the rural areas but was a central part of the competitive system in the urban areas as well. In this respect baseball was different from the other games in that such matches maintained a place far longer. This was reflected by the degree to which non-league teams outnumbered league teams. In Victoria in 1889, non-league teams outnumbered league teams nine to three.[96] A similar pattern was to be found across the country: Saint John, 60 to 9 in 1895; Winnipeg, 100 to 26 in 1905; and Montreal, 150 to 71 in 1915.[97] Thus, baseball was significantly different from the other sports in that its movement toward league competition came at a slower rate.

Obviously, too, baseball differed from the other sports in its American orientation. From the first adoption of the New York rules in 1876, Canadian baseball always maintained a strong link with the United States.[98] The form and nature of the American presence varied both geographically and over time, but it was an ongoing influence. While other sports promoted East-West relations through the promotion of national championships, baseball always followed North-South lines: the Maritimes with the New England states, Ontario and Quebec with adjacent states; the Prairies with Minnesota and North Dakota; and the West Coast with the state of Washington. This connection, in its most visible form, was reflected in the newspaper coverage given to the American professional leagues. Between 1895 and 1915, over 50 per cent of baseball coverage in Halifax, Montreal, Toronto, Winnipeg, and Edmonton was devoted to the U.S.-based leagues.[99] In terms of actual contact it was most pronounced in the acquisition of franchises in the U.S. professional leagues. The first city to gain a franchise was Toronto (1886), followed by Montreal (1897), Winnipeg (1902), and Victoria and Vancouver (1905).

For the smaller towns and cities contact was maintained through competition against American teams. These took the form of challenges, exhibition games, or league competition. The first of these international contests were in Ontario in the 1860's. In the 1870's these competitions spread through western Ontario and Quebec. For example, in August, 1872, the Boston Red Stockings visited Montreal and beat a local team, 63-3.[100] By 1874, the Guelph Baseball Club had gained such a reputation that the *Acadian Reporter*, hardly a local newspaper, commented on its victories over American opposition.[101] The famous Tecumsehs of London played a return match against the Hartfords of Brooklyn in front of 2,800 spectators in May, 1877.[102] In both Windsor and Montreal, teams competed regularly with teams from the neighbouring states. Throughout the 1880's and 1890's these contacts were maintained and expanded until teams from all parts of Canada were playing teams from neighbouring states. In the late 1880's and early 1890's, visiting college and town teams from Vermont, Maine, and Massachusetts were regular visitors to the larger towns of Nova Scotia and New Brunswick. Teams from Saint John, Fredericton, Moncton, and Halifax reciprocated by journeying south.[103] In 1895, Le Club de Baseball du National of Montreal visited Plattsburgh, New York.[104] Teams from Winnipeg regularly played teams from Fargo, North Dakota, Crookston, Minnesota, and other towns. On the West Coast, in 1889, the Victoria Amities received a visit from a Port Townsend team to help celebrate the Queen's birthday at Beacon Hill Park in front of 8,000 spectators.[105] Later in the year, the Amities undertook a tour during which they visited Port Townsend, Portland, Seattle, and Tacoma.[106] Throughout the latter years of the nineteenth century there was a continual flow of teams back and forth across the border. In the border towns the contact was even greater, teams often competing in international leagues. Such was the case early in the twentieth century in Windsor and Sault Ste. Marie.[107] However, it must be emphasized that the intensity of the interaction varied: the further one was removed from the border the weaker the American presence became.

In the early 1900's with the expansion of local teams and competitive opportunities, the American presence became limited to professional and semi-professional teams in Ontario, Quebec, Manitoba, and British Columbia. In other provinces, American touring teams appeared frequently. The nature of these teams is illustrated most vividly in the 1905 tour of the Boston Bloomer Girls. Travelling in a special railcar and accompanied by their own brass band, half a dozen young women and three male professionals journeyed through New Brunswick, Nova Scotia,

Quebec, and Ontario in August and September, playing local teams in large and small towns.[108] In the same year, an Edmonton team played a visiting theatrical company, the Hottest Coons in Dixie.[109] There were a variety of types of tours: in 1914 an American women's team beat the boys from Wolseley, Saskatchewan;[110] in 1915, two coloured teams, the Harvard Red Sox and Cuban Giants, toured Ontario and Quebec;[111] in British Columbia, the Alabama Giants paraded through Kamloops with their own orchestra and male quartet before beating a local team.[112] Canadians thus were always aware of the American roots of baseball.

Money, in the form of prizes or payment for services, has always been an essential part of sport. In the developmental years of organized sport, it played a pivotal role and served as the main mechanism for differentiating between amateurs and professionals.[113] The money problem, or professionalism, pervaded baseball more than any other sport. Not only were there professional and semi-professional teams, but money was also part of the game through the whole hierarchy of baseball, from the Toronto professional team to the community teams in Manitoba and Saskatchewan. This pervasiveness of money served to alienate baseball from the mainstream of amateur sport. In baseball, money was never regarded as an unmitigated evil; in fact, it was a part of the game, and the majority of tournaments and challenges involved money prizes. From this central root of money two divergent branches developed: full-blown professionalism on the one hand and the emergence of amateur baseball early in the twentieth century on the other. The professional or money element, then, was central to baseball's development.

The development of semi-professional teams and players imported from outside the local area serves to illustrate the depth to which the professional element reached. The first instance of imported players occurred in 1873 when Guelph brought in two players from the States.[114] This soon spread to teams in London and Stratford. By 1878, there was a short-lived Canadian Baseball Players Association and, according to one source, the first professional player in Toronto was Bob Emslie who, in 1878, was paid the grand sum of $1.50 a game.[115] During the 1880's the payment of money spread across the country and professionals and amateurs played on the same teams. In the Maritimes, there were teams with pros in Fredericton, Moncton, Saint John, and Halifax.[116] The nature and extent of professionalism is exemplified by the Saint John Amateur Athletic Association. During the 1889 season, the team played forty-five games against touring U.S. teams, local competition, and other teams in New Brunswick and Nova Scotia. The Saint John team included nine professionals plus several amateurs. The total wages for the season were $2,260.72, with the payments varying from $25 to $475.[117] This practice continued during the 1890's but all but disappeared in the early 1900's. By 1905, the players on the Saint John team were being paid on a percentage basis only.[118] By 1915, Halifax, with two pro teams, was the only city in the Maritimes offering professional baseball.[119]

The example of the Maritimes is not an isolated one. A similar pattern can be seen in British Columbia during the same period. In 1889, the Victoria Amities accepted a challenge from Port Townsend to play for $1,000. Later in the year they joined Port Townsend and Vancouver in a tournament in Kamloops in which the home team was accused of "importing players from Minneapolis."[120] Professional teams flourished in Victoria and Vancouver and, in 1905, joined a fully professional league. The experience of Ontario and western Quebec was different. Full professional baseball arrived much earlier with the entrance of Toronto into a U.S. league in 1886. This was followed by the emergence of semi-professional leagues in the smaller towns and cities of Ontario. In Ontario, professionalism, or payment, ran deeper. It was evidenced in the desire of small communities to have the best team, which led to the importation of players. In 1889, the Canadian Atlantic Railway Baseball Club of Ottawa secured players from Vermont and New York to bolster the local "battery."[121] The village of Lifford, near Peterborough, imported players from Toronto and Peterborough in 1895.[122] By 1905, Spencerville, champions of the Saint Lawrence Counties, included players from four neighbouring towns and one from as far away as Hamilton.[123] In Sault Ste. Marie, the baseball club claimed that its third baseman had been lured to Chapleau by the offer of a job.[124] Thus, payment in one form or another permeated the small and large towns of Ontario and, in fact, all of Canada.

One of the attributes that tied ice hockey, football, soccer, and lacrosse together was the development of local, provincial, and national organizations. By 1915, they all, to some degree, fell under the jurisdiction of the Amateur Athletic Union of Canada. Baseball was different. A cursory examination of newspapers from the 1870's might lead one to the conclusion that baseball must have had a sophisticated organizational system. There were a variety of local, provincial, and national championships – at least, teams claiming such titles. They varied from the Amateur Championship of Western Ontario in 1889 to the Indian Championship of British Columbia, to the baseball championship of the Saint Lawrence Counties in 1905.[125] Added to these were a bewildering array of village, district, city, and provincial championships. The reality was that there was no organization and each was a strictly local affair, rarely involving more than ten teams. This is illustrated, in 1905, in the formation of the Province of Quebec Amateur Baseball Association. It consisted of twenty-seven clubs, twenty from the city of Montreal and seven from the immediate environs.[126] It was provincial in name only. The central reason for this state of affairs was the lack of permanence and continuity of teams and leagues. Prior to 1900, few teams lasted for more than a few years, many only existing for a single season. Of 163 intra-city leagues that sprang up in fifteen towns and cities across Canada from 1889 to 1915, only four – in Saint John, Peterborough, Ottawa, and Toronto – had any degree of longevity.[127] Thus, from the grassroots level, there was little stability.

The reasons for this apparent instability are difficult to identify; they may lie in the composition of the social groups who played, or in the lack of middle-class involvement, or in the lack of institutional promotion of the game. The experience of Vancouver in 1915 may have been typical of baseball across the country. Lacking any leadership, the players formed a commission to run the city leagues. In Vancouver, the game was organized and run by the players, not by ex-players and older men as was the case in other sports. In this case, there would be a lack of continuity because of the yearly turnover of executives, as old players retired and new ones moved in. Whatever the reasons for organizational instability, just prior to the war the first signs of relatively permanent local and provincial organizations emerged. Interestingly, there is little evidence of organization east of Manitoba. Only in Toronto, with the formation of the Toronto Amateur Baseball Association in 1913, is there any indication that an organization tried to organize all of baseball within a certain locale. In the West, the Winnipeg Amateur Baseball Association had been formed to co-ordinate the game in the city;[128] Saskatchewan was a step ahead with the formation of the Amateur Baseball Association of Saskatchewan; in Alberta, tentative discussions were taking place within the Alberta Branch of the AAUC with the object of forming an Alberta Amateur Baseball Association.[129] Thus, baseball in the West at last began to move within the orbit of amateur sport. Yet this lack of organizational structure does not appear to have hindered the popularity and health of the game. It was, by 1915, undoubtedly the most widely played game in Canada – surely a telling comment on amateur sport.

In yet another respect baseball was different from the other sports. At some time during the nineteenth century groups from all levels of society took to the baseball diamond to demonstrate their prowess either in exhibitions, challenges, or leagues or for charity. Barbers, butchers, bankers, doctors, lawyers, engineers, spinners, dyers, mechanics, actors, and hotel workers all played baseball. It was promoted by colleges, universities, schools, churches, temperance societies, unions, factories, commercial enterprises, banks, and theatres. Baseball was the only game played by all Canadian social classes. However, there were distinct regional differences in who played. In Victoria the educational institutions maintained a central position in the game throughout the 1875-1915 period. On the other hand, in Ottawa the government offices always fielded teams and sponsored leagues. The working class was always present on the baseball diamonds of Saint John – longshoremen, foundry workers, conductors and motormen on the city railway, and others played on any spare ground they could find. Thus, baseball was characterized by local variations, and because of this it becomes virtually impossible to give an accurate picture for the whole of Canada.

There were, however, certain groups whose presence in other sports is more difficult to ascertain. In particular, there was significant participation in baseball by the working class, black Canadians, and French Canadians. Nowhere was the working-class presence more visible than on the baseball diamonds at union picnics, at tournaments, and in the popular challenge matches. The origins of baseball in Ontario lay within the pre-industrial working class,[130] and by the early 1860's the game was firmly rooted in working-class life in Hamilton.[131] In the 1870's it spread to the industrial towns of Ontario. In Montreal during the same period the majority of teams were located in working-class districts.[132] In all probability, working-class players were the majority of professionals and semi-professionals.

In Saint John throughout the nineteenth century, numerous teams challenged each other to play on the wharfs, corner lots, and any available ground. In these instances they tended to play against like groups: conductors versus motormen; spinners opposing dyers;

the longshoremen of the North Wharf against those of the South Wharf. Such contests were also part of the baseball environment in Montreal (1889-1915), Peterborough (1889-1895), Toronto (1875-1915), Simcoe (1889-1895), Goderich (1895), Winnipeg (1889-1915), and Brandon. These teams were characterized by a lack of permanence. Only with the development of leagues were the conditions created for stable organization. Leagues, with identifiable working-class teams, only emerged during the 1900's. Toronto, as usual, led the way with the inauguration of a Commercial League in the mid-1890's, although it is doubtful if this embraced truly working-class teams. Other commercial and mercantile leagues developed in Montreal (1905), Saint John (1905), Winnipeg (1905), Regina (1915), and Edmonton (1915). The only unequivocally working-class leagues were the manufacturing leagues in Montreal and Ottawa that emerged in 1915.[133] Thus, in terms of leagues, one of the hallmarks of organized sport, there was little evidence of substantive working-class involvement.

Another group, noticeable by its absence from the sporting scene, took to the baseball diamonds: the French Canadians in both Quebec and Manitoba. Although French-Canadian involvement in sport prior to the turn of the century was extremely limited, their involvement in baseball can be traced back to 1872 when the Jacques Cartier club was formed in Montreal. This club only lasted for one season but was followed by the Firefly and Saint Jean Baptiste teams in 1879, the Jeune Canadiens (1881), the Canadians of Ste. Cunegonde (1882), and the Patriot Baseball Club in 1884. This latter club gives us some idea who the young French-Canadian ballplayers were.

> The Patriot Baseball Club composed of young French Canadian lawyers and law students held their first practise on Sunday and had a large muster. Owing to the fact that the members are mostly old scholars of the large French Canadian schools where baseball is the favourite sport owing to the number of American students.[134]

This does suggest the route by which baseball entered French-Canadian life. The popularity of the game in the schools and colleges is born out by references to it being played at Saint Laurent College and Saint Mary College in Montreal and Nicolet College in Trois-Rivières (1876).[135] In these instances, baseball was limited to intra-college competition or games against other colleges. The first evidence of real growth occurred in the 1890's in Montreal. By 1895, teams had emerged in the French wards of the city and in neighbouring towns such as Joliette, Valleyfield, Lachute, and Saint Jerome.[136] During the next twenty years, the game spread to the far corners of the province – Rivière-du-Loup (1905), Coaticook (1905), and Lac Saint Jean (1915). However, there was one significant difference in baseball as played by the French Canadians. While the anglophone teams rapidly adopted the league system of play the French remained tied to the challenge system. By 1915, in Montreal, seventy-one teams were playing in seventeen leagues, the majority anglophone. Yet, during the week of June 1-8, over 142 teams issued challenges or announced games, and the vast majority of these were French. The French maintained an attachment to the form of competition most closely associated with rural life. This was not because they did not have the time, for many of the teams played weekly games. It was most likely their attachment to rural values that determined their choice.

One other group – black Canadians – graced the baseball diamond. The first evidence of "coloured" participation occurred in 1869, when a tournament in London, Ontario, included a class for "Colored citizens of U.S. and Canada."[137] However, the Maritimes was the only area of sustained involvement, where there were coloured teams in Saint John and Fredericton in 1889.[138] A few years later the Eurekas of Halifax played the Victorias of Truro for the coloured championship of Nova Scotia.[139] In 1905, the Royals of Amherst played Saint John for the championship of New Brunswick and Prince Edward Island.[140] It would appear that baseball retained a position among the black population. At the same time it perpetuated racial discrimination.

If baseball was a measure of American influence then that influence pervaded Canada and Canadian society. No other game reached into all areas and social groups of Canadian society. At the same time, no game was so recognizably identified with an alien culture. While players and spectators from all walks of life played, watched, and read about baseball, the game lay outside the mainstream of amateur sport. In addition, its organizational development was fragmented. Even by 1915, the organization of baseball was in an embryonic condition. Rejected by amateurs because of its links to professionalism and money, baseball was, by 1915, the summer sport of Canadians.

The period 1867 to 1914 witnessed significant changes in the nature of Canadian sport. By 1914, organized sport with leagues, championships, organizations, and standardized rules reached into all parts of Canada, rural and urban, French and English, East and West. It permeated all levels of society, providing common ground for Canadians of widely differing socio-economic and cultural backgrounds. However, its domination of the sporting life of Canada was not total. Traditional practices died hard and pre-industrial games and forms of competition exhibited a great degree of resiliency. The rural areas continued to favour exhibition games, challenge matches, and tournaments. Baseball and cricket rooted in pre-industrial game forms retained many of the earlier practices. As well, the French Canadians, eager participants in sport by the second decade of the twentieth century, remained attached to exhibition and challenge matches. Thus, organized sport across the nation was influenced by local conditions and the existence of different ethnic groups.

It is possible to identify some distinct developmental patterns that provide the basic elements necessary for an understanding of Canadian sport. First, in terms of the origins of various sports and the subsequent domination of national organizations, was the central role of Montreal. Without exception the games created in Canada were born and nurtured in Montreal. The domination of Montreal was soon challenged, however, by Toronto and the growing numerical strength of Ontario. While sport originated in Montreal, its real growth was rooted in Ontario. The Toronto-Montreal rivalry, eventually won by Toronto in 1909 with the founding of the AAUC, was one of the identifying characteristics of Canadian sport. At the same time, in the eyes of the developing Prairies and the East and West coasts, Ontario and Quebec domination of sport was an increasingly thorny problem. Canadian sport was transported to the Prairies by Ontario immigrants who took with them their newly acquired games. Thus, sport flowed across the Prairies with the railway and the tide of settlers. Sport in Manitoba and the Northwest Territories was given a different colour by the tide of British immigrants with their attachment to soccer and cricket. The West Coast and the Maritimes were subject to different influences. In each case, they were outposts of strong British influence in the form of garrisons and, in the case of British Columbia, immigrants. Neither ice hockey nor football gained a strong foothold in B.C. prior to the First World War. As for the French Canadians, their involvement parallelled the development of significant working-class participation. They adopted ice hockey and baseball with great enthusiasm but did not join the national amateur organizations that developed. The French, then, remained different from their anglophone counterparts. One factor was common across Canada – the domination of the large urban areas, especially with respect to the development of national organizations. This urban domination gave a particular pattern to Canadian development. Outside of Ontario and Quebec, organized sport tended to be dominated by one or at most two cities in each province. Hence, we have a picture of a Canada dominated at the highest level by Montreal and Toronto, while at the next level the various provinces were dominated by one or two cities. This was Canada.

Within the context of sport dominated by various provincial centres, did the term "Canadian" have any real meaning? The answer depends, to a large extent, on the criteria used to define "Canadian." If we measure "Canadian" by those sports created by Canadians, certain distinct patterns are evident. Ice hockey and Canadian football were created, developed, and promoted by the anglophone middle and upper class of Montreal and Toronto. Canadian football was a large-town phenomenon, for the most part limited to Ontario and western Quebec, but ice hockey was played across the length and breadth of Canada. Its phenomenal development in the late 1890's may have been due as much to the lack of alternative games as to its suitability. Unlike Canadian football and lacrosse, each of which fared less well, ice hockey faced no opposition – there were no other winter games. Perhaps more important to the history of Canadian sport were the creation and domination of amateur sport organizations by Montrealers and Torontonians. The various national bodies were created by Canadians. This was particularly important in the development of the AAUC. Many of its leading supporters came from the ranks of ice hockey, lacrosse, and Canadian football. Notable by their absence, or reluctance, were the organizers of soccer and baseball. Amateur sport in Canada was created by Canadians, in particular, by anglophones from Montreal and Toronto. Thus, if we accept a definition of "Canadian" based in organizational terms, a view of domination by Ontario and Quebec is a reality.

On the other hand, if we measure "Canadian" by the degree to which games were played, a different perspective emerges. By 1914 there were only two truly Canadian sports – ice hockey and baseball. Baseball had a much longer history than ice hockey, having been played across the country since Confederation. Ice hockey, on the other hand, was strictly limited until the 1890's, when it experienced great growth. In fact, the dominant position of baseball was even greater than hockey since it faced formidable rivals in soccer, cricket, lacrosse, rowing, and many other sports. Ice hockey had no rival except curling. By this definition, baseball was truly Canada's national sport. No other sports were played across the country and exhibited such steady and sometimes spectacular growth. Soccer and cricket experienced uneven development, ebbing and flowing in popularity. They depended on a continuing supply of British immigrants. Only in the Canadian private school was cricket given any strong support and thus it was as a society game that it had any degree of permanency. In fact, cricket experienced significant decline while soccer experienced many ups and downs. Such a perspective provides a picture of a dominant winter game born and bred in Canada and an American summer game overshadowing a variety of games whose success depended on a continuing flow of immigrants.

A final measurement of "Canadian" is the degree to which the game was played or watched by Canadians. In this case, only one game comes close to the criterion – baseball. All others drew their support from particular groups. Amateur sport drew its strongest support from the white-collar segment of society. Until the turn of the century, sport was essentially anglophone. The working class and women, although maintaining some presence, were, for the most part, relegated to the sidelines. Organized team sport, then, did not permeate all levels of Canadian society; in terms of participation, it was limited to specific groups in specific locations. Ideally one should have been an anglophone, white-collar worker, and Protestant located in an urban area. This combination of characteristics fit only a small proportion of Canadian society.

Canadian sport cannot be characterized by a single definition. By 1914 it reflected the complexity of Canada and Canadian society. There were regional variations, differences between urban and rural, and ethnic differences. What can be said is that amateur sport, which exerted such a powerful influence on all sport, was a creation of the anglophone, Protestant middle class of Ontario and Quebec. This group of people created the organizations that exerted the influence.

4

The Growth of Organizations and the Development of Amateurism

By 1914, nearly every village, town, and city across Canada could boast a variety of sporting teams. For the most part, these teams lived a brief existence before succumbing and being replaced by other teams. In most instances they remained purely local concerns, providing recreation and leisure activities for an increasing number of Canadians. However, from as early as the 1850's, there is evidence of a more serious purpose to sport – the crowning of a champion. From baseball in the 1850's to lacrosse in the 1860's, to football in the 1870's and ice hockey in the 1880's, the emergence of teams in various cities and provinces led to a proliferation of so-called "champions." These "championships" were primarily regional, but sometimes organizations attempted to establish more broadly based championships and laid claim to the title "Champion of Canada." The activities of these organizations brought some degree of cohesion to the growing chaos in sport. While the 1880's and 1890's witnessed the emergence of local and provincial organizations across the country, a group of so-called "national" organizations played the most important role in the development of amateur sport. Within this small group of organizations Canadian amateur sport was forged. Without denying the importance of local and provincial organizations, we must now turn to the national organizations.

An understanding of the origins and development of these organizations is important on two counts. First, the men who created and controlled the organizations determined the foundations of amateur sport and the framework within which it would be played. They determined the rules to be followed, the form of the game adopted, who should or should not play, and the all-important definition of an amateur. In other words, they created the structure of sport and articulated its underlying rationale. Their greatest, and possibly most destructive, contribution was the definition of an amateur, which served to exclude large segments of Canadian males from participating in amateur sport. This provided a focus of agreement for amateur sportsmen across the country and served to dampen the forces of regional discontent and the drive for autonomy of individual sports. These forces of regional discontent and autonomy underlay the second reason for the importance of understanding the origins of the organizations. The history of the truly national organizations reveals the geographical and social foundations of Canadian amateur sport. In particular, groups of men from Montreal, Toronto, and some of the larger Ontario towns were at the centre of the movement to create national organizations, so that the history of the growth of these organizations is central to an understanding of Canadian amateur sport – they created the structure and ideology that has influenced amateur sport to the present day. The history of these national organizations also illustrates particular Canadian patterns of development.

Local and provincial organizations were central to the development of sport in certain localities but rarely did they have an impact beyond their immediate geographical area. Those organizations that laid claim to being "national" had the potential for impact on the Canadian scene. As Table 4 indicates, during the 1880's a number of national organizations emerged. During the next thirty years various others were founded. By the outbreak of World War I at least twelve organizations claimed to have jurisdiction over particular sports. This limited number of organizations provided a degree of coherence to Canadian sport.

A number of factors were common to all the organizations. In every case the stimulus to organization came from within the upper and middle classes. Lawyers, bankers, university professors, doctors, businessmen, newspapermen, and civil servants held the majority of executive positions. Thus, amateur sport was organized within the context of the values of the middle class, and these values proved a common bond among sportsmen across Canada and served to soften regional aspirations for autonomy. Not only were the organizers middle class but they were drawn from the urban areas. Without exception, the organizations were formed in central Canada, in particular, Montreal and Toronto. By the first decade of the new century Winnipeg also began to play a significant role on the national scene. Finally, with one or two notable exceptions, the organizations were national in name only,

Table 4
National Sport Organizations, 1867-1914

Organization	Date Founded	Location of Original Membership	Date National
National Lacrosse Association *became*	1867	Ontario and Quebec	
National Amateur Lacrosse Association	1880		
Canadian Association of Amateur Oarsmen	1880	Ontario and Quebec	
Canadian Wheelman's Association (Bicycling)	1882	Ontario and Quebec	1890*
Amateur Athletic Association of Canada *became*	1884	Ontario and Quebec	
Canadian Amateur Athletic Association *became* Amateur Athletic Union of Canada	1898 1909	Ontario and Quebec	1909
Canadian Lawn Tennis Association	1884		1900*
Canadian Rugby Football Union	1884	Ontario and Quebec	
Canadian Lacrosse Association	1887	Ontario	
Canadian Cricket Association	1892		1892
Royal Canadian Golf Association	1895	Ontario and Quebec	1910*
Canadian Canoe Association	1900	Ontario and Quebec	
Canadian Amateur Swimming Association	1909	Montreal	1914
Dominion Football Association (Soccer)	1912		1912
Canadian Amateur Lacrosse Association	1914		1914
Canadian Amateur Hockey Association	1914		1914

*Approximate date.

their membership being drawn from Ontario and anglophone Quebec: not until the twentieth century was there significant expansion beyond the boundaries of central Canada. Therefore, the use of the title "Canadian" or "National" served to obscure the reality that they were, for the most part, the exclusive preserve of the urban, anglophone middle class of central Canada – a far cry from truly Canadian organizations.

The differences between organizations served to distinguish those that were peripheral from those that were central to the development of mass sport. In the first place, there was a clear distinction between those created to organize and co-ordinate the competitions of members and those whose objective was control. Lawn tennis, golf, cricket, and canoeing were the preserve of a small, select group of middle- and upper-class Canadians. If any of the officially organized sports drew from a wider social base, they were the team sports of lacrosse, soccer, and ice hockey. Even in these sports, the organizations were national in name only prior to 1910. At the same time, the emergence of professionalism between 1895 and 1905 was instrumental in the creation of the first truly national organization in 1909, the Amateur Athletic Union of Canada. The AAUC, with representation from every province and by 1912 embracing 1,300 clubs and over 100,000 individual members, was the most important and powerful organization in amateur sport. In fact, its jurisdiction was such that a majority of the individual sport governing bodies were affiliates and even those that remained outside its jurisdiction could not ignore it. Its power permeated all sport.

THE AMATEUR ATHLETIC UNION OF CANADA

On Saturday evening, November 27, 1909, the first annual meeting of the Amateur Athletic Union of Canada was held, appropriately, in the King Edward Hotel, Toronto.[1] This represented both a beginning and an end: the beginning of a new era, during which the AAUC became the absolute arbiter of amateur status in Canada, and the end of a period of nearly unbelievable chaos in the world of sport. It was one of those pivotal moments in history when decisions are taken that determine the road to be followed in the foreseeable future. It signified not only the establishment of the underlying principles of amateurism but also a shift in the locus of decision-making in amateur sport. Thus, the AAUC stands at a crossroads in the history of sport in Canada. To understand its full significance and the forces that led to its formation, it is necessary to turn to the 1870's, for during that decade the spectre of professionalism was first addressed by sport organizations. In particular, the actions of the Canadian Association of Amateur Oarsmen (CAAO) in 1880 and the formation of the Amateur Athletic Association of Canada (AAAC) in 1884 provided the foundations upon which all subsequent confrontations with professionalism were based.

The history of rowing in Canada can be traced back to the early 1800's when, because of the limited number of oarsmen, the dividing line between amateurs and professionals was never a major stumbling block to participation. By the late 1860's and 1870's, with the expansion of both professional and amateur rowing, the question of distinguishing between different competitors became a real concern. The event that signified the real beginnings of amateur rowing was an action taken by the Toronto Argonaut Rowing Club in 1872. In that year, the Argonauts inaugurated a revolutionary practice, the buying of boats by the club for its members. The provision of shells, clubhouses, and training and social facilities ushered in the era of amateur rowing clubs. The Argonauts were joined by two Toronto clubs and one each from Hamilton, Belleville, and Windsor. Then a number of amateur clubs were seeking competition.

This development was parallelled by the rise of professional rowing to its greatest heights. The 1870's and 1880's were the finest years for professional rowing throughout the world. Canadians were at the forefront, with the Paris crew of Saint John, New Brunswick, George Brown of Herring Cove, Nova Scotia, and the incomparable Ned Hanlan of Toronto rowing for the world championship on courses in England, France, Australia, the United States, and Canada. Therefore, during the 1870's the number of races and regattas held on the waterways of Canada increased. This growing popularity and international contact led to expressions of concern over the differences between amateurs and professionals. A direct result of this concern was the formation of the CAAO in 1880. The most important action taken at the first meeting was an attempt to define what an amateur was. The following definition was incorporated into the group's by-laws:

An amateur is one who has never assisted in the pursuit of athletic exercises as a means of livelihood, who rows for pleasure or recreation only and during his leisure hours, and does not abandon or neglect his usual business or occupation for the purpose of training more than two weeks during the season.[2]

In terms of rowing, this definition effectively achieved the required differentiation between amateurs and professionals, and the subsequent history of rowing was one of relative harmony between professionals and amateurs. However, the importance of the definition rests not so much in the history of rowing as in the fact that it was the first definition of "amateur" developed by Canadians. As such, it was used as the basis of all future definitions and consequently was crucial to the growth of amateur sport in Canada. Its importance lay in the fact that it failed to do what it set out to do, that is, define what an amateur was. What it did was to say what an amateur was not. This negative approach to amateurism became the Canadian approach to the problem of professionalism. The definition and approach were the foundation stones of a small but important organization formed in 1884, the AAAC.

The founding meeting of the AAAC was held in the rooms of the Toronto Fencing Club on April 11, 1884; the decisions that determined its course until 1909 had been taken in the months immediately preceding the inaugural meeting. The idea of a national amateur athletic association was the brainchild of a small group of Montrealers who were members of the Montreal Amateur Athletic Association (MAAA), formed in 1881. These dedicated amateurs were concerned with the increasing evidence of professionalism in sport, in particular on the lacrosse fields. They banded together in what appeared to have been a deliberate effort to guide amateur sport down their own chosen path. In November, 1883, three leading sportsmen, W. Maltby, H. Becket, and H. Paton, sent a circular to various athletic clubs in the Dominion inviting them to attend a meeting at the clubhouse of the MAAA on December 14, 1883, for the purpose of forming a national association.[3] Twelve clubs endorsed the idea but because of the shortness of notice only five attended, one from Toronto and four from Montreal. In fact, the meeting was dominated by members of the MAAA since two of the clubs were affiliates of the MAAA and another was comprised of MAAA members.[4]

The December meeting, which was little more than a meeting of MAAA members, took actions that ensured that the proposed organization would be a replica of the MAAA and reflect the values of its membership. The first was the establishment of a committee to draft a constitution and by-laws for the governance of the organization. Three Torontonians, one from Ottawa, and five from Montreal were voted onto the committee. The meeting then voted that the constitution should be drafted by the Montreal members and submitted to the others for approval. The Montrealers then sought to ensure that the association should only be open to clubs that accepted their views on amateur sport. George R. Starke and Angus Grant, both of the MAAA, moved and seconded

> That the membership of the Association shall be limited to amateur athletic clubs and to such clubs as shall hold during each year one outdoor athletic meeting containing at least three events open to amateurs. They shall also have embodied in their bylaws, the definition of an amateur as adopted by this association.[5]

The passage of this motion guaranteed that the membership would be strictly limited. In particular, it discriminated against powerful clubs, such as the Shamrock Lacrosse Club, while allowing membership to its rival, the Montreal Lacrosse Club, which was affiliated with the MAAA. Thus, amateur sport was to be the exclusive preserve of a particular social group. This was reinforced by the requirement that member clubs must incorporate what was, in effect, the MAAA definition of an amateur.

When twelve Ontario and six Montreal clubs met in Toronto in April, 1884, to form the AAAC, the Montreal constitution and by-laws were passed without change. The only challenge came from Hamilton and Kingston, who wanted to have the location of the annual championship decided at the annual meetings. The power brokers, Montreal and Toronto, joined to crush the challenge, 25-4, and thus the original draft alternating the championship between Montreal and Toronto was adopted. The acceptance of the committee's definition of an amateur and the Montreal by-laws laid the foundations of amateur sport and power for the next twenty years. In adopting the definition of an amateur, the association followed the exclusionary precedent set by the CAAO rather than attempting to define what an amateur really was:

> An amateur is one who has never competed for a money prize, or staked bet or with or against any professional for any prize,

or who has never taught, pursued, or assisted in the practise of athletic exercises as a means of obtaining a livelihood.[6]

This definition was incorporated into all future definitions.

The by-laws, adopted by the meeting, served to institutionalize Montreal power. Article V, relating to executive membership, gave the MAAA control of the association. Since the MAAA was represented by three separate clubs, Article V, which allowed "Not more than two members of the executive committee" to be elected from one club, meant that the executive could, as happened, include up to six members from the MAAA. In addition, the MAAA in effect was able to veto any new members as a result of Article VI, which required that new members must gain the approval of two-thirds of the executive. Finally, Article IX, which gave extra voting members to clubs with over 100 members, ensured that the MAAA had a block of nine votes, and this effectively gave it control of the AAAC. It is difficult to escape the conclusion that the creation of the AAAC was no accident but rather a well-conceived plan to create a so-called national body run by members of the Montreal Amateur Athletic Association.

A final insight into the real objectives of the AAAC organizers is contained in the organization's stated objectives. Ostensibly, the AAAC was formed to organize track and field competition in Canada. However, as the official report of the inaugural meeting revealed, in the minds of the delegates there was some confusion over the actual objectives of the organization. The official report included a revealing passage that stated:

A number of cricket, football, lacrosse and bicycle clubs appointed delegates to the meeting thus concluded under the misapprehension that the association was intended to cover all aspects of sports. The end of the association, as was made clear by several speeches during the meeting is simply to regulate such athletic sports in Canada as are not now under the control of other associations, the aim of the Canadian Amateur Athletic Association is mainly to cover amateur competitions on the cinder track.[7]

Was the organization to control track and field, or did it aim to consider the broader question of amateurism? Not one of the twenty-four clubs attending meetings in 1883, 1884, and 1885 had as its declared function the promotion of track and field. Here was an organization theoretically created to control a sport of which not one of the member clubs' main orientation was that sport. Whether Maltby, Becket, Grant, Paton, and Starke recognized this or not, within a short time the main thrust of the organization was the protection of amateurism. At the first annual meeting on September 27, 1884, the main report dealt with nine applications for reinstatement of amateur status. The die was cast, and the central function of the AAAC became the supervision of amateur sport rather than the promotion of track and field.

Appropriately, William L. Maltby became the first president of the association and that indefatigable worker in the cause of amateurism, Hugh Wiley Becket, the secretary. Montreal controlled both the executive and the council. During the first two years the only clubs represented at each of the meetings were the three powers in amateur sport, the MAAA, its affiliate the Montreal Snow Shoe Club, and the Toronto Lacrosse Club. The two-to-one split between Montreal and Toronto reflected the reality of power in Canadian sport. Despite the challenge of Toronto, Montreal reigned supreme, and, through the MAAA, placed an indelible imprint on amateur sport. Although this changed during the next two decades as the distribution of power altered, nothing can detract from the foundations laid by the MAAA and men like William Maltby and Hugh Becket.

From its inception in 1884 until 1906 the Amateur Athletic Association of Canada was a small organization limited for the most part to Ontario and Montreal. Supposedly created to control track and field in Canada, the membership was drawn from a far wider segment of the sporting community, with lacrosse, snowshoe, rowing, skating, and hockey clubs joining the two or three amateur athletic associations. Throughout its history it was plagued by instability of membership. Because of this, the two organizations with continuous membership were influential in determining the policies adopted by the AAAC. The MAAA, the sole continuing member from its beginning, was the most influential and powerful amateur organization in Canada. Not far behind in power, prestige, and continuous service was the Toronto Police Amateur Athletic Association (1885). So the natural rivalry of Toronto and Montreal was present. In addition, with few exceptions, the association included only Ontario and Quebec clubs. In fact, the membership was even more localized with Toronto and Montreal dominating throughout the 1890's. While Toronto membership was dispersed among a variety of different organizations, the Montreal contingent was invariably dominated by the MAAA, so that the AAAC remained to a large extent closely allied to the MAAA until the fatal confrontation of 1906.

Although in terms of numbers there was little change between 1884 and 1906, the twenty-two-year period can be divided into two distinct eras, 1884-1896 and 1897-1906. During the first period, any claim to being a national organization was simply a figment in the minds of the organizers. Apart from the temporary affiliation of three Maritime clubs in 1886 and 1887 and of the British Columbia Lacrosse Association in 1893, the membership was drawn entirely from Ontario and Quebec. Yet, as we will see, there was some justification for the national title.

The main objective of the association was to cover track, which until then had no central organization to codify rules and control meets. More intriguing, because of its nebulous nature, was the aim of regulating other amateur sports not under the control of other associations. The question was, what sports? The obvious ones – lacrosse, soccer, football, rowing, and bicycling – all fell under the control of other organizations and thus lay outside the jurisdiction of the AAAC. To answer this question, then, we need to turn to the actual actions of the AAAC to see how its mandate was interpreted in the real world of amateur sport.

The AAAC faithfully controlled amateur competition on the cinder track and in this sphere it could, with some justification, claim to be a national organization. In terms of active involvement in track and field, this was limited to holding the annual championship that alternated between Toronto and Montreal. Its other function was as an information centre on the organization of track meets, and in this role it was recognized as a national body: letters of inquiry from all over the country were sent to the AAAC. However, this was a weak justification for claiming to be a "national" organization. The executive was aware of this deficiency and took concrete, but unsuccessful, steps to remedy the situation. In 1890, the secretary, W.S. Weldon (MAAA), reported on one such effort:

> Your local committee deemed it advisable to draft a circular and distribute it among the various clubs in the Dominion, with a view to soliciting their membership.... This was duly done and some one hundred clubs and associations communicated with, but up to the present we regret to say that no apparent results have been attained.[8]

For whatever reason, over 100 clubs throughout Canada saw no merit in joining, a rather illuminating comment on its "national" aspirations.

By far the most important function of the new organization was as a regulator and arbiter of amateur status, an objective that was stated at the first meeting. The AAAC promoted itself as the ultimate arbiter of amateur status in sports other than track and field. In fact, the question of reinstatements was practically the sole concern of executive meetings between 1886 and 1888. Of the sixteen executive meetings held in either Montreal or Toronto, twelve dealt exclusively with reinstatement of amateurs and only three had substantial portions of the meetings devoted to other concerns.[9] Even in the day-to-day work of answering correspondence, between 1890 and 1894, 103 of the 315 letters were concerned with amateur status.[10] This willingness, in fact, eagerness, to arbitrate questions of amateur status paid the greatest dividends between 1890 and 1896, when a most important precedent was set. The two premier lacrosse leagues, the Canadian Lacrosse Association and the Five-Team League, were beset by dissension over the question of professionalism. By the early 1890's the discussion had reached such a pitch that it threatened the integrity of the game. Both organizations turned to the AAAC to act as an impartial arbitrator on questions dealing with amateur status. The case of the Five-Team League was rather suspect in that the majority (three clubs), after defeating a motion by the Toronto and Montreal lacrosse clubs to have the AAAC act as an arbitrator, capitulated under the threat of withdrawal by the two clubs. What made it suspicious was the fact that both clubs were also members of the AAAC while the others were not. Hardly the impartial act of gentlemen! However, the precedent had been set – two larger organizations recognized the jurisdiction of the AAAC in matters of amateur status. This established the real foundation of a national amateur organization as the central controlling body for all sport.

Parallelling these moves to expand its area of jurisdiction were internal actions initiated by the MAAA to expand the role of the organization. In 1892, a subcommittee composed exclusively of MAAA members submitted an amendment to the constitution:

Article 2 Objects. The object of this association shall be the encouragement of systematic physical exercise and education in Canada. The advancement and improvement of athletic sports among amateurs.[11]

Although numerically weak, the AAAC was led by men with a lofty and, as it turned out, accurate vision of the growth of amateur sport and the need for an organization to lead in its development. As so often happened in Canadian amateur sport, the foresight of the Torontonians and Montrealers was not heeded. It was to be early in the twentieth century, when conditions in amateur sport overtook them, that clubs and leaders across the country recognized what some members of the AAAC had recognized in 1892.

In November, 1896, the annual meeting translated into words the actual work the association had been doing for the past twelve years and implemented the changes suggested by the 1892 subcommittee. At that meeting the constitution was revised to incorporate the actual function and change in role. Article II, Objects, was revised to include the following:

> The advancement and improvement of athletic sports among amateurs. The establishment and maintenance throughout Canada of a uniform test of amateur standing and uniform rules for the government of all athletic sports within its jurisdiction.[12]

The objects by this time had changed from regulation to advancement and improvement, and from track and field to an undetermined number of amateur sports. Perhaps the lack of a clearly defined list of sports reflected the precarious status of the association. The new, expansionary, and grandiose objective of being *the* amateur association in Canada was built on an inadequate and ever-changing base of clubs centred on Montreal and Toronto. At the same time, these objectives provided the association with a focus and direction that was to remain unchanged – that of being the central governing body of all amateur sport.

The changes, incorporated within the revised constitution of 1896, were reflected in practice during the ensuing years. In 1898 the organization changed its name to the Canadian Amateur Athletic Union (CAAU) to bring it into line with its American counterpart. Of greater significance was the action taken in 1902 to reduce the confusion over the sports the CAAU claimed to control:

> This Union recognizes all athletic sports, and claims jurisdiction over all track and field athletes, as well as those taking part in the following: basketball, bicycling, bowling (ten-pins),

handball, hockey, lacrosse, skating, snowshoeing, swimming, wrestling and rowing.[13]

At last, the constitution reflected the underlying objectives of the union. Instead of such nebulous terms as "all athletic sports within its jurisdiction," the CAAU had taken the final step in its claim to be the amateur governing body for Canada. Fundamental to the jurisdictional claim was its attempt to usurp the rights of other associations, in particular bicycling, lacrosse, and rowing. Obviously, its power and status within the world of amateur sport depended on the CLA, Five-Team League, CAAO, and DWA (Dominion Wheelman's Association) acquiescing to this usurpation of their powers. The tacit acceptance of CAAU jurisdiction by the lacrosse associations made it appear that the CAAU had won its battle to be the supreme arbiter of amateur status.

Yet, by 1906, the CAAU was a powerless organization limited to parts of Ontario and Quebec. The question is, why did this happen? The answer lies in the changing conditions within the world of sport, which destroyed the fragile foundations of the CAAU while allowing it to rise phoenix-like from its own ashes. At last, the conflict betweeen amateur and professional had reached such a degree of intensity that some solution had to be found. Whatever the solution, it was bound to establish the framework for the future development of sport: the actions taken at this juncture had an impact far beyond their apparent importance.

Even as the AAAC was revising its constitution in 1896, the problem of professionalism in amateur sport was escalating at such a pace that within six years it would become the only meaningful issue facing the CAAU. The denouement came in lacrosse and hockey. The signs that conditions were deteriorating were already present in the late 1890's. In 1897, the AAAC handled forty-seven cases of professionalism, mainly in lacrosse, a significant increase over earlier years.[14] The association could not ignore the growing signs of professionalism on the playing fields and took various steps to meet the threat. First, it increased the number of general rules from three to eighteen. This *ad hoc* approach to the problem attacked the symptoms but not the causes. The rules dealt with such things as athletes participating in meets conducted by companies, incorporated bodies, and individuals; competing when under suspension; Sunday competition; and professional contests at amateur meets.[15] The hasty improvision of rules to meet contingencies when they arose also characterized the CAAU approach to the problem and was highlighted in the 1902 redefinition of an amateur:

> An amateur is a person who has not competed in any competition for a staked bet, monies, private or public or gate receipts, or competed with or against a professional for a prize; who has never taught or assisted in the pursuit of any athletic exercise or sport as a means of livelihood; who has never, directly or indirectly, received any bonus or a payment in lieu of loss of time while playing as a member of any club, or any money consideration whatsoever for any services as an athlete except his actual travelling and hotel expenses, or who has never entered into any competition under a name other than his own, or who has never been guilty of selling or pledging his prizes.[16]

In actuality, nothing changed in the definition apart from the addition of further restrictive categories to meet the new evasions as they arose.

This approach did nothing toward solving the real problems. The CAAU efforts were characterized by a rigid adherence to the principle of pure amateurism, which equated any contact with professionals or with money, no matter how small the sum, as being sufficient cause to professionalize the individual, his team, and his opponents. The unyielding CAAU stance led to the confrontation that determined its future. In large part, the CAAU owed its increasingly powerful position in the world of amateur sport to the CLA and the National Amateur Lacrosse Union (NALU), both of which had delegated their authority on matters of amateur status to the CAAU.[17] Without this delegation of authority the CAAU would have remained a relatively powerless organization. By 1900, the situation in both leagues was such that the open professionalism of individual players was being accepted. Still relying on CAAU jurisdiction, both approached the CAAU to allow amateurs and professionals to play together on the same team without professionalizing everyone. The CAAU remained adamant in its position and refused even to consider the question. There were no negotiations or discussion. The two lacrosse leagues could not reverse their stance, with the result that by 1904 most of the senior teams had been professionalized by the CAAU. The CLA and NALU had no option but to terminate their agreement with the CAAU, thus removing the basis of its power. By its inflexibility on amateurism it lost everything that had been gained in the last twenty years. William Starke's comment that, by 1906, the CAAU was "a weak, uninfluential body, with a membership confined almost exclusively to the Province of Ontario" was, on the surface, an accurate assessment of the situation.[18] At the same time, conditions were ripe for the creation of a central association to bring some coherence to the increasingly chaotic situation. The lacrosse situation was limited to Ontario, Quebec, and British Columbia, but the recognition of the need for a central organizing body was countrywide. All that was required was an organization willing and able to provide the expertise and leadership, and the CAAU contained such expertise and men.

From 1896, the organization had actively promoted the development of provincial associations to affiliate with the parent association. Until 1906 these efforts had been in vain, but in that year, in a continuing effort to make the CAAU national in practice as well as theory, the president, Captain P. Gorman, went on a tour of the Maritimes, Manitoba, the Northwest Territories, and British Columbia.[19] For once, the CAAU made the right move at the right time – conditions were propitious to the enterprise and the tour was rewarded with unexpected success. Clubs across the country flocked to join the association. In one year the membership rose from thirty-six to 465.

Why should this particular initiative fall on fertile ground when repeated efforts in the past had met with no response? First, the acceptance of open professionalism in lacrosse and the inauguration of the first professional hockey league, in 1904, made visible what had been hidden from view. Open professionalism had come to the two major organized Canadian sports. This served as a catalyst to the rising concern over professionalism and the future of amateur sport across Canada. Thus, Captain Gorman embarked on his crusade at a time when all amateurs were concerned about the future of their sports. Their concern was increased by the consequences of different sport organizations accepting different definitions of amateurism. A player could be a *bona fide* amateur in soccer and baseball yet, just as legitimately, a professional in lacrosse and hockey. The potential effect of this was nothing short of catastrophic since many players participated in more than one sport. Therefore, the sport governing bodies were confronted with an increasingly chaotic situation in which, despite efforts to the contrary, the dividing line between amateur and professional was becoming less clear. The organizations were now willing to sublimate temporarily their own aspirations in the face of more pressing needs. One of the most obvious solutions was the creation of a central organization to bring order out of chaos by providing a definition of an amateur that would apply to all amateur sport. The CAAU was ready, willing, and able. Its moment of triumph was at hand.

The years 1906 to 1909 were the best in CAAU history as clubs, sport governing bodies, and amateur athletic associations hastened to join. Early in 1907 the influential soccer governing body, which controlled 203 clubs, applied for affiliation. More important to the long-term growth of the union was the affiliation of the first provincial association, the Maritimes Amateur Athletic Association, which had been formed in 1888 and had long maintained an independent status. In 1907, it succumbed and applied for affiliation. In 1908, the CAAU moved to form other provincial associations, which resulted in the formation of the British Columbia, Alberta, Saskatchewan, and Quebec branches of the CAAU. A truly national organization was taking shape. By 1909, the CAAU claimed 900 clubs and associations with over 60,000 additional members, a far cry from the thirty-six clubs of 1906. At this moment of phenomenal growth the CAAU was rent by internal dissension that at first appeared to threaten the existence of the organization. The so-called "Athletic War" that raged from February 1, 1907, until September 6, 1909, was, in fact, the final factor in the creation of a strong, centralized, national association.

The Athletic War signalled the end of Montreal domination of amateur sport and the beginning of a more broadly based organization, although in the pre-war era it was dominated by Toronto. The battles were fought over the perennial problem – the playing of amateurs and professionals on the same team. As ice hockey and lacrosse proceeded down the road to full professionalism, the MAAA, a club that could claim to be truly amateur, had increasing difficulties in fielding competitive teams in ice hockey and lacrosse. Unwilling to follow the hypocritical practices of many of its opponents, who used various dodges to avoid being classed as professionals, the MAAA, in 1904, proposed a change in the CAAU constitution. This change would allow amateurs and professionals to play together without affecting the amateur status of the players.[20] The reaction of outraged indignation was predictable. The proposal was soundly defeated, but this did not end the affair. By February, 1907, the differences had become so acute, and the possibility of a solution so remote, that the Montreal association severed relations with the CAAU and formed a rival association, the Amateur Athletic Federation of Canada (AAFC). The AAFC claimed the same powers and jurisdiction as the CAAU except for one notable exception: "All Clubs are to employ one or more professionals who are to play – but they must be declared."[21] They were joined by twelve clubs from the province of Quebec and thus the Athletic War began.

In fact, the war, in one sense, was over before it began. Although it gained some adherents, the AAFC remained a small Quebec-based organization while the CAAU went from strength to strength. Yet the CAAU leaders took the threat of the AAFC so seriously that they found it necessary to come to a joint agreement over the composition of the 1908 Olympic team. This was due solely to the immense power and prestige of the MAAA, which until this confrontation was the most powerful athletic organization in Canada. Using the tactic that had been used in the past – withdrawal (1871, 1880, 1892, 1897) – the MAAA hoped to prevail upon the CAAU to change its position. At the outset, the CAAU consisted of thirty-six clubs and thus the chances of success attending the Montreal exodus, with one-third of the members, would appear to have been good. Nobody could have foreseen the revolutionary increase in membership that took place in 1907. By the end of the year, the numerical power had shifted to the CAAU. Still, the position of the MAAA was such that it could not safely be ignored. Thus the compromise of 1908.

There is no saying what would have happened if the Montreal association had not committed the unforgivable sin of going back on its word. Such an action could not be countenanced by "gentlemen." At the 1908 Olympic Games in London the Montrealers made their fatal error of judgement. Since both the AAFC and the CAAU claimed jurisdiction over Canadian track and field a compromise had to be reached over the composition of the team to represent Canada in London. On November 30, 1907, Colonel Hanbury Williams, a representative of the British Olympic Committee, and P.D. Ross of Ottawa met with representatives from the two organizations and the compromise was reached to pave the way for the Canadian team to travel to London. After arriving in London, the AAFC representative, Leslie Boyd of the MAAA, lodged a protest against the amateur status of Tom Longboat, a CAAU-sponsored runner. The protest was not allowed but reaction in Canada was instantaneous. Sporting men across Canada were aghast at the "Baseness and treachery of the action."[22] After agreeing to give full support to the Canadian team, the AAFC had reneged on its agreement. This was ungentlemanly conduct, unacceptable to the majority of amateur sportsmen. Whatever the previous status of the AAFC, the tide now turned strongly against it. The Canadian Olympic Committee withdrew its support of the two organizations and gave full support to the CAAU. Even within the AAFC some members were appalled at this conduct, withdrew from the organization, and on October 29, 1908, established a Quebec branch of the CAAU.[23] It would appear that the AAFC was finished as an effective power, yet such was the power and prestige, apparent or real, of the MAAA that in February, 1909, James Merrick, the CAAU president, approached the MAAA with regard to the amalgamation of the two organizations into a new amateur body. This was effected and resulted in the formation of the Amateur Athletic Union of Canada (AAUC) on November 27, 1909. In effect, it was the CAAU of 1906. More important than the political power struggle was the fact that the cause of pure amateurism won out.

A major question is to what extent and in what ways was the new organization different from its predecessors. In both composition and administrative structure the AAUC was different, as was reflected in J.G. Merrick's report to the first annual meeting.

The old Constitution of the CAAU had to be disregarded in its entirety, because it had been drafted to suit the requirements of an organization confining its energies practically to the district of Toronto and Montreal. In our plan for the government of amateur sport, we have provided for the government of athletics from coast to coast and have carefully considered not only the representation of each section of the country, on the Board of Governors; but also the attitudes of the National body towards Dominion organizations that were interested in the direction of some particular branch of athletics.[24]

The most significant change was representation from each province; it was a truly national organization. In addition, the administrative structure provided for the provincial associations and sport governing bodies to have considerable autonomy. However, on the important issue of amateur status, the AAUC remained the ultimate authority and thus retained the real power. In this, very little had changed. The actual decision-making power still lay in the East, but in Toronto rather than Montreal. The first executive illustrated this. The three most important positions were held by Torontonians: president, James G. Merrick; secretary, N.H. Crow; and treasurer, J.J. Ward. Although the AAUC was the first truly national organization it was still dominated by central Canada. This was to become an increasingly thorny problem as the century progressed. Finally, in one most important respect nothing had changed – the rigidity of the definition. The basic philosophy of the new organization was founded on the same principles of pure amateurism as were its predecessors. Although the definition of an amateur adopted by the union was structured differently it contained all the clauses of the 1902 definition plus one further restrictive category aimed at those individuals who "promoted an athletic competition for personal gain."[25] If anything, the position adopted by the AAUC was even more severe, stating that "An athlete guilty of any of the above offenses can never be reinstated."[26] Thus, any individual who ran for money, pursued athletic exercise as a livelihood, received money for loss of time, sold or pledged his prizes, or promoted an athletic competition for personal gain was forever a professional. This basic tenet of amateurism, once a professional always a professional, was a rigid, harsh system of social as well as athletic discrimination. The rigidity of this definition and the inflexibility of successive executives of the AAUC sowed the seeds of dissension that were to plague the organization in the post-World War I era.

In the years preceding the war, the AAUC moved to consolidate its position as the sole authority in matters pertaining to amateur athletics. During this era, one of the greatest in the history of Canadian track and field, it effectively brought a degree of stability to the Canadian track and field scene. The culminating act of its involvement in track and field was the establishment of the Canadian Olympic Committee in 1913 under the aegis of the AAUC. With regard to the two major Canadian team sports, lacrosse and ice hockey, the AAUC recognized the impossibility of solving the problems besetting the games within the context of the existing sport governing bodies and moved to create separate sport bodies modelled on the AAUC with a central organization and provincial affiliates. At the 1912 annual meeting a motion was passed: "That representatives from the different provinces meet on Monday and take up the question of forming a National governing body for lacrosse."[27] The result was the formation of the Canadian Amateur Lacrosse Association in 1913. Although it could claim 243 affiliates, the CALA was never truly national because in many areas, such as the Maritimes, lacrosse was not popular. In 1914 the AAUC promoted the formation of a similar organization for ice hockey. This move met with great success and thus began the history of the powerful Canadian Amateur Hockey Association.

While the organization was moving to consolidate its position in amateur sport, the artificial identity of interest with the larger sport governing bodies began to disintegrate over the definition of an amateur and the aspirations for autonomy. The rigid definition of an amateur caused soccer authorities considerable concern since many of their players had been or had played against professionals in the old country. In addition, the highlight of the Canadian soccer season, and a source of revenue for the association, was the visit of professional teams from England or Scotland. After the formation of the Dominion Football Association in 1912, the soccer clubs withdrew from the AAUC. Similarly, the Canadian Wheelman's Association, with a more liberal interpretation of amateur rules, withdrew in 1913. The battle lines that were to dominate the 1920's had been established. The rigid definition of amateurism, the autonomy of individual sport governing bodies, and an increasing resentment of eastern domination were to be the focal point of dissatisfaction in the post-World War I era.

Central to the history of the AAAC/CAAU/AAUC was the problem of differentiating between an amateur and a professional. The day-to-day work of the association, the executive meetings, and the deliberations of the annual meetings all reflected concern over how to keep amateur sport pure. These concerns culminated in the Athletic War, which result in an overwhelming victory for the conservatives of amateurism. Their legacy was a continued antipathy, on the part of amateurs, between themselves and professionals. This has remained a fundamental aspect of amateur sport.

What was there within professional sport that stimulated this implacable dislike on the part of amateurs? (Rarely did the professionals comment on the amateurs.) Why should an amateur be so "superior" or different from a professional? The more closely one considers these questions, the more difficult it becomes to provide a rational answer. There is no doubt as to what was unacceptable about professionalism – the reasons were given many times by different individuals. As Major Macauley, a leading exponent of amateurism in Montreal, proclaimed in 1901, he abhorred professionals because "they were men who made sport their business."[28] When sport became work it was unacceptable.

A second universally deplored characteristic was the acceptance of money in any shape or form. Finally, amateurs claimed that work plus money equalled violence, ungentlemanly conduct, and unethical practices. In other words, because sport was a man's work for which he received remuneration it was inevitable that the athlete would demonstrate unacceptable behaviour in various forms, a rather interesting analysis if one considers that many of the leading exponents of amateurism were businessmen for whom making money was a prime consideration!

The logic of the argument used by the amateurs was rather difficult to follow. Obviously, within an emerging industrial society in which both money and work were worshipped with a religious passion, the acquisition of wealth through work could not, in itself, be regarded as evil. The only argument that could stand up to any critical examination was the assumption that when sport became work it inevitably led to cheating, hippodroming (fixed games), violence, and ungentlemanly conduct. Without doubt there was some justification to this line of reasoning, for professional sport does have a fair share of unacceptable behaviour. But just as obvious to the impartial observer was the fact that the playing fields and ice rinks of amateur sport were not devoid of the behaviour attributed to professionals. It certainly appeared that this was an example of selective perception. As will be seen, the real reasons for the amateurs' disdain of professionals lay in a complex of deep-seated and perhaps subconscious values within the amateur movement itself.

THE PHILOSOPHIC BASIS OF AMATEURISM

The focal point of the whole amateur movement, as we have seen, was the definition of amateurism. Since the definition of 1909 incorporated the statement of 1884, its origins assume a vital role in understanding the problem, which was not peculiar to Canada. Both Britain and the United States were struggling, at the same time, to provide workable definitions. This fact alone served to make the task more difficult, for Canadians invariably turned to these sources for guidance and advice. The difficulties being experienced by the English were surprising because the word "amateur" had been used without fuss or fanfare since the end of the eighteenth century.

Amateurism evolved from the lifestyle of the leisured aristocracy of eighteenth-century England. The patterns of behaviour, the attitudes, and the values that eventually formed the foundations of the amateur code were inculcated in children through example and education in both the family and the school. A child's early years were spent in the home where he was treated by family and servants in the manner befitting his rank. At the age of eight, he attended one of the prestigious Public Schools, such as Eton or Harrow, where he was moulded into a gentleman by learning the subtle patterns of behaviour that differentiated him from the rest of society. The designation "gentleman" was not equated with money, which for the majority was simply an accepted part of life. This attitude was clearly demonstrated in a letter written in 1879 to the Montreal Lacrosse Club: "That no one was qualified to play as an amateur who made a profit of his services. The meaning of this being that a gentleman should not be debarred from playing as such by his poverty."[29]

Sport played a central role in the life of a gentleman, the hunt, horse-racing, and cricket being the centrepieces around which social gatherings were focused. Sport was more than just the playing of games, it was a vehicle for demonstrating that the person was a gentleman. The chase and the cricket field were locations for demonstrating courage, perseverance, fair play, and honesty – abiding by the letter and, more importantly, the spirit of the law. Such behaviour was expected of a gentleman. The strength of the system was that it was never formally enunciated in written form, the value system and patterns of behaviour being transmitted by example through the family, school, and other social institutions. This gave the system an exclusiveness that practically guaranteed that outsiders would be unable to gain access.

Although the ideology was not formally written down, it is possible to discern the basic attributes that eventually formed the amateur code. Central was the idea of individual responsibility. A gentleman was responsible for his own actions. Thus, the imposition of an official, referee, or umpire would impugn his reputation as a gentleman. This emphasis on form did not mean, as some more recent amateurs have claimed, that winning was not important. It was still the most important aspect of a game. One was expected to sacrifice everything but honour in order to win. Fearlessness, reckless heroism, sublimation of individualism, acceptance of pain – all were expected of young gentlemen. The delicate balance between winning with or without honour was demonstrated in a Canadian context in a statement issued by the Montreal Lacrosse Club in 1870.

> We further notice that we have for the past 3 years striven to inculcate, a growing regard for the strict observance of sporting rule and precedent. Nothing goes further to promote enjoyable sport than this scrupulous observance of custom. We do not believe in sacrificing spirit to letter, nor do we encourage quibbling and petty advantage seeking, but like to see the strictest legality compatible with honour sought and accorded.[30]

The letter of the law must not be emphasized at the expense of the spirit. The spirit was a set of attitudes inculcated in the young aristocrats since childhood and reinforced throughout life by family, schoolmasters, and, more importantly, the close friends of their peer group.

In England there was no definition of an amateur because there had been no need. Amateurism, as it came to be known, was part of a way of life within a closed social system. Success or failure depended on the ability of the system to impose meaningful sanctions on individuals who transgressed the bounds, the black sheep of the families. As the nineteenth century progressed and first the middle class, then the workers, threatened the exclusive playing fields of the aristocracy, it became necessary to institutionalize, in written form, the value system – thus the attempts to define the amateur code. That the English had great difficulties and failed to come up with an adequate definition did not bode well for Canada.

There is no doubt that Canada received the value system and the idea of amateurism from Britain. They were transmitted by the military, the private schools, and the universities. Middle-class immigrants educated in the English Public Schools added to the tide of English ideas. However, what was brought to Canada was a part, not the whole, the ideology without the social system. On the one hand, Canadians accepted with open arms the idea of building character and using the playing fields for the demonstration of desirable social characteristics; on the other, Canada lacked an essential ingredient, a landed aristocracy. In an editorial on outdoor sports in 1875, a writer commented: "we lack that portion of the population which in England devotes large leisure to the cultivation of everything physical, manly and plucky."[31] The Canadians, therefore, were in a vacuum, attempting to create something that was rooted in a different social system.

At first, the lack of a clearly defined leisure class, or a closed social system, was not a hindrance since the early participants in sport were, for the most part, drawn from a select social group. The real problems arose when groups with different origins, ideas, and expectations began to invade the playing fields in the 1860's and 1870's. At that moment the move to define an amateur developed and gathered strength. In searching for assistance, the Canadians looked to the United States and England. In 1878, the Montreal Lacrosse Club, the leader of the amateur movement, wrote to the Marylebone Cricket Club and the New York Athletic Club for advice. What emerged from this exchange was a rejection of "An English definition of an amateur" on the very grounds that were fundamental to English amateurism.[32]

> Our principle objection to the definition is to the concluding words of it. We do not propose to make this a peg whereon to hang a string of worn out platitudes on the dignity of labour and so forth. But to us, as Canadians, it does seem peculiar that the honest young mechanic who spends his leisure time in healthy recreation, should be classed as a professional and excluded from amateur competition.[33]

The rejection of the social system meant that the administrators were left with an ideology. They faced a difficult task, that of operationally defining implicit patterns of behaviour. This was achieved, in lacrosse for instance, by simply listing undesirable behaviour as it appeared on the playing field. It was acceptable to state what was unacceptable but unacceptable to codify laws to control behaviour – the individual was responsible for his own actions. To establish rules in such a way as to remove responsibility from the individual would be to impugn his honour. This was reflected in a plethora of comments in the newspapers to the effect that everything would be all right "if only the players would play the game." The result was that Canadians were coping with a problem that was insoluble within the framework of the accepted value system. They could not define what an amateur was, legislating for behaviour was unacceptable, but, at the same time, there were no meaningful sanctions to impose on recalcitrants. The answer was the definition of amateurism in the constitutions of the CAAO and the AAAC. By 1884, an embryonic exclusionary system provided the foundation stone of all future definitions. Unfortunately, in so doing, the organizers of amateur sport, either consciously or unconsciously, failed to solve the real problem of defining the ideology itself and of developing a meaningful system to implement it. Instead, a system was created that effectively excluded professionals. This had never been difficult, but in doing this it excluded large segments of the population and thus sowed the seeds of a class-based amateur code. The impact of this on the growth of sport – amateur, professional, and commercial – is, because of its pervasiveness, impossible to estimate.

This paradox was reflected in the changes incorporated into the definition between 1884 and 1909. Canadians accepted without question differentiation between vocation and avocation, the use of money as the defining criterion, and the equalization of competition. Only in the underlying assumption that an amateur was a gentleman, an individual with leisure and education, was there some hesitation on the part of Canadians. It was not so much the Amateur Rowing Association of England's belief that an amateur was a gentleman that was questioned but rather the phrase that banned "artizans, mechanics, and labourers."[34] Canadians could not accept this blatant class definition. From the outset they expressed concern over the "honest workingman." But even in this, the adopted definition was restrictive in that the honest workingman was someone who accepted the values of the middle classes. In other words, it applied to those workers who accepted the ideology of "sport" and acted like "gentlemen" on the playing fields. What eventually emerged within the AAAC and its successors was a definition based solely on the dual criteria of work and money.[35] The nature of the changes can be seen most clearly in the successive additions to the definition of an amateur, and in the fact that no part of the previous definition was eliminated:

1884: An amateur is one who has never competed for a money prize, or staked bet or with or against any professional for any prize, or assisted in the practice of athletic exercises as a means of obtaining a livelihood.

1896 (add): Or who has never entered any competition under a name other than his own.

1902 (add): private or public gate receipts ... who has never, directly or indirectly, received any bonus or a payment in lieu of loss of time while playing as a member of any club, or any money considerations whatever for any services as an athlete except his actual travelling and of selling or pledging his prizes.

1909 (add): promoted an athletic competition for personal gain.[36]

There was nothing in the definition that explicitly stated what an amateur was; the position of the organization did not change at all from 1884 to 1909. For whatever reason, the arbiters of amateurism were unwilling or unable to state in clear, unequivocal language what an amateur was.

But why was there this steadfast adherence to a position in the face of massive changes within society and sport? The first answer can be found in the underlying intellectual foundations of Western society, in the dualism of mind and body. Since the Greek philosophers first propagated the division of a being into a mind and body, there has been an implicit assumption in Western society that the mind is superior to the body. In the hands of the Christian church this position was sometimes advanced to the point that body and sin became synonymous. As a result, the belief that the mind is superior to the body has become an assumption requiring no verification. For any individual, social group, or society, games or any physical activities could not be important in themselves. Games must be instruments for the achievement of some other goals. Since work was the basis of Victorian society and play was unimportant, a diversion from the real meaning of life, making a vocation out of something that by definition was divorced from the mainstream of life was intellectually unacceptable to the educated middle class. Thus the harsh, vitriolic, and apparently paranoic condemnations of professional sport by educators, churchmen, and intellectuals. This attitude was clearly demonstrated in an editorial in the *Montreal Star* on November 29, 1890, on the athletic craze sweeping English and American universities:

> We do not think this kind of thing can last very long. Whatever is greatly overdone exhausts itself with more or less rapidity, and the athletic business will, we doubt not, illustrate the law. Within reasonable limits, there will not only always be room for athletics, but they will constitute a valuable part of a young man's education. Let the end in view, however be physical health, grace and efficiency, not the more noisy triumphs of the hour. Let us make athletics tributary to life, and not subject life to athletics.[37]

This value system was promoted and inculcated in the youth by educators, churchmen, philosophers, historians, and writers – in short, by the educated segments of society and by the institutions that played such a large part in the transmission of cultural values. There is no denying the pervasiveness of this value system through all parts of society influenced by the churches and schools. However, the strength of its hold varied according to the proximity of individuals and social groups to these institutions. For the majority of Canadians in the nineteenth century, formal education and theology were the exception rather than the rule. An acceptance of the value system based on a superior mind and inferior body doomed them to an unfulfilled life. For the pioneers in Ontario and the Prairies, physical prowess made the difference between success and failure; the body was certainly important. Games were important in themselves, not as means to some end determined by the middle classes. The consequence of this for amateur sport was an antithetical approach based on the opposite values to those preached by the exponents of pure amateurism. Thus, the set of assumptions accepted by a particular group with reference to the relationship between the mind and body is critical to an understanding of the meaning of a game for that group.

In order to understand amateurism, it is necessary to recognize two different levels. First, within a societal context in which a game or sport cannot be important, it must be an avocation, diversion, recreation, or amusement – a break from the main function of life. Second, within a group, a sport club, it can be very important, an all-consuming interest, but only as a means to an end. To an amateur, a game cannot be important in the overall view of life. This approach was illustrated most vividly in the continuing assertion by amateurs that sport must be an avocation. Victory in any game, even a national championship, could not be overemphasized; in fact, victory ultimately was not important. The logical conclusion of this was that the competition itself lost its meaning and became, as it did for aristocratic Englishmen, a social display. Emphasis on victory *per se* was replaced by striving for victory, and thus the contests could be heated and hard fought. The process was important, not the end result. This, of course, could only take place in conditions of equality, and hence arose the amateur concern over equality of competition and the claims that professionals had an unfair advantage. This whole attitude was summed up, in 1911, in a letter from an English gentleman to the *Toronto Globe*:

> Sport is a fundamental essential not only of English life but also of human life itself, and the question that confronts us today is this – upon what can we better build up and establish the character and physique of the future builder and maintainer of Empire than upon the foundation of sport in its highest and noblest form? Of course there are those who would pooh pooh the idea altogether of anything so serious as human character being formed and strengthened and established by the training that forms the life's work and object of the accomplished sportsman. Indeed, many people maintain that, so far from building up character, it debases and demolishes it. I not only do not agree with such a ridiculous verdict, but I honestly believe that the very reverse is the truth. Of the two modes of building up a man of fine character – sport or literature – I say, without a moment's hesitation, give mc the man brought up to be a sportsman. That is the kind of man who, in the past, conserved the idea of Empire; that is the man who has established and who maintains the British Empire as the most marvellous political fact ever known in the long history of humanity and the world.[38]

This rather chauvinistic letter is a classic exposition of pure amateurism: sport is a means to an end and within that context can become an all-consuming concern, central to life itself, but only to develop the leaders of future generations. While the concept of amateurism remained unchanged, the whole structure and basis of sport was changing from pre-industrial sport forms to modern organized sport. Individually and collectively, these changes increased the probability that the central objective of any contest would be victory. Changes within the competitive structure, rewards, and administrative structure made it increasingly difficult for individuals and groups to adhere to the principles of sport, that is, playing the game for values other than victory. This was reflected in a decrease in challenge matches, an increase in leagues, and the development of local, provincial, and national championships. All these factors increased the likelihood that victory could become the sole motivating criterion. Parallelling this shift was an increase in the value of rewards, both extrinsic and intrinsic, given for victory.

At the highest level, professionals like Ned Hanlan were rewarded with substantial purses. Perhaps even more important was the increasing value placed on sport within the community. Again, the adulation heaped upon Ned Hanlan and other oarsmen illustrates the importance attributed to sport by segments of the community. Finally, the growth of bureaucratic structures increased the distance between players and administrators, thus increasing the likelihood of different value systems existing within the same organization. What all these changes indicated was a shift from a pre-industrial to an industrial society. Sport, no longer the exclusive preserve of a small elite, began to reflect the capitalistic industrial society of which it was a part. The predominant values of this type of society emphasized monetary rewards and victory at any cost. It was unreasonable to expect that sport would be the reverse of this set of values. Yet this was exactly what dedicated amateurs expected: behaviour on the sporting field was to be the reverse of behaviour in business life – co-operation instead of competition, means rather than ends.

What happened to amateur sport? It experienced great expansion and change. Many observers of the amateur scene commented on the deleterious effect of championship competition, the impact of increased rewards, and the entrance of new groups into sport. Nearly without exception, these observers failed to recognize the relationship to fundamental changes within society itself and attributed the evils to the example of professionals. In one sense they were right – many of the things that were anathema to amateurs were found in professional sport, but what escaped the majority was that, in one sense, amateur sport had been professionalized through changed competitive structure, increased prizes, and increased bureaucratization. Within the amateur movement, groups emerged that did not accept the ideology of pure amateurism. For many individuals and groups acquisition of the championship became all-important. Thus, victory rather than striving for victory became the primary concern. At the same time, the age and social distance between administrators and players increased, creating a potential communication gap between the two groups and a void between the stated objectives of the organization and behaviour on the playing field. Accentuating the problem was a breakdown in the homogeneity of the social groups participating in amateur sport. These groups, especially those in soccer and baseball, brought to amateur sport a set of values antithetical to those contained in the rigid definition of amateurism. The entrance of the working classes into organized sport, still in its infancy in 1909, signified the infusion, at the playing level, of a new value system – one in which sport was important for itself and victory the ultimate test. For men caught in the bind of the meaningless, unfulfilling work of the new industrial factories, sport was central to life itself instead of being simply a diversion. By 1909, then, the amateur movement existed in a social and physical environment far removed from 1884.

Why did the amateurs fail to respond to the new conditions? Why did they not seek a realistic solution instead of maintaining a rigid adherence to the tenets of pure amateurism? The answer of the decision-makers, of course, was a rigid adherence to the ideology laid down in 1884. The victory of 1909 was a glowing tribute to the ultra-conservatives of amateur sport – nothing had changed. In one important sense nothing had changed – the social and educational background of the sport administrators remained the same. The first executive of the AAUC in 1909 was drawn from the same section of society as the first executive of the AAAC in 1884 – educated, anglophone, upper middle-class.[39] Maltby, Becket, and others were replaced by Dr. F.J. Tees, a professor at McGill University, Dr. H.D. Johnson, a doctor from the Maritimes, J.G. Merrick, a Toronto lawyer, and N.H. Crow, an official in the Treasury Department. No wonder there had been no change in the definition of an amateur – the new executive was new in name only. They were men who had the time to devote to an avocation and who, throughout their lives, had been imbued with the ideals of pure amateurism. The importance of this lies in the understanding that while amateur sport on the playing field had expanded far beyond the narrow base of 1884, the representation in the board room had remained stagnant. Sport had expanded across the country, but the amateur representatives from across Canada had not changed. Amateur sport at the administrative, decision-making level was still the exclusive preserve of the elite.

Even on the playing field, early expansion was from the top down rather than from the bottom up. Entrance to organized amateur sport was severely circumscribed, open only to individuals from certain social groups. Until the expansion of intra-city leagues, around 1910, it was necessary to belong to some organizations that promoted sport. Nearly without exception, these organizations – private schools, universities, high schools, churches, the YMCA – were purveyors of middle-class values, and the creators of amateur sport, the anglophone, educated middle class, kept a close rein on the growth of sport. Rather than democratization we witness embourgeoisement. Within this context, it was virtually impossible for the participants to accept any other definition of amateurism that one based on the belief that it was an avocation.

The above analysis indicates that amateur sport was created, developed, and administered by the middle class, who accepted a particular set of ideas with reference to the place of sport in life. Due to the nature of the institutions most clearly identified with the promotion of sport in the late nineteenth and early twentieth centuries, the amateur idea was implanted firmly in large numbers of new adherents. However, undesirables, from a variety of viewpoints, were invading the playing fields from the beginning, and an analysis of the actions of sport governing bodies leads to the conclusion that, consciously or not, their actions were aimed at specific groups of people. It is clear from the successive additions to the definitions of an amateur that the amateurs were attempting to exclude individuals for whom sport was a vocation, or those who accepted money, or those who believed that the game and victory were important in themselves. More important were the logical consequences of the definitions – which segment of society was affected by "loss of time" or would need to "sell or pledge" their prizes? Obviously, it was those who could not afford to compete as pure amateurs, for whom regular days off work were not feasible.

The period 1896-1902 witnessed the addition of the greatest number of restrictions to the definition of an amateur; coincidentally, there was also a significant increase in the number of new groups entering the fields of amateur sport. Interestingly, no concern over professionalism was evidenced in those sports that remained the exclusive preserve of the middle and upper classes. Curling, one of the most popular winter sports, was never tainted by professionalism. In golf and tennis, professionals were hired to perform clearly defined duties while retaining a position of recognized social inferiority. Basketball, which experienced rapid growth but no professionalism, was played exclusively within the YMCAs, churches, and educational institutions where the amateur code was firmly entrenched. Finally, the claim that payment of money allowed a man to practise more frequently, thus destroying the basic equality necessary for amateur competition, will not bear critical examination. Prior to the twentieth century, there were no full-time professionals in lacrosse, ice hockey, or soccer. How then could a man who had to work all the week find more time to practise than the middle-class amateurs? It is difficult to escape the conclusion that amateurism was, at least in part, simply a system of class discrimination. The amateurs were trying to restrict entry to those individuals who had been imbued with their idea of sport. In many ways this is one of the strongest pieces of evidence in support of the existence of an antithetical value system, in which games and victory were important in and for themselves.

What then was the significance of the conflict between amateurism and professionalism? It was certainly the most significant aspect of conflict in the history of sport prior to 1914 since its outcome set sport on the path it was to follow at least until the 1980's. By failing to solve or even attempt to solve some very real problems, the amateurs avoided the real issues facing sport. Simply, the amateur/professional conflict symbolized the emergence of mass sport with its conflicting social and ideological bases. Mass participatory sport and professional spectator sport were direct outgrowths of the change from a pre-industrial to an industrial society. In this social and physical environment it became increasingly difficult to maintain the values of amateur sport – playing the game for the game's sake, striving for victory rather than victory itself. The whole thrust of society was toward the capitalistic ethic of maximization of profits and victory at any cost. With the entrance of new social groups onto the sporting fields, the amateur movement assumed a pivotal and increasingly important role. Created by and for a select social group, the amateur leaders were unequal to the challenge of a new society. By rigidly maintaining their commitment to an ideology rooted in pre-industrial society and gaining most of their recruits, until the twentieth century, from institutions that propagated their ideal, they continued to control the direction of amateur sport. For whatever motivations, the amateur movement placed upon itself a class connotation. By failing to address the problems of mass sport, the amateurs ensured that the only ones who gained access to the sporting fields for the most part accepted their value system. From 1884 to 1909, amateurs simply restated the basic position that sport was an avocation and could not be important within the total context of life. Here was an organization, which by 1913 boasted 130,000 members, that was predicated on the assertion that it was not important. What, in fact, their rigorous definition propagated was exactly the things they abhorred most – hypocrisy, circumvention of rules, and under-the-table payments.

THE MONTREAL AMATEUR ATHLETIC ASSOCIATION

The foregoing must not be taken as a condemnation of the amateur administrators of the period, many of whom were dedicated men whose value system was engrained, but rather as a comment on the way Western society reacted to the emergence of the masses as a significant and important part of society. At the same time, individuals and groups committed to the amateur ideal made suggestions that, if implemented, would have solved some of the problems that later faced both amateur and professional sport in Canada. It is most appropriate, therefore, that we should conclude our consideration of amateurism with the most important athletic organization in Canadian sport history prior to World War I – the Montreal Amateur Athletic Association.

From its inception in 1881, the MAAA provided leadership, competitive teams, Olympic champions, and presidents and executives of various national and provincial organizations. More important to this discussion is the fact that the MAAA was one of the few organizations to recognize the problems facing amateur sport and recommend actions beyond a simple adherence to pure amateurism. Prior to 1900, the MAAA was recognized as the most ultra-amateur group in Canada, maintaining an unwavering stance on the amateur code. In 1897 it embarked on a futile attempt to save amateur sport. During this battle it became evident that a central tenet of the MAAA was opposition to hypocrisy. What really upset the Montrealers was the existence of pseudo-amateur teams that retained their amateur status by employing a variety of dodges to circumvent the spirit of the law while legally remaining within the law.

At the same time, the MAAA was concerned about placing competitive teams on the lacrosse field and hockey rink. During the early years of the twentieth century, the MAAA apparently reversed its position on pure amateurism by advocating the playing of professionals and amateurs on the same team, the only restriction being in the number of professionals and the fact that they should be declared. This apparent about-face resulted in the Athletic War of 1907-1909. In reality, this was not a reversal of position but a logical step within the framework of the philosophy of the MAAA. In its unsuccessful attempts to save pure amateurism, the

MAAA, unlike many amateur organizations, faced the reality – the failure of the amateur bodies to control effectively professionalism in amateur sport. The MAAA, most perceptively as the future of amateur sport has shown, recognized that amateur sport at the highest level would be plagued by pseudo-amateurs. The Montrealers realized that victory was important, that national titles were coveted, and that clubs would take the steps necessary to acquire them. To the MAAA the only way to avoid a hypocritical stance and remain competitive was to allow amateurs and professionals to play together; thus, its philosophy, more honest than most, demanded the solution its leaders recommended. If these two points had been accepted, that victory was important and hypocrisy undesirable, the history of amateur sport in Canada may have been very different. Accidentally, the MAAA had also proposed the only path to purely Canadian professional sport. High-level professional sport was impossible in Canada without the availability of the U.S. market. Joint amateur and professional teams may have prevented the exodus of hockey players and hockey franchises to the U.S. in the 1920's.

As we have already seen, the MAAA failed in its efforts by being defeated overwhelmingly by the formation of the AAUC in 1909. This ensured that the fundamental problems underlying sport would remain – nothing had been solved. The future of amateurism was based on the victory of the pure amateurs in 1909. The scene was set for the denouement of 1936, when the CAHA disaffiliated from the AAUC and thus destroyed the foundation of the AAUC's power.

5

The Growth of Professional and Commercial Sport

One thing common to sport at all levels was money. For the amateurs, it served as a mechanism for differentiating between themselves and others. For the professionals, it was the end product of their labour, providing their livelihood. For entrepreneurs, it was the *raison d'être* for building facilities and promoting athletic competition. For organized sport, as it spread across the country, it became the criterion for success or failure. And for the social elite, it served as a vehicle for maintaining their exclusivity. In other words money, the focal point of industrial capitalism, permeated all levels of sporting activity and gave to sport one factor that tied everything together. In its most attenuated form, the centrality of money was reflected in the growth of commercialism and professionalism. This chapter focuses, first, on the various manifestations of commercialism, of the use of sport "to yield an income." It then considers the origins of professionalism before moving to the ultimate combination, the growth of professional-commercial sport. By the First World War, professional-commercial sport, with its removal of individual freedom, had moved to centre stage.

COMMERCIALIZATION

The 1870's and 1880's witnessed a significant increase in the number of sport teams, spectators at games, and the variety of sports being played. As organized sport began to take shape two separate yet related responses occurred. First, the new sport organizations found it increasingly difficult to remain financially viable. As cities grew, pressure on space increased, land prices skyrocketed, and traditional locations disappeared; thus it became increasingly expensive to maintain grounds for sport. One of the answers to this problem lay in the recognition that sport could be utilized to yield an income. In other words, sport, as a spectacle, had potential as a marketable commodity. One of the sites of commercialization was therefore the amateur sport clubs themselves, the vocal opponents of commercialization. The second response lay with individuals and groups that recognized the financial potential in providing facilities for sporting participation and who moved into the market to provide these facilities. The central question of money inexorably pushed sport toward commercialization. Unless clubs and sports were supported by the membership, or were associated with other institutions that provided funding, or had external sources, they were forced to generate income or cease to exist.

Evidence of commercialization can be found across Canada in the late 1870's and early 1880's. However, it developed first in the larger urban centres before spreading into the smaller communities. As with so many events in sport, the earliest signs of commercial development were to be found in Montreal. Once again, Montreal provided an example of the processes to be observed in the other cities and towns at a later date.

Commercialization focused on the provision of facilities for both spectator and participant sport. In the years leading to Confederation space was readily available for any sporting activity on the plots of spare ground to be found in any town or city. There was no real need for specialized facilities. It was the social elite who first erected athletic facilities for their own private use. The first was a curling shed in 1838.[1] During the 1840's and 1850's other facilities were added – a racquet court, the Garrison Grounds, McGill College Grounds, and the first sport ground, the Montreal Lacrosse Grounds. In 1862, the wealthy citizens of Montreal banded together to form a joint stock company to build the Victoria Skating Rink. These were, indeed, the playgrounds of the wealthy and so they remained until the 1870's when the rapid expansion of the city placed increased pressure on space and clubs faced rising costs, increased taxes, and soaring land costs. These pressures forced some clubs to abandon their grounds to developers while others were forced to look for ways of generating income to meet the rising costs. The different responses and consequences were illustrated most vividly in the histories of two institutions, the Montreal Gymnasium and the Victoria Skating Rink.

The Montreal Gymnasium, at the corner of Mansfield and Burnside, was formed in the 1860's as an incorporated company. In addition to the gymnasium, it included a reading room, bowling alley, and billiard room. It was, therefore, a social club rather than simply an exercise facility. By the early 1870's its financial condition was not healthy. The treasurer's report to the 1873 annual meeting stated that income exceeded expenditures by a mere $90. In every succeeding year discussion centred on finances and the possibility of keeping the gymnasium open without making it available to outside groups. Temporary relief came in 1877 when some members, who were affiliated with the Montreal Lacrosse Club and the Montreal Snow Shoe Club, persuaded these clubs to rent the social facilities for club rooms. This stopgap measure failed to save the gymnasium – it was bankrupt by 1881. The premises were taken over by the newly formed Montreal Amateur Athletic Association, and so the gymnasium became the head-quarters of the most powerful athletic organization in nineteenth-century Canada. This was the end of the private company; it had failed to react to the new conditions. Interestingly, a group of snowshoers, many of whom were involved in the affairs of the gymnasium, promoted a new undertaking, the Athletic Club House, on fourteen acres of the Côte de Neige Road with a capital investment of $25,000 in $10 shares. It was opened in July, 1885, with the express object of acting as a rendezvous for snowshoers. During the next ten years it was the centre of many good times. However, it collapsed in the mid-1890's for the same reason as the gymnasium.

The Victoria Skating Rink, opened in 1862, met a different fate. This enterprise was supported by the social and business elite of Montreal. In 1862 it had a capital investment of $20,000. During the 1860's, fashionable skating parties, masquerades, tournaments, showshoe races, lacrosse on ice, and various other activities filled the winter evenings for the members of the club. Despite this heavy use during the first three months of the year, the financial condition of the rink gave cause for concern. This was due to the fluctuation in the popularity of skating and its lack of use during the remainder of the year. So narrow was the margin of safety that one bad year brought cries of anguish from the shareholders. By 1873, faced with increased taxes and costs, the profit margin had decreased to a bare $967.80 or 4.8 per cent of the capital. This did not meet with the approval of the investors. The report of the eleventh annual meeting of the

Victoria Skating Club pinpointed one of the major problems. "Another season has passed without being able to turn the rink to good use in the summer."[2] The ensuing years reflected a change in policy by the rink management. First, in winter the rink was opened to other amateur groups. Perhaps more important was the promotion of summer activities. On August 6, 1878, one of the largest gatherings to grace the Victoria Rink attended a reception for the great Ned Hanlan. The success of these innovations was reflected graphically, no doubt to the pleasure of the shareholders, in the annual reports of 1883 and 1884. A $5,459 profit in 1883 was followed by an even larger profit in 1884 of $9,544.56, a 47.7 per cent return – a reasonable investment. The Victoria Rink did, however, remain exclusive, participants and spectators being drawn from the middle classes. Even so, the winds of change, unrecognized at the time, were already present in the form of the increasingly popular hockey games. Within ten years the Victoria Rink became more famous for hockey than it ever had been for skating, and the social elite withdrew their support and moved into other fields where their exclusiveness could be maintained.

More central to the process of commercialization were the changes in the use of the private athletic grounds. The Montreal Cricket Grounds, McGill College Grounds, and Montreal Lacrosse Grounds were joined by the Shamrock Lacrosse Grounds in the late 1860's. All these were located in the exclusive English-speaking St. Antoine's Ward on the west side of the city. The four locations became the focal points of a variety of athletic contests. In the late 1860's and early 1870's they became the venues for lacrosse, football, baseball, and showshoeing; the annual athletic meets of various societies; and, most surprisingly, a variety of professional contests. The presence of professional competitions on the grounds of amateur clubs, who repeatedly condemned professional contests, pinpointed the basic reality facing the clubs – financial stability. Financial problems forced the clubs, except for McGill University, to accept any offers to rent the facilities. Since all were located on prime property in the West End, tax hikes made it increasingly difficult for the clubs to retain them. By 1876, taxes on the Montreal Lacrosse Grounds had risen to $2,500. In 1878, the less wealthy Shamrock Lacrosse Club was forced to move west into the less costly suburbs. This was the first of many moves. By 1889 only McGill, because of its unique position, retained its original grounds.

The histories of the MAAA and the Shamrock Lacrosse Club illustrate the precarious balance between financial stability and insolvency. Both moved to Westmount, but then their experiences were different. Although the MAAA gained significant revenue from the high-profile lacrosse and football games, its financial viability was based on a large social membership who used the grounds for skating in winter. The Shamrocks, on the other hand, did not have strong financial backing and were heavily dependent on gate receipts. As a result they were forced to move yet again, this time to the northeast of Montreal where land was cheaper. Thus, the commercialization of amateur sport was only a partial answer to the problem of athletic facilities.

The second evidence of commercialization lay with individuals and groups who recognized the potential profit available in providing facilities for participation. As early as the 1850's, enterprising individuals swept the snow off the ice of the St. Lawrence River and the basins of the Lachine Canal and charged people a fee to skate on the cleared ice. As the population shifted inland, the rinks moved from the river to open spaces in the heart of the city. In 1880, the *Montreal Star* commented that the "rinks on the river are not doing such a good business as they had done in previous years, the many city rinks proving too strong an opposition."[3] This move away from the river was initiated in the mid-1870's and by 1880 there were nine rinks in the city.[4] During the 1880's the number of rinks increased dramatically, reaching a high point in the early 1890's. At many of the rinks, bands were in nightly attendance, carnivals and masquerades were held, and skating races were run to attract participants and spectators. The rivalry between the proprietors was fierce, with owners resorting to ethical and unethical methods to increase their share of the profits. On several occasions the ice was hacked to pieces during the night. Others, such as the Winter Garden Rink, attempted to improved their competitive edge by installing electric lights. None of these initiatives was of a permanent nature since the various rinks were often taken over for building purposes.

However, two rinks were different in social composition and permanence, the covered Victoria and Crystal rinks. The origin, development, and social orientation of the Victoria Rink have already been discussed. The Crystal Rink was different. From the outset it was a commercial enterprise. In November, 1878, Samuel Robertson took over an old rink, covered it, and opened for business early in 1879. Robertson promoted hockey in addition to the masquerades, dances, and social skating. An astute businessman, he did not make the same mistakes as the management of the Victoria Rink. From the summer of 1879, the rink was used for both professional and amateur sport. For example, in 1882 seven separate events were held at the rink. On April 3, a sixteen-hour go-as-you-please race for professionals was commenced. During the next four days the professionals competed for four hours a night. Other professional contests were held on May 18, June 26, and September 2-8. Other professional and amateur meets were held in June and September. On September 5 a boxing exhibition was held. It ended in a riot when the crowd broke into the ring and fought until the ring collapsed. From the beginning, Robertson's primary concern was to make a profit, and consequently he ignored the niceties of the differentiation between professionals and amateurs. The Crystal Rink was a successful commercial enterprise, predicated on the promotion of participation, professional performers, and spectators, a precursor of modern organized sport.

One of the most popular commercial and professional enterprises was billiards. There were numerous tables throughout the city and an extensive system of local, provincial, national, and international competitions for both amateurs and professionals. Unfortunately, very little is known of the growth and development of the game except to attest to its undoubted popularity.[5] Given extensive newspaper coverage during the 1870's, billiards was one of the few sports that was played and watched by all segments of the community, rich and poor, French and English. At one level, it was played at the prestigious English and French social clubs, at the first-class hotels such as the Windsor Hotel, and in the homes of many prominent Montrealers. At the same time, the game was condemned for its close association with drink, gambling, and the tavern. It is indisputable that many billiard rooms were associated with a wide spectrum of taverns but it is also true that between 1869 and 1884 at least six billiard halls, devoted exclusively to the game, existed in Montreal, from Messrs. Dions Boudoir (1869) to Alphonse's Billiard Hall (1884). Billiards crossed ethnic boundaries and in the French-Canadian Dion brothers produced two of the finest players in the world.

More important to the growth of sport was the opening of commercial facilities used solely for sporting events, which can be taken as a reasonable indicator of the spread of sport throughout a wider social base since, in every instance, the investment was based on large numbers of participants or spectators. Prior to 1870, the only regularly scheduled horse race was the Annual Steeplechase held by the socially prestigious Montreal Hunt Club. The locations for these annual events were various farms in the vicinity of Montreal. An increase in challenge matches in trotting and the organization of the Montreal Turf and Trotting Club in 1870 indicated an increased interest in horse-racing. The extent of this surge of interest can be measured by the actions of three tavern owners, Messrs. Emonde, Decker, and Lepine, who opened three tracks, Fashion Race Course (1870), Decker Park (1871), and Lepine Park (1871). Subsequently, the three tracks became the focal points of horse-racing in the Montreal area. The Montreal Turf Club held its biannual meets at one of the courses. More important to the financial stability of the tracks were the numerous challenge matches, flat races, ten-mile buggy races, twenty-mile races, trotting matches, handicap events, and other events that proliferated in the years after 1870.

The owners of the tracks became involved also in the active promotion of both flat- and harness-racing. The impact of commercialization was vividly illustrated in the actions of the owner of Decker Park. For the inaugural meet in July, 1871, the enterprising Mr. Decker obtained concessions from the Grand Trunk and Vermont Central Railroad companies and the Canadian Navigation Company – return tickets for a one-way fare. By 1873, Decker had incorporated suggestions for improvements in the form of the race cards, a telegraph board, a clerk of the course, and jockeys riding in colours. Also during the early years, horse-racing alone could not provide enough revenue to make the tracks profitable, so they were rented for various athletic meets. This was especially the case during the first half of the 1870's, when professional runners, snowshoe and lacrosse clubs, and a variety of organizations holding annual picnics rented the grounds for their own purposes. Thus, throughout this period, while horse-racing was developing, the race tracks were used as multi-purpose athletic facilities.

The foregoing examples of commercialization were, for the most part, aimed at a middle-class audience and were supported by middle-class money. These facilities were not yet available to the majority of the population who laboured for six days. This effectively excluded them from attending the weekday and Saturday entertainment. Provisions were made by entrepreneurs to fill this void with facilities and entertainment on Sundays. Despite persistent complaints about "Sabbath desecration," Sunday was the day of recreation for many Montrealers.[6] The events were located without exception in the predominantly working-class areas of the city and thus it appears logical that the majority of the supporters were drawn from this class. At the same time, they crossed ethnic boundaries and provide one of the few instances in which French- and English-speaking Canadians attended the same events.

These sporting entertainments were the antithesis of the amateur sports popular among the middle class of St. Antoine's Ward. Often violent, involving bloodletting and pain, the games were practised for financial gain and immediate pleasure and not for the demonstration of desirable social qualities. Invariably involving gambling and drinking, these "debauched spectacles" focused on the working-class areas of St. Cunegonde, St. Jean Baptiste, and St. Mary's wards or just outside the city boundaries, in the purview of more amenable councils.

The periodic railings against Sabbath desecration provide a fascinating insight into the nature of this Sunday subculture and the popularity of these entertainments. The summer of 1870 was the high point of the velocipeding craze that aroused the ire of the editor of the *Montreal Star*, who expressed frustration at being unable to control the Sunday activities taking place at Mile End, just beyond the city limits.[7] On Sunday, May 22, 1870, nearly 5,000 spectators gathered to watch the velocipede champions Pacquette and Alard. Swearing, drinking, and betting accompanied this three-heat race.[8] During the same year, crowds of up to 4,000 attended velocipede races, acrobatics, prize fights, cockfighting, and clog-dancing in St. Henri and St. Jean Baptiste wards and in Guilbault's Gardens within the city boundaries. The problem became so acute that the city council held a special meeting to consider steps to be taken to prevent desecration of the Sabbath and the excessive drinking associated with it. No action was taken.[9]

In the ensuing twenty years the Sabbath question was prominent on several occasions. In 1871 the issue was raised over prize-fighting and velocipede-racing in St. Henri and Rond St. Jacques and Sunday entertainments in Viger Gardens.[10] The city council, in November, 1873, passed a motion "That power should be obtained to pass bylaws for the better observance of the Sabbath."[11] By 1878 complaints were being made about the "unruly mobs congregating on Sunday in the villages of St. Henri and St. Jean

Baptiste in connection with sports openly carried out in both villages."[12] Crowds of over 3,000 attended these regular Sunday afternoon athletic events. Large crowds also watched the Sunday horse races on the Lachine Canal in Côte St. Paul in 1880.[13] In 1884, saloons, billiard rooms, and skating rinks were doing a thriving business and in the early 1890's attention turned to the skating rinks and the increasingly popular game of hockey.[14] There was, indeed, a thriving Sunday entertainment industry that catered, to a large extent, to the working class. Significant segments of this group were not overcome by their hours of work and living and working conditions but rather, with their one free day a week, found momentary pleasure and an escape from reality in these spectator events where they could swear, gamble, drink, and enjoy the companionship of other like-minded individuals. In short, this was a vivid and telling rejection of the value system of the work-oriented middle class.

One further activity was the illegal sport of cockfighting. Throughout the second half of the century, cockfighting faced an active campaign by the RSPCA to suppress it, yet despite several prosecutions it continued to exist.[15] The twenty-two fights prosecuted between 1860 and 1895 were located without exception in working-class areas: near the Lachine Canal, by the tanneries in St. Henri, and on the border of St. James and St. Mary's wards.[16] Twenty-nine of the forty-three participants prosecuted were blue-collar workers. Although the majority of fights were organized by particular ethnic groups, there was some interaction between the French and English, certainly more than in middle-class amateur sport.

What general conclusions can be drawn from this brief review of the commercialization of sport in Montreal? First, and most important, was that money was basic to all sport, amateur as well as commercial. The recognition that sport was, and indeed had to be, a marketable product became common during the 1870's and 1880's. Although public and institutional sponsorship did develop later, the money motif has remained central to organized sport. Underlying the rhetoric of amateurism and the various justifications of sport was the stark reality of financial viability. Amateur sporting clubs, commercial facilities, and professional spectator sport were all predicated on a sound financial base. The foundations of organized sport, then, were unequivocally commercial. Sport had become a marketable commodity.

Perhaps even more telling than its development in Montreal is the degree to which commercialization permeated Canada. Although the evidence is fragmentary, some tentative conclusions can be drawn. Commercialization was evident across the country and had permeated down to relatively small villages. From the urban centres of Montreal and Toronto to the villages of Summerberry, Saskatchewan, and Bear River, Nova Scotia, the "solid, respectable citizens" and various entrepreneurs provided a variety of facilities whose existence was based on making a profit. During the 1880's the first signs of nationwide commercialization appeared. This parallelled significant developments in the growth of organized sport: increased numbers of teams, organizations, and leagues. Commercialization, in other words, was related to increased demand.

Also during the 1880's, urban centres developed and the beginnings of the pressure on land were felt. This was graphically illustrated in Brandon, Manitoba, in 1889, only eight years after its founding. In an editorial the *Brandon Daily Sun*, commenting on the availability of sport grounds, stated:

> Instead of having proper grounds the clubs have to content themselves with any vacant spot in the neighbourhood large enough to permit its use. Up to the present they have not been disturbed, but there is little doubt that the grounds now used for these purposes will be required for building purposes this year.[17]

Brandon, like many other Canadian towns, was caught between the past and the future. The traditional locations were disappearing as a result of growing pressure on land and, in some cases, legislation. Sportsmen across Canada were forced to look for alternative venues. Invariably this entailed a financial outlay plus ongoing sources of revenue. The result was a kaleidoscope of short-lived facilities and teams. Some stability was provided by certain groups, in particular the middle class and entrepreneurs. In the larger towns and cities, the middle class joined together to provide athletic grounds for a variety of sports. These associations frequently took the form of amateur athletic associations and modelled themselves on the Montreal Amateur Athletic Association. In many cases the associations purchased their own grounds, as was the case with the MAAA. In 1884 the Peterborough AAA purchased grounds on Ashburnham Road, which soon became the centre of sporting activity in the town.[18] Later in the decade, the Ottawa AAA paid $14,000 to construct a gymnasium to add to its substantial holdings.[19] Not all these initiatives met with success. The experience of the Saint John YMCA was replicated many times across Canada. After expending considerable sums of money to improve its grounds on Wentworth Street, the YMCA was forced to forfeit the grounds in 1895 because of ongoing financial problems.[20] Thus, across Canada, various middle-class organizations provided athletic facilities, but they, too, were subject to the basic requirement of all sport – financial viability.

In the larger cities individuals and groups banded together to form joint stock companies to erect commercial sporting facilities. As early as the late 1870's some "solid citizens" of Winnipeg invested in Dufferin Park.[21] Perhaps more indicative of commercial interest were three events in widely separated Canadian cities. During the period 1890-93, the Winnipeg Street Railway Company invested in River Park and Elm Park, both sites of sporting activities.[22] In 1897, the Toronto Ferry Company went a step further and bought the stadium at the Toronto Islands in order to promote professional baseball. Similarly, in Vancouver, when a baseball franchise was awarded to the city a Recreation Park Co. Ltd. was floated with stock of $30,000. Its objective was to build a stadium for professional baseball.[23]

Although these enterprises were limited to the larger urban areas, two types of facilities were to be found across the whole country – ice rinks and race tracks. It appeared that every village, town, and city by the turn of the century could boast of these sporting facilities. However, they varied considerably in quality, some ice rinks being little more than a sheet of ice cleared of snow while some race tracks were located in hospitable farmers' fields. At the same time, there were certain clear developments – covered ice rinks with accommodation for spectators and race tracks with stabling facilities and grandstands. In both cases these were business enterprises supported by individuals, joint stock companies, or the community. The interesting fact is that they were to be found in small towns and villages as well as in the larger cities. A comment made in the *Digby Weekly Chronicle* in 1895 probably applied to the smaller towns across the country: "Rinks are not generally profitable in our local towns."[24] Consequently, many rinks continually flirted with financial disaster. Success depended on unpredictable weather and clientele. In spite of these difficulties and the generally short-lived nature of such

Hockey on Henderson Lake, Lethbridge, Alberta, c. 1912. Courtesy Glenbow Archives, Calgary / NC2-685.

undertakings, continual efforts were made to provide the facilities for what was soon to be recognized as Canada's national sport.

The origins of the first ice rinks lay within the upper middle class who formed semi-commercial rinks in order to enjoy skating, masquerades, and balls. Thus, the creation of ice rinks preceded ice hockey. The first covered rink was constructed in Quebec City in 1852.[25] This was followed by rinks in Montreal (1862), Halifax (1863), and Saint John (1864); the social elite were providing for their own leisure time. By the early 1870's there were a dozen covered rinks in Canada.[26] Rinks proliferated in the larger towns during the seventies. Perhaps catering to a different clientele were the outdoor rinks, opened in Toronto as early as 1876, with skaters at the Royal and St. George's skating rinks being entertained by the bands of the Queen's Own Rifles and the 13th Hussars.[27] Further west, in Winnipeg, the first rink, the Victoria Rink, was opened in 1875.[28] In the East, in 1884, the Halifax-Dartmouth area boasted at least five rinks that hosted masquerades, amateur skating races, and mass skating.[29] The pervasiveness of the rinks is illustrated by Chatham, Ontario, certainly no metropolis, but by 1884 this southwestern Ontario town had a commercial skating rink.

By the 1890's the rapid expansion of ice hockey and curling stimulated the growth of covered rinks in the smaller towns of Canada. In 1893 the citizens of Portage La Prairie, Manitoba, subscribed $3,000 for a rink.[30] Edmonton, in 1895, had one rink that was serviced by three waiting rooms.[31] The Sault Ste. Marie, Ontario, Rink Company's facility was the site of the first professional hockey game in Canada in 1904. The inhabitants of Summerberry, Saskatchewan, formed a joint stock company in 1906, and the Liverpool, Nova Scotia, rink built in 1912-13 cost $6,000.[32] Across the country, communities, groups of investors, and individual entrepreneurs invested in ice rinks. The one common variable was the requirement that they be financially viable. Therefore, by the outbreak of the war, commercial ice rinks were a familiar institution across the land.

HORSE-RACING

The commercialization of horse-racing was complex, its roots lying deep in the fabric and structures of society. Its history reveals the difficulty of defining "commercial" since money was always central to the sport as prize money, gate receipts, side bets, or formalized gambling. One thing that made its history different was its relationship with everyday life. The horse was of central importance in nineteenth-century Canadian life – as a beast of burden, as a method of transportation, as an industry, and as a race horse. It was necessary to the economic foundations of the society. Men raced horses for fun and profit from the eighteenth century, and no corner of British North America was immune to the passion for the horse. As with so many sports critical changes began to occur during the 1880's, although to some leading Canadian sportsmen the 1870's were the best years for the sport. The reasons are quite clear. Mr. Miller, MP for South Grey and mover of a Bill to Prohibit Gambling in 1910, stated that thirty years earlier horse-racing was "More sportsmanlike, and was carried on with less commercialization than it is today."[33] Hugh Paton, a prominent Montrealer, in evidence before committee, stated that "in 1875 he raced his horses for the honor of the thing."[34] The perceived reason for the idyllic years was demonstrated clearly by E. King Dodds, editor of the *Canadian Sportsman* for forty years and an acknowledged expert on racing, in his reminiscences about racing at Woodstock, Ontario, in the 1870's.

> Men did not pronounce judgement on the success of a meeting by the amount of money they won and turfmen were ready to gather together and enjoy a pleasant social time, open a cold bottle and not shout 'thief, thief' when beaten.[35]

Thus, in the minds of certain Canadians, the unhappy state of affairs in 1909-10 was due to the commercialization of the sport. This was, however, a gross oversimplification and biased perspective. Commercialization had always been a part of the sport, and the problems that precipitated an unprecedented two-day debate in the House of Commons on April 6-7, 1910, were rooted in the social structure of Canadian society and the impact of urban-industrial society on that system. In fact, all the elements of commercialization were present in Canadian horse-racing prior to 1870.

Horse-racing, in a structured sense, was a British phenomenon, in particular, a British upper-class phenomenon. Therefore, it was no accident that racing arrived with the British troops in the eighteenth century. From that time the military took horse-racing with them wherever they went. Horse-racing was popular at all the military garrisons. Halifax, Quebec City, and Montreal could all point to horse-racing in the eighteenth century and were to remain centres of the sport. Racing soon spread beyond the boundaries of the military and into the countryside. During the 1820's and 1830's French Canadians adopted horse-racing and developed an extensive network of races.[36] In Upper Canada, British immigrants had brought horse-racing with them – Toronto in the 1830's and Sandwich in 1838 hosted race meetings. The 1840's witnessed an expansion in the number of organized races across Upper Canada. By the early 1850's, the inhabitants of the Hudson's Bay Company settlement at what was to become Winnipeg celebrated the Queen's birthday with horse-racing.[37] Out on Vancouver Island, Beacon Hill had already become the site of horse-racing in Victoria. By Confederation, few areas of the country did not celebrate May 24 with horse races.

Early horse-racing was characterized by its irregularity. There were no racing calendars. Clubs organized for a year or two, then fell by the wayside. At the same time a degree of permanence was created, albeit not on a sound basis. In such larger centres as Quebec, Montreal, Toronto, and Halifax it was unusual for a year to pass without at least one meet. Clubs did emerge, even though they led a transitory existence – Toronto Turf Club, Western Racing Association in Windsor, Montreal Trotting Club, and others. A number of factors became basic to the commercialization of horse-racing. First was the involvement of the wealthy and the social elite. From the outset, horse-racing was regarded as part of the social lives of the leisured classes. Second, racing provided a location where all segments of the population met, although their roles were clearly differentiated – the wealthy were the owners and the workers the spectators. Third, and most important, was the central role of money. Prize money, gate receipts, and wagers always lay at the heart of racing. Invariably the races were for a purse and/or a wager. In the Ste. Hyacinthe races held on August 7-8, 1849,[38] the purses for the four races were provided by merchants and hotel keepers, the turf club, the proprietor of the race course, and the St. Lawrence and Atlantic Railway. These represented four elements involved in the development of commercial racing: business interests, in particular taverns, the wealthy and socially prominent through the jockey clubs, the proprietors of the race courses, and transportation companies. Different combinations of these groups were central to the development of racing across Canada.

It would be erroneous to suggest that horse-racing could be encompassed under a single rubric. Sponsorship, type of racing, and form of competition all exhibited differences, some of which became more pronounced as the century progressed. The most prominent and prestigious events were those associated with the turf clubs and the military garrisons. Located for the most part in the larger towns, the clubs were closely related to racing in England, which was dominated by the landed aristocracy. These races were usually flat or steeplechases and were the precursors of the thoroughbred racing that developed later in the century. They remained within the purview of the social elite. The social elite were also involved in trotting and pacing in both summer and winter. However, in this instance the racing was more widespread in both a geographical and social sense. Trotting and pacing were more closely related to horse-breeding, an industry that become increasingly prominent and important with the settlement of Upper Canada. Soon, nearly every small town boasted a yearly agricultural fair. The popularity of these fairs is illustrated by the existence of fairs in the early 1850's in the small villages and towns of Amherstburg, Sandwich, and Leamington in Ontario. Racing thus became an integral part of the agricultural scene, providing a format for testing the strength and endurance of the horse. Since tests of strength were central the form of competition varied, with the trotters and pacers most often racing a number of heats, usually the best three out of five. This type of racing was most popular in French Quebec and agricultural Ontario. While the differences between flat-racing and trotting were noticeable it is important to emphasize that there was no clear line of demarcation, with meets often incorporating a combination of flat-racing, trotting, pacing, and steeplechases.

The first significant changes occurred in the 1860's, and these eventually led to the development of the thoroughbred horse-racing industry. In 1860, the first Queen's Plate was held in Toronto, thus initiating a sporting event that has continued to the present day. During the first fifteen years the Plate was run at various tracks throughout Ontario. This was the great era of racing at Barrie, at the old Cataraqui track at Kingston, and at the Newmarket track in London. There was a lively thoroughbred racing scene in Ontario. Two events, though, served to retard the development of thoroughbred racing, the withdrawal of the garrisons in the early 1870's and the hard times in horse-racing following the American Civil War.[39] Eventually, many tracks, such as those at Barrie, Whitby, Kingston, and London, were closed, but thoroughbred racing was kept alive by a small group of sportsmen in Ontario.[40] The decline in thoroughbred racing was offset by the growth of trotting and pacing, which now moved to centre stage. At this juncture it was possible to distinguish three distinct trends in horse-racing, each of which threw a different light on the commercialization of the sport. First was the development of the thoroughbred horse-racing industry. Second, the 1870's and 1880's witnessed the beginning of commercially operated race tracks. Third was the nationwide development of more broadly based flat-racing, trotting, and pacing.

The early 1880's saw the formation of a number of new jockey clubs. The Ontario Jockey Club, the Province of Quebec Turf Club, and the Manitoba Turf Club were all formed in 1881.[41] In all cases the leaders were drawn from the most socially prominent members of the community. Other clubs were formed during the next few years: a British Columbia Jockey Club, the Quebec Turf Club, and the Connaught Park Jockey Club of Ottawa in 1889; the Hamilton Jockey Club in 1893; and the Windsor Racing Association in the early 1890's.[42] Some were short-lived but a small group of Ontario and Montreal clubs formed the nucleus for the future development of thoroughbred racing. The most important of these was the Ontario Jockey Club, with its avowed objective to clean up racing and promote the development of thoroughbred stock. Thus, a small group of extremely wealthy and prominent Ontarians provided the leadership in bringing some structure and coherence to thoroughbred racing: Joseph E. Seagram, distillery owner, leading horse breeder, and for many years MP for North Waterloo; William Hendrie of Hamilton, one of Canada's captains of industry, who started an association between the Hendrie family and horse-racing that has continued to the present day; and Dr. Andrew Smith, principal of the Ontario Veterinarian College in Guelph for forty years.

As commercial interests threatened the purity of thoroughbred racing the socially prominent moved to protect their own interets and the purity of the sport. In 1895, led by the Ontario Jockey Club, a number of clubs in Ontario and Quebec formed the Canadian Jockey Club. Appropriately, the first meeting was held at the headquarters of the Ontario Jockey Club in Toronto, on May 23, 1895. The eventual composition of the council of the Canadian Jockey Club reflected the focus of thoroughbred racing and the basis of power, with Ontario having eight members and Quebec four. The representatives were from Toronto, Hamilton, Windsor, Montreal, and Quebec City.[43] One of the objectives of the CJC was to control the breeding of thoroughbred race horses through the creation of breeding books. This served to solidify the power of a small group of wealthy owners. In this, the wealthy moved to protect and enhance their investment by ensuring their own control of the development of thoroughbred horses. Perhaps more important was its impact on racing itself since it served to limit high-level racing to distinct locations. In many cases, the tracks were owned by the jockey clubs – Woodbine in Toronto by the Ontario Jockey Club, the Hamilton track built by members of the Hamilton Jockey Club in 1893, and Bluebonnets in Montreal opened by the Montreal Jockey Club on June 4, 1907. In the early 1900's, thoroughbred racing was limited to a circuit of tracks: Woodbine, Hamilton, Montreal, Windsor, and Fort Erie. By 1905 this circuit offered eighty-seven days of racing with total prize money of $228,868.

The hegemony of the CJC was threatened by the intrusion of other interests into its exclusive domain. This challenge was reflected most graphically in the expansion of the racing calendar, in particular in Victoria, Vancouver, Windsor, and Fort Erie. By 1909 the number of racing days in Vancouver had expanded to sixty days. In the East, the two less prestigious tracks, in Windsor and Fort Erie, benefited from legislation in the United States banning race-track betting, which effectively ended racing there. Windsor profited from its proximity to Detroit and, in 1909, increased its calendar to sixty days. Horse-racing now threatened to move beyond the purview of the socially acceptable and prominent members of society. The final threat came with the expansion of off-track betting. By 1909, it was estimated that over $22 million was bet in Canada. This combination of expanded track schedules, the intrusion of American interests, and the perception of excessive gambling among the populace led to the unprecedented two-day debate in the House of Commons on April 6-7, 1910.

In 1910, Mr. Miller introduced a private member's Bill "To amend the criminal code so as to prohibit betting on race tracks." The third reading of the Bill on April 6, 1910, precipitated the debate. Late on Thursday, April 10, the Bill was defeated. But that was not the end. Five days later the Bill was allowed to stand on the order paper in the hope of a compromise, which was reached, and the amended Bill was passed into law. The debates and the ensuing compromise revealed the true motivations behind the Bill – on the one hand, an absolute condemnation of public gambling, and, on the other, the protection of the business interests of a small group of horse owners and jockey clubs and of the rights of the upper levels of society to gamble and wager. The original Bill aimed to outlaw all betting both on and off the race tracks. While there was nearly unanimous agreement on the evils of gambling and the need to curtail it, the original Bill was defeated because the majority of MPs were unwilling to legislate against betting at the race tracks. The compromise of April 15, 1910, allowed betting at the track while banning all off-track betting. It also restricted thoroughbred racing to two seven-day meets at each track officially sanctioned by the CJC. Further, it prohibited the development of new tracks in towns or cities of under 15,000. In effect, this achieved the creation of a monopoly of thoroughbred racing and betting. While the jockey clubs were not allowed absolute freedom to control their own affairs they were given wide powers over the sport. What emerged from the debates was the fact that horse-racing, despite disclaimers to the contrary, was a most successful and profitable commercial enterprise.

The concerns of the majority of MPs were revealed in the opposition to the Bill. J.B. McColl, MP for Northumberland and the leading spokesman in opposition to the Bill, stated the concerns quite clearly: "There are no opponents to the leading features of this Bill but there are opponents to thc drastic, extreme, unjust, and unfair provisions of the Bill."[44] Even the supporters of the Bill did not want to destroy horse-racing, only undesirable tracks. Again, as McColl argued:

> When I am arguing in favour of race track associations of jockey clubs I mean those conducted by the class of men who are in that business for the sport that is in it, and not race tracks that are conducted purely for business purposes or perhaps for gambling purposes.[45]

The upshot of this line of argument was that the MPs were eager to close down off-track betting and all tracks except those of a small, select group. There was little pretence that both racing and gambling were seen to be the exclusive preserve of a certain group of people. "Now the Woodbine race meet is essentially a social and sporting event, attracting many of the best people in Canada with race track bookmaking as an attraction and as a principal financial support."[46] To ensure the viability of thoroughbred racing, it was essential to maintain the income derived from gambling. At the same time, it was wrong for anyone else to gamble. The opponents of the Bill argued that the imposition of restrictions on race-track gambling would "seriously effect if not destroy the noble sport of horse racing."[47] This would have serious consequences for the breeding of light horses in Canada and depreciate the property of racing associations and jockey clubs.[48] The interests of the wealthy and socially prominent were at stake, essentially their right to "sport."

The idea that horse-racing was a "noble" sport devoid of commercial connotations will not bear critical examination. Thoroughbred racing, especially at Woodbine, Hamilton, and Bluebonnets, was a commercial operation generating significant returns on investment for a select group of horse and race-track owners. In 1893, the Hamilton Jockey Club was incorporated with a paid-up capital of $4,050. By 1910 the assets were worth $225,000 and the net profit on the capital of $4,050 was $70,000.[49] A substantial portion of the income was derived from bookmakers, who paid $74,800 for betting privileges in 1909.[50] Not only did the members of the OJC, MJC, and HJC get a substantial return on their investment; many also were among the leading thoroughbred breeders, in particular, Joseph E. Seagram, the Waterloo distiller who saddled twenty Queen's Plate winners between 1891 and 1935, and William Hendrie of Hamilton. In fact, the majority of the eighteen Canadian thoroughbred owners were associated with the most prestigious tracks.[51] Thus the OJC and its equivalents in the other four centres were successful enterprises and the full force of parliamentary power was marshalled to protect the interests of this elite of Canadian society.

In the years leading to the First World War thoroughbred racing remained under the control of the tracks mentioned above. Although there was some thoroughbred racing on the West Coast, it was isolated from the important meets in the East. The powerful eastern tracks moved toward further commercialization with the installation of pari-mutuel betting machines at Windsor in 1914. The elite retained their hold on the commercially profitable, but socially exclusive, thoroughbred racing.

If headlines, column inches, and prestige were the only criteria it would be fair to conclude that thoroughbred racing was the dominant form of horse-racing. However, if another set of criteria is used a different picture emerges. Replace social prestige with actual participation, replace Ontario with Canada as a whole, and there is little doubt that thoroughbred racing was not the most popular form of racing in Canada. At one time or another, every village, town, and city witnessed horse-racing. Challenge matches, head-to-head competition, races in heats, races on the main street, races on river and lake ice, and race courses were to be found from coast to coast. Far more pervasive than thoroughbred racing were the numerous flat, steeplechase, trotting, and pacing races. These activities were more strongly rooted in rural life and the needs of that life. The races tended to emphasize strength and endurance rather than speed. Races were frequently over distances of four or five miles and often entailed winning heats. Because of its lower profile it is extremely difficult to disentangle the history of this "other" racing, but it permeated to every corner of the country and every social class. During the 1890's it was popular among the miners of Cape Breton; in 1893 a Roman Catholic priest was instrumental in building a track in Judique, Nova Scotia; in French Canada annual races were held in Joliette, Beauharnois, Valleyfield, and other villages; and agricultural fairs in Ontario and on the Prairies invariably included horse-racing. Perhaps its position relative to thoroughbred racing is most accurately captured in the Ontario racing schedule for 1895. During that year six thoroughbred meets were held at four different tracks for a total of thirty-nine racing days. Summer and winter trotting, on the other hand, included ninety-two meets at seventy-two locations for a total of 135 racing days – a telling comparison.[52] This "other" racing, for the most part trotting and pacing, reveals the degree to which horse-racing penetrated the lives of ordinary Canadians.

The history of trotting and pacing is characterized by significant differences from thoroughbred racing and by one underlying similarity. Unlike thoroughbred racing, there was no concentrated effort to form a national association. Trotting was mainly local and at best regional. Few efforts were made to form even provincial associations. Second, there was no strong inter-club structure linking the various clubs together; although turf clubs and driving park associations proliferated, few existed for a prolonged period. Associated with the weak club structure was the fact that for the majority of clubs there were only one or two meets a year. This, in turn, had an impact on the financial viability of the organizations. One bad year could spell disaster. Thus, the history of trotting is characterized by instability and impermanence of organizations. Nonetheless, trotting was a commercial enterprise. Money was central to the sport in prizes, gambling, and breeding fees. Even more than thoroughbred racing, trotting faced attacks from the protectors of public morals for perceived corruption, bad management, and race-fixing. Throughout the nineteenth and early twentieth centuries it was always regarded as a shady business, not suitable for gentlemen.

Until the late 1870's it was impossible to discern clearly the separate development of trotting. As with sport in general, the immediate post-Confederation era saw significant changes that were to continue until the First World War. Perhaps the most important change was the increased commercialization. This focused on the building of race tracks. In the larger cities, such as Montreal and Toronto, these were commercial tracks. The three tracks opened in Montreal in 1870 and 1871 were the forerunners of many others.[53] From 1870, Montreal was never without commercial tracks that sponsored and hosted all sorts of racing. There was a Lepine Park until the turn of the century. One of the most popular with the trotting fraternity in the 1890's was the Jacques Cartier Ice Track on the river at the foot of Jacques Cartier Square. Bel Air (1889), Bluebonnets, Montreal Driving Park, Dorval, King Edward, and DeLorimer all served Montrealers in the early years of the twentieth century. Only in Toronto was there a similar pattern, with Dufferin Park and Thorncliffe accommodating the trotting fraternity.

No other cities or towns could boast fully commercial tracks, but semi-commercial facilities associated with agricultural fairs and/or exhibitions did develop. These emerged in the larger cities and towns across the country in the late 1890's. The Halifax Exhibition Grounds were "governed and controlled by an exhibition commission which is appointed by the provincial government, the City Council of Halifax, and the Farmers Association of Nova Scotia."[54] At approximately the same time, the Parc de l'Exposition was opened in Quebec City. Even earlier, in 1889, horse races were held on the Agricultural Grounds track in Winnipeg. On Vancouver Island, racing moved from its traditional location at Beacon Hill to an Oak Bay location in the 1890's. During the next twenty years under various names – Bowker Park, Stanley Park, and Willows – it remained the centre of racing on Vancouver Island. This fragmentary evidence suggests that in the larger urban centres in the late 1890's different groups promoted the development of permanent sites for racing. In some instances the stimulus came from government, in others from various turf clubs and driving park associations, and in others from the agricultural societies.

The final evidence of commercialization comes in the form of the driving park associations that sprang up across the country but were particularly strong in the Maritimes and Ontario. In many instances the associations were directly linked to particular driving parks. By the mid-1880's all the major urban centres in the Maritimes had driving parks that hosted annual meets for the next thirty years. In New Brunswick, Moncton, Fredericton, Woodstock, St. Stephen, Saint John, and Sussex all boasted driving parks and annual meets. Similarly, in Halifax, New Glasgow, and Charlottetown annual trotting races were held. Other venues were less stable. Calais, Maine, Bridgetown, Cape Breton, Kentville, and Digby, in Nova Scotia, Shediac, New Brunswick, and many others sponsored meets at least once during the 1890's. Trotting was to be found in all corners of the Maritimes, although its stability appears to have been directly related to the size of the town.

The development of commercial tracks, permanent locations, and driving parks suggests that a degree of stability and continuity was creeping into trotting. Such was, in fact, the case and this was clearly evidenced in the emergence of annual meets that continued for a number of years. In Ontario the movement commenced in the 1870's with annual meets being held in Port Perry (1871), Ottawa (1875), Peterborough (1875), St. Catharines, and Hastings (1886). As has already been mentioned, this developed in the Maritimes in the early 1880's. In French Quebec annual trotting races were held in the small towns around Montreal. By the mid-1890's, St. Jean, St. Lin, Joliette, St. Pie, and many others hosted annual meets.

By the late 1880's race tracks dotted the landscape of Canada. In fact, this was the beginning of a period of substantial development in trotting, mainly at the local level. The nature of the changes is illustrated by the areas from which various meets drew their horses, by the various attempts to develop circuits, and by the few efforts to establish regional and national organizations.

One of the most interesting insights into trotting and its commercial importance is the degree to which various meets attracted horses from different locales. By this measurement trotting was principally local or regional. The size of the purse

Winter Racing on the North West Arm, Halifax, 1904.

determined the distance from which horses were attracted, and large purses invariably were to be found in large towns. In 1895, the proprietors of the Jacques Cartier Ice Track in Montreal, Messrs. Remi Arbour, Dan Donnelly, and E. Aubry, offered $9,000 in purse money to be raced for on February 5-8.[55] As a result, ninety-eight horses from nineteen towns were entered. The majority came from within a 300-mile radius – four from Ontario towns, seven from the province of Quebec, one from Vermont, and six from New York. However, one horse came from as far away as Baltimore, Maryland.[56] Similarly in the Maritimes, the Halifax Exhibition of 1905 attracted 112 entries from twenty towns, most from within a 200-mile radius and three from Massachusetts.[57] As the size of the town and the prize decreased the radius from which the trotters were drawn decreased: Peterborough (1889), a seventy-mile radius; St. Stephen, New Brunswick (1895), a seventy-mile radius; and Springhill, Nova Scotia (1905), from New Brunswick and Nova Scotia. Even at this level, though, trotters were travelling significant distances. It was not until the prize money and towns were small that the meets became purely local concerns. Simcoe, Ontario, in 1889 attracted horses from ten towns and villages within a thirty-mile radius; Lucan, Ontario, a thirty-mile radius; Grenfell, Saskatchewan (1895), all from Grenfell; and Digby, Nova Scotia (1905), all from within a few miles of Digby. Thus there was a complex system of trotting meets starting at the local level and moving up to the more prestigious regional meets. But only on rare occasions did horses from the Maritimes race in central Canada or vice versa. Prior to the Great War, trotting had not developed beyond regionalism.

The regional focus is illustrated by the various attempts to develop circuits. The creation of a circuit implied a need or desire on the part of owners to establish a mechanism for ensuring regular competition. When this occurred, trotting truly had become a commercial enterprise. One of the first signs appeared in 1884, when a preliminary meeting of men interested in forming a trotting circuit to embrace the leading Canadian cities was held in Montreal.[58] During the next few years initiatives were undertaken in the Maritimes, Quebec, Ontario, and Manitoba to form circuits. The move to create some regular competition was general, but in each instance it was regional. In 1888, a circuit was organized to include the principal Nova Scotia and New Brunswick tracks. In March of the following year a Maritime Provinces Trotting Association was formed and a circuit of meets was to be held at Halifax, Truro, Moncton, Fredericton, St. Stephen, and Saint John between August 28 and September 25. This initiative failed when the circuit folded in September because not enough horses were entered.[59] Almost seventeen years later, on March 2, 1905, the secretaries of the driving park associations of Nova Scotia and New Brunswick met to form a Maritime Horse Breeders Association to establish a circuit from June 30 to September 20.[60] In this instance it included six New Brunswick tracks and two in Nova Scotia. Similar initiatives were undertaken in Quebec, where the major venues were the commercial tracks in Montreal, Jacques Cartier in the winter and Lepine Park in the summer. Various efforts were made – in 1891, 1895, and 1901 – to create circuits embracing towns in the eastern part of Ontario and western Quebec. None achieved any degree of permanence. On the Prairies, a Manitoba and North West Racing Association was formed in 1890 embracing Moosomin, Calgary, Grand Forks, and Winnipeg. Circuits proliferated on the Prairies in the early 1900's, from local ones like the Minnedosa circuit (1905) to the Western Canada Fair and Racing Association, which included eight cities between Brandon in the east and Edmonton in the west. All these circuits illustrated the continuing efforts to organize competition in order to provide a sound commercial base. At the same time, the failure to create any relatively permanent circuits indicated an underlying weakness. For whatever reason trotting owners were unable to

Edmonton Fair, 1905. Courtesy Provincial Archives of Alberta, photo no. B8875.

create an organization whose authority they were all willing to accept.

The failure to create organizations was the final blow to the systematic development of trotting. No one group or body of men had the expertise and political strength to create a national organization to provide the necessary cohesion. The need was recognized by the owners and the race tracks and various efforts were made to associate with United States-based organizations. Only later did a Canadian association develop, and even then regional differences effectively split the organization as the Maritime owners affiliated with the U.S. Trotting Association.

From the outset, trotting always had commercial overtones. Money was central and at the heart of many of its problems. Trotting, however, unlike its thoroughbred counterpart, did not turn into a capitalistic endeavour in which profits, despite protestations to the contrary, were always central. Instead, it maintained contact with its base, the mass of society, and perhaps served a more important role in the lives of ordinary people.

PROFESSIONALISM

Although the development of professionalism was closely related to commercialization it is possible to trace its development before the athletes lost control of their freedom and became employees of business enterprises. During the 1870's and 1880's, prior to the emergence of professional team sport, athletes in rowing, running, and bicycling first recognized the possibility of making a livelihood from their athletic prowess. Although men had competed against one another for wagers and prize money for many generations, by the 1870's a market had been created that allowed a man or woman to earn a living from sport. The development of urban-industrial society, the invention of the telegraph, and the increased popularity of the daily newspaper created the conditions necessary for the emergence of professional athletes. Thus, it was no accident that professionalism first saw light of day in Montreal and Toronto.

Perhaps the first real developments in professionalism occurred when individuals and groups recognized the financial potential to be derived from touring around the larger urban areas. It is possible to identify a number of individuals who toured the various picnics, fairs, and Caledonian Games held annually in central Canada. A number of runners passed through Montreal in the early 1870's: the champion runner of England participated in the Orphans Picnic in 1870;[61] Donald Dinnie and James Fleming, the great Scottish athletes, competed at the Caledonian Games in the early 1870's; the aging Deerfoot challenged the local champion, Keraronwe, in 1872; and John Raine of Ottawa was a perennial contestant from 1872 to 1884. Others, such as John Scholes, the Toronto tavern keeper, and his rival Nurse also graced the Montreal scene. The touring professionals were an ever-present, although infrequent, part of the sporting scene. They were viewed with disfavour by the amateurs, who levelled accusations of cheating and hippodroming at all professionals. These accusations were not unfounded because professionals often competed under aliases to create better betting odds, and fouls, appeals, disputes, and dishonesty were not uncommon. However, it would be wrong to place all the blame on the professionals, as Deerfoot's visit to Montreal in August, 1870, illustrated. In a letter to the *Montreal Star*, Deerfoot made this plea:

> Being a stranger in the city of Montreal and having to contend against your acknowledged champion, Keraronwe, I hope that the sporting gentlemen of Montreal will see that I have fair play and a clear course – that is all I ask.[62]

His fears were well founded; the forty-five-year-old Deerfoot was beaten in the three-mile race after being hooted by the crowd at the start and physically impeded at the finish.[63] This typifies the problems facing professionals throughout the 1870's, and such difficulties were to become increasingly prevalent in the twentieth century as winning became more important.

The next step in the development of professional sport occurred when professionals toured in a group competing among themselves in various cities. For this to happen, a circuit of cities with facilities and entrepreneurs willing to provide prize money had to exist. These conditions were to be found only in Montreal and Toronto. Even then, two cities were hardly enough to provide sufficient support for the touring professionals, but the proximity of the two cities to the urban centres on the eastern seaboard of the United States made such touring possible. Thus, these early professionals established a pattern that was to characterize Canadian professional sport, an identity with and dependence on U.S. markets.

The first of the professional spectacles was the go-as-you-please walking contests that swept North America and Great Britain from 1879 to 1882. As the name suggests, go-as-you-please contests involved individuals walking or running around a track over a set period of hours or days. The winner was the one who covered the greatest distance in the set time. Several professional contests were held in Perry's Hall and Guilbault's Gardens in the early 1880's; one example will suffice to illustrate the characteristics of pedestrianism. In May, 1882, a Grand Pedestrian Contest in Montreal, comprised of walking four hours a night for four successive nights for a purse of $1,000, attracted professionals from Ottawa, Montreal, Toronto, London, England, Elmira, and Keesville, New York, and Indians from Oka and Caughnawaga.[64] Even more interesting was the advent of women pedestrians, whose contests were over a defined number of miles or a relatively short number of hours. One of the most hardy of these was Miss Monahan of Montreal, who started in 1879 and was still attracting crowds in 1882.

The pedestrians were followed by the bicyclists. In March and April, 1882, a group of professionals visited Toronto and Montreal for a series of races on their high-wheeled penny-farthing cycles. The amateur Montreal Bicycle Club sponsored a three-day exhibition at the Crystal Rink in April. During these days there were races varying in length from five to 100 miles, each involving two or three of the riders, who included the champion, Professor Rollinson, T.W. Eck of Toronto, S. Gratton of Chicago, and the champion lady bicyclist, or so she was styled, M'lle Louise Armaindo. M'lle Armaindo, the professional name of Louise Bresbois, a native of St. Ann's Ward in Montreal, was greeted with scant respect on her first appearance in her native city. During her race against T.W. Eck she was "pulled off her bicycle by a zealous individual who tried to drag off a coat she was wearing as she went by at full speed."[65] The life of this early female professional was not an easy one.

The arrival of circuit professionals making their living by moving from city to city signified the development of some of the necessary conditions for the growth of mass sport. Most important was the existence of a group of people willing and able to support spectator sports. By the early 1880's, these conditions existed only in Montreal and Toronto. Giving further substance to the contention that the early 1880's witnessed significant changes in sport was the growth of professional teams. During the period 1879-1886 the first professional teams in Canada were founded. The first to play in a U.S.-based league was the Toronto baseball team that joined the International League in 1886. Again, the precedent set by Toronto was to be the pattern followed by the majority of successful Canadian professional teams, that is, participation in American-based leagues. The arrival of professional teams, more than anything else, indicated that conditions were right for the development of mass sport.

The increasing visibility of professionals was parallelled by the involvement of entrepreneurs in the promotion of sport as a spectacle. This was directly related to the availability of facilities with controlled access. At first these were limited to the private athletic grounds and a variety of other institutions whose primary function was not related to sport. Several multi-purpose facilities were used by entrepreneurs and touring professionals to host contests. The most important of these was the tavern, which at times served as the location for running races, horse-racing, cockfighting, and boxing contests. On other occasions, tavern keepers sponsored various sports, snowshoeing and horse-racing in particular. For the professionals, both local and touring, the taverns served as the headquarters in which all the arrangements for their matches were finalized. Among the professionals using the hotels were the boxers and wrestlers who travelled to various cities. In this instance, the taverns could not serve as the location for the actual competition, this falling to other general-purpose halls built in the second half of the century. Having no national organization, clubs, or specialized facilities, boxers and wrestlers had to look elsewhere. Throughout the late 1870's and early 1880's, bouts were held for so-called championships of cities, Canada, and even the world for stakes of from $250 to $1,000. Between 1877 and 1884, six boxing bouts were held in Montreal at the Theatre Royal, Nordheimers Hall, Union Hall, Hall of the Canadian Institute, and the Mechanic's Hall. Various wrestling bouts were held in the same locations in 1872, 1876, 1879, and 1884. In this era of emerging professional spectator sport, the promoters were forced to use venues not specifically constructed for athletic spectacles. The use of such halls is indicative of the embryonic state of professionalism at the time.

The existence of professional sport outside of Montreal and Toronto is more difficult to ascertain. Competition based on the challenge system and involving money prizes was basic to sport across the country. Touring and circuit professionals were less common, however. Toronto and Montreal apparently were the only Canadian cities to serve as regular stops on the North American circuit. There is no evidence of touring professionals, of the stature of those who visited these two cities, in the Maritimes, Manitoba, or British Columbia. The only other professionals were relatively local ones or itinerants who drifted into town and attempted to make some money against the local champions.

The question remains as to whether professional sport touched the lives of Canadians outside the major urban centres. Certainly the go-as-you-please craze of the early 1880's visited the smaller towns of Ontario, but whether they were professionals or not is a moot point. Men were given money for playing baseball in Guelph, Brantford, and Hamilton in the mid-1870's. A skating race at St. Thomas, Ontario, offered a purse of $500 in 1884, and a walking race in London in 1887 paid $100. The circuit of Caledonian Games, which touched most of the Scottish communities in Ontario, attracted the great Scottish professional, Donald Dinnie. Many of these examples demonstrate the difficulty of defining exactly what a professional was. The definition created by the amateurs simply obscured the problem by making it a black-and-white issue. Obviously, many men who competed for money once or twice a year were no more full-time professionals making a living from sport than the most pure of amateurs. Thus, it is impossible to determine the extent of professionalism outside the large cities. Full-time professionals were (and are) an urban phenomenon that has never filtered down to the rural hinterland. This symbol of modern sport was conceived and nurtured in the cities of Montreal and Toronto.

TEAM SPORT

Perhaps the most visible and far-reaching example of sport as a marketable product is professional team sport. At this juncture, athletes being paid to perform and entrepreneurs seeking a marketable commodity joined forces. When entrepreneurs bought the talents of players and employed them to make a profit, professional commercial sport had come of age. The path to fully professional teams was tortuous, beset with many false starts, financial failures, and collapsed franchises before any degree of stability was attained. As will be seen, professional franchises flourished only under certain circumstances. The different routes to success are illustrated in the histories of two sports, baseball and ice hockey. Each demonstrated a different path to professionalism while being subject to the same basic requirement – financial viability.

Baseball

The case of baseball is most revealing because of the difficulties encountered in differentiating between an amateur and a professional. If one accepted the definition of an amateur used by the AAAC (1884), the OHA (1890), and the AAUC (1909), then anyone who accepted money in any form or who played with or against a professional was himself a professional. Using this definition the majority of baseball players from the 1850's on were professionals. Money and contact with money was never, in baseball circles, regarded as an unmitigated evil. In fact, money in the form of payment for services, payment for lost time, prizes, and gate receipts permeated all levels of the game. In some respects, then, all baseball was professional. To sharpen the focus it is necessary to delimit the definition further. Only when the player's occupation during the summer was to play baseball can we really say professional baseball had arrived. Using this definition, the history of baseball in Canada reveals that there were levels of professionalism in Canadian baseball related to the salaries of the players, the length and geographical scope of the schedules, the stability of the franchises and leagues, and their relationship to the United States. Thus, the history of professional baseball in Canada can only be understood by examining these various levels.

Baseball in Canada began in southwest Ontario in the 1850's. Guelph, Hamilton, Woodstock, and Ingersoll were hotbeds of the game throughout the 1860's. During the 1870's certain events moved the Canadian game closer to its American counterpart. The first was Guelph's hiring of two American professionals in 1873, and the second was the acceptance of the New York rules in 1876.[66] High-level Canadian baseball was unerringly drawn toward the U.S. During the late 1870's and early 1880's baseball moved toward fully professional teams. Perhaps the first league was the short-lived Canadian League formed in 1884 and comprised of three Hamilton teams and one each from Guelph and London. Each team included American players. However, it was disbanded in June in favour of an all-Canadian, Western Ontario Baseball League. More important to the long-term development of professional baseball was the entry, in 1885, of a team from Toronto, the second largest city in Canada. It joined Hamilton,

Guelph, and London in a new Canadian League. The entry of Toronto was critical because it alone exhibited the basic requirement for a successful franchise – population. The Toronto Baseball Club was formed as a joint stock company with $5,000 in stocks. During the first season it employed nine players, seven Americans and two Canadians.[67] Interestingly, the league teams played more exhibition and challenge matches than league games – the old, rural traditions died hard. In December, 1885, Toronto and Hamilton withdrew from the Canadian League to join the American-based International League. This move, incidentally, provoked a lawsuit by the Canadian League, which it lost. Thus, in 1886, Toronto embarked on a century-long affiliation with U.S.-based leagues.

  In many respects, the late 1880's were the most active years of professional baseball in Canada as professional teams sprang up from coast to coast. However, only in Toronto, Hamilton, and London were they affiliated with leagues. The development of professional teams across the country was rooted in the traditions of baseball, with competitions of an exhibition or challenge nature. This was the case in Nova Scotia and New Brunswick, where teams of American professionals and Canadian amateurs played forty- to fifty-game schedules against each other and against college teams from Maine, New Hampshire, and Massachusetts. Saint John hired nine U.S. players for a total of $2,200 in 1889. Similar teams were also active in Fredericton, Moncton, and Halifax.[68] In the same year, the Canadian Atlantic Railway Company baseball team of Ottawa hired players from New York, Vermont, and Montreal to play against a number of U.S. opponents.[69] Even Calgary in the Northwest Territories could boast a professional team in 1889.[70] In British Columbia there were thriving professional teams in Victoria, Vancouver, and Kamloops. These teams, stocked with players from Portland and Minneapolis, played in a series of tournaments throughout the Pacific Northwest in the summer of 1889. In fact, this was the high point of this type of baseball. In the Maritimes the professional teams fell on hard times. By 1905, the Saint John players were on a percentage basis, and professionals there disappeared entirely before the war. In Ontario, Quebec, Manitoba, and British Columbia they were replaced by a more permanent and stable form of organization – professional leagues.

  The entry of Toronto and Hamilton into the International League in 1886 ushered in Canadian involvement in professional leagues.

By the outbreak of the war, at least eighteen Canadian towns and cities had experimented with professional baseball, only five with any long-term success. The Canadian professional baseball experience thus was one of instability, with short-lived leagues and franchises. Their histories pinpoint the necessary conditions for success. First, there was a direct correlation between stability and size of population. It was no accident that those cities with any degree of continuity included the four largest cities in Canada. Toronto, except for a short break in the early 1890's, boasted a professional team from 1886; Montreal, 1897; Winnipeg, 1902; and Victoria and Vancouver, 1905. Since the fundamental objective of baseball was profit, an adequate supply of spectators was a necessary condition of success. Only in the larger cities was the base large enough to offset the loss of spectator interest during losing seasons. Even though most of the professional clubs appealed to community spirit, as soon as a franchise became unprofitable it moved to what were perceived to be more fertile grounds. Towns and cities like Guelph, Woodstock, and Ingersoll, although hotbeds of baseball, could not build up a reserve of goodwill or cash, and so their flirtations with professional leagues were doomed to failure. The second condition of success was affiliation with a U.S.-based league. None of the Canadian-based leagues survived for more than four or five years. This was due, in part, to the fact that the Canadian leagues were invariably rooted in the smaller towns. In the final analysis, profit was directly related to the size of the market, and this was only to be found in specific cities: the factors that have plagued professional sport in Canada down to the present day were the same ones that determined the success or failure of the early professional baseball teams.

The entry of Toronto and Hamilton into the International League signalled the beginning of an association with the only really stable professional baseball league in which Canadian teams participated, and even the International League struggled for six years before disbanding because of financial problems in 1891. Its history was one of great instability at first, with franchises being distributed among eighteen cities. Most of these were in New York but three were Canadian. Hamilton and London, hotbeds of the game since the 1860's, struggled to survive but finally succumbed to financial failure. Toronto was the only one with any degree of financial stability. After the International League was reformed as the Eastern League in 1894, Toronto was offered a franchise the following year. Thus began a long association with this league based in the northeastern states of the United States; it was not plagued by the same degree of instability, with only seventeen cities operating franchises in twenty-two years. After 1897, five of the teams remained the same. Toronto was joined by a Montreal team in mid-1897 when the Rochester franchise moved there after its ballpark was destroyed by fire. Although there were yearly discussions about unprofitable franchises the league was remarkably stable.

The association of Toronto and Montreal with the Eastern League does not exhaust the history of Canadian participation in American-based leagues. There were two other efforts, both of which faced great instability. Winnipeg, the gateway city to the West and a city with great aspirations, flirted with professional baseball with a city professional league in 1886, but the experiment failed.[71] This was followed, in 1889, by discussion about a league with U.S. teams in Minnesota and North Dakota. Although this failed to materialize, it contained the essential ingredient for a successful professional league – association with the U.S. Finally, in 1902, Winnipeg had a fully professional team.[72] Although the Winnipeg Maroons maintained a professional team, the leagues and the teams changed. Sometimes it was a U.S-based league and on other occasions a Western Canada League. For example, in 1907 the Northern Copper League disbanded and was reorganized the following year with teams from Winnipeg, Brandon, and Duluth-Fargo. By midsummer Duluth-Fargo dropped out and Winnipeg had lost $3,100.[73] Brandon had four highly successful seasons, but at the first evidence of financial problems the club disbanded (1911). Professional baseball on the Prairies was plagued by instability; it always lived on the edge of disaster.

The other professional league was the North West Baseball League formed in 1905 with teams from Washington, Oregon, and Victoria and Vancouver in British Columbia. Again, this league was unstable and experienced shifting franchises. Franchise owners were forced to reduce player salaries and thus provoked player strikes. By 1915 the financial losses overcame the Victoria franchise, which was forced to disband in mid-season.

A survey of the three principal leagues does not exhaust the story of professional baseball in Canada. The area to the west of Toronto, the birthplace of baseball in Canada, did not give up its interest in professional baseball and was the site of successive attempts to promote the professional game. Most of the initiatives were short-lived and in every instance one or more of the franchises were in financial difficulty. This makes it impossible to provide a coherent history, but it is possible to identify one or two general characteristics. First, all of the leagues incorporated franchises in at least one or two of the following cities: Hamilton, Guelph, London, and Brantford. Second, from 1884 to 1915, there was a Canadian Baseball League, although its composition and status varied. At times it was a professional league and at other times an amateur league. Between 1892 and 1895, the league consisted of four amateur teams from Toronto and Hamilton. By 1898, it had become a professional league with teams from St. Thomas, Hamilton, London, and Chatham. This disbanded in August, 1899. By 1902, the amateur Canadian League was replaced by a professional Western Ontario Baseball League. It was finally placed on a more stable footing in 1911 when a 110-game schedule for each team was adopted. The new league included Guelph, Brantford, Hamilton, London, and St. Thomas. They were joined, in 1912, by teams from Ottawa and Peterborough. However, the league was Canadian in name only – all members of the Ottawa team in 1915 were American.[74] Even at this level, professional Canadian baseball was dominated by the United States.

Hockey

Although the road to professional hockey led to the same destination – large cities and the American market – the route followed was very different. Unlike baseball, the professionalization of hockey was directly related to the growth of amateur hockey. Thus, its development must be seen within the context of amateurism, in particular the actions of the Ontario Hockey Association and the Eastern Canada Amateur Hockey Association. The OHA fought tenaciously to maintain control of top-level amateur hockey and protect hockey from the evils of professionalism. One of the consequences of this was that the top amateur teams were the equal of and perhaps better than the professional teams that developed in the first decade of the twentieth century. As a result, the battle for spectators was not one-sided because the top amateur teams provided real competition for the professionals. Of course, the purity of the top amateur teams was open to question. Accusations of professionalism became an annual ritual early in the 1900's. This dogged pursuit of shamateurism, pseudo-amateurs, and semi-professionalism eventually forced some top "amateur" teams to declare themselves professional and hence ushered in the real development of professional ice hockey in 1910.

The furore over the intrusion of the professional element in the ice rinks of eastern Canada began in the mid-1890's when ice hockey witnessed a significant expansion in the number of teams and in the groups playing hockey. This led to the development of ice hockey as a spectator sport and to increased commercialization. However, unlike baseball, the first evidence of commercialization was evident in amateur hockey when the executive councils of the OHA and the ECAHA recognized the financial potential of the high-profile championship games. Therefore, since professional ice hockey did not have a monopoly of the highest-calibre players, it faced a powerful protagonist in the battle for spectators. The real development of professional ice hockey in Canada began when the Montreal Wanderers won the last amateur Stanley Cup in 1908 and subsequently declared their professional status. The history of professional ice hockey prior to 1914 therefore falls into two distinct eras, pre- and post-1908.

In January, 1910, with the formation of the National Hockey Association (NHA), professional hockey finally came of age. Prior to this date, the development of professional teams and leagues defied all the prerequisites for establishing sound and stable professional enterprises. The initiatives, prior to 1908, lay outside the two major cities, Montreal and Toronto, and outside the location of the highest level of amateur hockey. Between 1893 and 1908, the Stanley Cup, the premier trophy in amateur hockey, was won on fourteen occasions by teams from Quebec and eastern Ontario, the area of the highest level of the game but not of professional hockey. This is not to say that the spectre of professionalism did not penetrate the two most prestigious leagues, the ECAHA and, after 1904, the Federal Hockey League. In fact, accusations of professionalism were rampant, but the authorities were able to avoid the consequences by collusion and evasion. Pseudo-amateurism and shamateurism were the order of the day, but because of hockey's roots in amateurism and the vested interests of clubs seeking the Stanley Cup, the premier amateur clubs were able to avoid the consequences of their actions.

The first professional league was the International Hockey League, which ran from 1904 to 1907. It was located in three small northern Michigan towns, Pittsburgh, and Sault Ste. Marie, Ontario. The league was the brainchild of a dentist in Houghton, Michigan. Except for its American location, the league defied the necessary conditions for successful professional sport – large population and easy access. The weakness in the league surfaced in the first full season. By March, 1905, the Sault Ste. Marie team was $1,500 in the red. The franchise was saved by the actions of the Sault Rink Company and ten promoters who raised $1,000 at the bank.[75] Throughout its brief history the league suffered financial problems, eventually succumbing in 1907.

This was not the only professional undertaking. Other short-lived initiatives met the same fate. By 1908 the Temiskaming Hockey League, formed in 1905, had become professional. In this instance, wealthy mine owners and industrialists, benefiting from the mining boom in northern Ontario, attempted to "buy" the Stanley Cup by forming teams in Renfrew, Haileybury, and Cobalt. For a few short years these towns became synonomous with the highest calibre of professional hockey before the owners found that the return on their investment did not warrant a continuance of their efforts. There was also a brief experiment with professional hockey in Winnipeg in 1907-08, but this, too, failed.[76] Perhaps the first truly Canadian professional league that lasted for more than one or two seasons was the Ontario Professional Hockey League (1908) based in industrial towns: Brantford, Berlin, Guelph, and Toronto. It, too, was plagued by shifting franchises, instability, and financial problems. All these leagues were located outside the stronghold of ice hockey in eastern Ontario and western Quebec. There would be no stability until open professionalism found root in this area.

Although the spectre of professionalism invaded the stronghold of hockey in the late 1890's, it was not until the formation of the Federal Hockey League in 1904 that there was any threat to the dominant position of the ECAHA. The formation of the FHL provided competition for the outstanding players. Slowly but surely, the two leagues moved toward open professionalism. In 1907, the ECAHA allowed professionals to play on their teams but insisted that the pros be declared.[77] When the Montreal Wanderers declared themselves to be professional after their 1908 Stanley Cup victory, open professionalism gained a foothold in Montreal. Subsequently, in 1909, the ECAHA removed the word "amateur" from its title. The 1909-10 season was critical to the growth of professional hockey. Soon after the commencement of the season, in January, 1910, the two major leagues, the Eastern Canadian Hockey Association and the new National Hockey Association, amalgamated and formed the National Hockey Association. It consisted of the Montreal Wanderers; a new French-Canadian team, the Montreal Canadiens; the Montreal Shamrocks; a team from Ottawa; and teams from Renfrew, Haileybury, and Cobalt. At last, professional hockey was established in the stronghold of the game. By the commencement of the 1912 season, the three small towns had disappeared, victims of rising costs. The league, now composed of two teams from Montreal and one each from Ottawa and Quebec City, was beginning to take shape. Hockey lacked only one final ingredient, a team from Toronto. In December, 1912, an artificial ice arena was opened in Toronto and two Toronto teams joined the league. In fact, the development of artificial ice was the most important single factor in ensuring the stability of ice hockey. Toronto and western Ontario, the heartland of organized sport, always lagged behind in ice hockey because the weather was just a little milder than in eastern Ontario and Montreal. Thus, the seasons were always highlighted by the concern over the availability of ice. While this greatly inconvenienced amateur hockey, it was the death knell of professional hockey since a week's warm spell could destroy the profits of an eight-week season. These problems were illustrated vividly in the history of the Ontario Professional Hockey League: ice conditions dominated the weekly league meetings. The opening of the Mutual Street Arena in Toronto provided the final foundation stone for the successful development of professional hockey.

Artificial ice was also responsible for the other major development in professional hockey, the formation of the Pacific Coast Hockey Association. This effectively destroyed the monopoly of the NHA and was instrumental in the creation of the NHL in 1917. In December, 1911, the first artificial ice rink in Canada was opened in Victoria, British Columbia. This was followed in January, 1912, by the opening in Vancouver of the second of the Patrick brothers enterprises. Ice hockey could now be played in the inhospitable climes of the West Coast. The year 1912 witnessed the formation of the PCHA by the Patricks, who soon raided the eastern clubs to recruit players. In 1915, the New Westminster franchise was transferred to Portland, Oregon, and thus the final requirement for successful hockey had been attained, a foothold in the U.S. market.

A glimpse of the two high-profile leagues based on the larger urban areas does not exhaust the history of professional ice hockey in Canada. By the early twentieth century, ice hockey had become recognized as Canada's national winter sport and its roots ran deep into small-town community life. Small towns across the country strove to promote high-level hockey and in seeking local, provincial, and national honours were willing to pay players to uphold the honour of the community. They faced strong opposition from the powerful amateur organizations such as the OHA and the AAUC. Small-town success was greatest in industrial and mining towns where the amateur tradition was not as solidly entrenched. The Ontario Professional Hockey League continued until after the 1911 season, when it split into two leagues, a Trolley League of four industrial towns to the west of Toronto and a Lakeshore League of three teams to the east of Toronto. Both died after one season. On the East Coast, pressure from the Maritimes Amateur Athletic Association forced a group of teams to form the Maritimes Professional Hockey League in January, 1911. During the next few years, it operated with a combination of teams from Halifax, Moncton, New Glasgow, Sydney, and Glace Bay. It, too, faced financial problems and unstable franchises. Finally, in 1912, another professional league was formed for one season in northwest Ontario with teams from Schreiber, Port Arthur, and Fort William. None of these leagues was solidly based and all, in the final analysis, were doomed to failure.

NED HANLAN, CANADA'S SPORT HERO

Clearly, the money motif was central to the growth of all sport, amateur as well as professional. This relationship and its importance to Canadian society as a whole is reflected in the emergence of Canada's first sport hero, Ned Hanlan. Professional sport was to provide the heroes of the future. Money, not how one played the game, was the basic measurement of capitalistic society. The emergence of high-profile sport heroes was anathema to the educated elite of Canadian society. To the intellectual leaders of Canadian society, it was incomprehensible that so much fame and fortune should be showered on professional athletes. The emergence of Canada's first real sport hero illustrates an underlying paradox that has plagued Canada and indeed Western society. How could something that was, by every accepted definition, inferior and unimportant be so important to so many Canadians from all walks of life? Thus, we must look to the success of Hanlan, "the Boy in Blue."

The recognition of Hanlan as a Canadian sport hero was directly related to the growth of urban-industrial society and the related technological changes. These social and technological changes created the necessary conditions for the emergence of sport heroes. A sport hero is not just an athlete who has performed outstanding athletic feats – such athletes are identifiable in every locality and era and are enshrined in the various halls of fame.[78] The very nature of sport, the physicality and impermanence of the act, makes it difficult to capture the essence beyond the bald statement of records, but a sport hero is one who transcends his or her own sport to become recognized within the nation as exemplifying basic national qualities. Although athletic prowess is basic, the extra qualities move these particular athletes beyond the boundaries of sport. This could only occur when sport had become a part of everyday life.

John A. Macdonald, Lester Pearson, the Group of Seven, and Stephen Leacock might be recognized by large numbers of educated people as important figures in the political and cultural life of Canada because their deeds or works have remained after they died. For this to occur, the works or deeds must remain visible. The deeds of historical figures have been perpetuated by historians, while the works of artists, literary figures, and musicians live on in visible form. In both instances, however, there must be those who, through writing and criticism, keep the names and works alive. In each instance, they are kept alive by an educated elite – historians, literary critics, university professors, and the like. Their views and ideas are then transmitted to successive generations through the educational institutions. The visible culture, therefore, is that whereby an elite tends to ignore the patterns of behaviour, lifestyle, interests, attitudes, and values of the vast majority of Canadians.[79]

Such figures as sport heroes would not be part of what an educated elite would consider important. In fact, sport has most often been considered frivolous, of no relation to the important things in life. Thus, the transmitters of culture have ignored sport as having no meaning beyond that of ephemeral amusement and diversion. The existence of sport figures, throughout history, is indisputable. In some instances they were enshrined, as were the victors in the ancient Olympics. Only during the last 100 years have conditions developed to allow for the emergence of truly national sport heroes. The telegraph and mass press in the second half of the nineteenth century were basic to the transmission of news across the continent and the world. All Canadians, for the first time, could become aware of the exploits of the great figures. What had not developed in the nineteenth century was a system of transmission from generation to generation. Every generation had its own sports figures, recognized by large segments of the population. These remained only as long as that generation survived and perpetuated the memory. They rarely held meaning for the next generation. This was due in part to the lack of means of transmission and in part to the difficulty of defining the characteristics of a great sportsman beyond the statement of games played, goals scored, money won. This whole process was illustrated in the case of Ned Hanlan, after whose death in 1908, nearly twenty years after his last race, there was an outpouring of genuine emotion and grief. He was so important that, in 1926, Toronto sportsmen erected a statue to the great oarsman. By the 1970's he was forgotten.[80]

It is doubtful if any Canadian, prior to Hanlan, can be considered a true sport hero, an individual with a national reputation and something more than a string of victories. However, two instances came close. The first was the Paris Crew from Saint John, New Brunswick, and it was the acquisition of the name "Paris Crew" that gave them their claim to fame.[81] Although other crews had been successful in regattas on the eastern seaboard of the United States, none had ventured across the Atlantic to compete against the crack amateur crews of Europe. In 1867, the province of New Brunswick donated $2,000 and the citizens of Saint John supplied $4,000 to send Robert Fulton, George Price, Elijah Ross, and Samuel Hilton to the international competition being held in conjunction with the Paris Exposition. Here was an unknown crew of working-class men, a lighthouse keeper and three fishermen, invading the exclusive rowing circles of Europe. The arrival of these "colonists" was greeted with an indifference amounting to scorn. They were given no chance of beating the four other crews, Boulogne, the Geslings of Paris, and the Western and Dolphin Rowing Clubs of England. To the astonishment of all, these unknowns beat the heavily favoured Geslings. Causing even greater dismay was their subsequent victory over three of the greatest clubs in the world, Oxford University, London Rowing Club, and the Leanders of London. The social inferiors had beaten the cream of Europe in an old-fashioned boat that outweighed the other boats by more than 100 pounds. The Paris Crew, for so they were known, received a tumultuous welcome on their return to Saint John. In addition, they were rewarded with substantial amounts of money, which caused them to lose their amateur status. They continued to gain fame during the ensuing four years. Despite their numerous victories, however, they failed to establish themselves as sport heroes. The time was not ripe.

The second example is also an oarsman from the Maritimes. The career of George Brown illustrates the thin line that divides a great athlete and a sport hero.[82] Between 1863 and 1871, George Brown, a fisherman from Herring Cove, Nova Scotia, established a reputation as one of the best oarsmen in the Maritimes. His chance for international recognition came in 1871 when the organizers of the Halifax Aquatic Carnival attracted the top scullers in the world. Brown rowed against Joseph Sadler, the World Professional Rowing Champion, over a five-mile course and lost by a scant four seconds. Between 1871 and 1874, he was perhaps the best professional oarsman in the world, but because of circumstances he failed to gain the recognition. Sadler successfully avoided meeting Brown, who, while waiting for Sadler, defeated all the leading American contenders. Sadler finally agreed to a match in 1875 but Brown suffered a fatal stroke while training for the race. He thus failed to gain the stature that would have made him a potential Canadian sport hero. He did, however, become a true Nova Scotian hero, a monument being erected to his memory in his native Herring Cove. The extent of his local fame can be gauged from the fact that in 1925, on the fiftieth anniversary of his untimely death, the *Halifax Herald* devoted two columns on the front page to his memory, while a memorial service was held at the Anglican Church in Herring Cove.[83]

Despite the undoubted success of the Paris Crew and George Brown, Edward "Ned" Hanlan was the only truly Canadian sport hero prior to 1885 and perhaps in the nineteenth century. Ned Hanlan's absolute domination of the professional rowing world from 1877 to 1884 made him a household name throughout Canada and the English-speaking world.[84] Born on July 12, 1855, in Toronto, Ned spent his youth working in his father's hotel on Toronto Island and spent his spare time rowing. He started competing in the Toronto area in 1873 and, over the next few years, established a formidable local reputation. The year 1876 signalled a major breakthrough when, at the centennial sculls held in Philadelphia, he defeated some of the world's best scullers. This victory led to the formation of the Hanlan Club, a group of local tavern keepers, businessmen, and civil servants who agreed to provide financial backing for the up-and-coming oarsman. In 1877, he won the Canadian championship against Wallace Ross of Saint John over a five-mile course on Toronto Bay. This ushered in an era of unprecedented success and domination of the professional rowing world. From 1878 to 1884, he won the Championship of America (1878), the Championship of England (1879), and the Championship of the World (1880) on the famous Thames River course from Mortlake to Putney in England. He successfully defended or won his titles fifteen times and rowed for prize money of between $2,000 and $5,000 per race. Hanlan rowed on all the great courses of the world, the Tyne, Thames, St. Lawrence, and Paramatta rivers.

Ned Hanlan remained supreme until 1884 when he lost, like a champion with no excuses, to William Beach on the Paramatta River in Australia. Although he continued to race, he never attained his former heights. His final championship match in 1888, appropriately against William Beach, ended in defeat, and he finally quit competitive racing in the early 1890's. Subsequently, Hanlan became a rowing coach at the University of Toronto and Columbia University and eventually became a respected Toronto alderman. He died on January 4, 1908.

During his era of true greatness, 1877-1884, Hanlan became a national hero, greeted by large crowds wherever he went. Crowds waited at the telegraph offices to hear reports of his races. Newspapers reported the preparations for the races and the races themselves in great detail. Ice rinks, buildings, and streets were named after him. Dinners, attended by leading Canadians, were held to honour Hanlan and gifts were showered upon him. Perhaps the place he held in the minds of Canadians was summed up most clearly by Thomas White, an admitted non-oarsman and non-athlete, at a reception given to Hanlan at the Victoria Rink, Montreal, in August, 1878.

> But I am an earnest Canadian. I love this my native country, and I rejoice at the success of those manly sports which, practised by the younger men of the country are certain to promote a manly national character.[85]

It was as a symbol of Canada that Hanlan became Canada's first sport hero.

What was the significance of Ned Hanlan to sport and Canada? In terms of sport he was the first to place Canada at the undisputed forefront in the world in any sport – he was without question the best in the world. Central to his whole stature was his run of successes from 1877 to 1884. Not only was Hanlan a winner but he came to be regarded as invincible, as superhuman. Unlike so many other sport figures, his period of domination, seven years, was long enough for his reputation and status to become well established. Success in itself, though, was no guarantee of heroic status. He had an additional attribute that added to the aura surrounding him – the way he achieved his victories was stamped with the individual style of Ned Hanlan. This was illustrated, most graphically, in the most important race of his life, the contest against Trickett on the Thames River, England, for the Championship of the World in 1880. A vast concourse of spectators lined the banks of the Thames to witness the race, but, even at this critical moment, Hanlan's flair for showmanship came to the fore. After pulling to an early lead, he began his usual exhibition of showmanship, waving to spectators, sudden spurts, clowning, and finally collapsing in the boat with 500 yards to go, only to stage a "miraculous" recovery when Trickett threatened to overtake him. Hanlan proceeded to row to an easy victory. It was this showmanship that provided the charisma so necessary for a sport hero. Rowing was a serious affair but he demonstrated that it was still possible to maintain one's individual identity. To rowing he brought spectators, international recognition, and success; to Canada, a new status for a new country.

The position of Hanlan within the world of sport was indisputable but the claim that he was important to Canada as a nation rests on less certain ground. Yet, recognizing the position of Canada at that moment in time, we may see that Hanlan provided the country with something no one else in any other field of endeavour was capable of doing. Canada was a young country struggling to find an identity independent of Britain and the United States. Certainly within the world at large, Canada was regarded as a colony of the mother country, subservient to it with no identity of its own. Within the English-speaking world, Hanlan placed Canada in a position it had never held, as a victor over the rest of the world. That he was an excellent ambassador was certainly to Canada's advantage. Always portrayed by the newspapers as a gentleman in victory or defeat and only slightly touched by the scandals that rocked professional rowing, he represented all the good things in sport. He went out of his way to emphasize his Canadian identity when many people referred to him as American. Hanlan was visible to the rest of the world while the rest of Canada remained a British colony on the other side of the Atlantic.

Within Canada itself, the victories of Hanlan, like the first Canada-Russia hockey series, provided a symbol that transcended provincial boundaries and gave the different parts of the country concrete examples of something Canadian. Psychologically, his victories provided a major impetus to the steps toward nationhood. Here was a Canadian beating the best British and Americans; the child was beginning to grow up. In how many avenues of life could Canada even claim equality with Britain and the United States? It is difficult to judge the real impact of Ned Hanlan on the majority of Canadians, yet he was the most important single symbol of Canada at that time – the greatest salesman of Canada.

If Hanlan was so important to Canada and Canadians, why has his name all but disappeared? The answer lies within the value system of Western society, which influences what the transmitters of culture perceive to be important. Basic to Western thought is the underlying belief that the mind is superior to the body. This has resulted in the relegation of sport to a frivolous concern that can have no significance in the real meaning of life. Thus, the purveyors and transmitters of the written word and the controllers of education determine the value system that the rest of society should accept. This value system was reflected most clearly in the attitudes of leaders toward the victories and recognition gained by Ned Hanlan. Goldwin Smith, in reaction to a suggestion to honour Hanlan, stated:

> It is not a question, as some would make out, between physical and intellectual worth, but between worth of any kind and that which is worthless.... No part of the affair is more offensive than the suggestion that Canada is indebted to a professional oarsman for redemption from obscurity and contempt.[86]

Of course, Goldwin Smith was right. Hanlan *was* rescuing Canada "from obscurity and contempt." Smith was also representative of the educated elite who were always first into print with their judgements based on their own elitist value system. The role of rowing and sport in the lives of the majority of Canadians was tacitly recognized in several *Montreal Star* editorials that called for Canadians to mend their ways and do "the right things." In May, 1880, prior to the Trickett race in London, the *Star*, in an editorial, which itself was significant, questioned the ultimate importance of rowing. The editorial suggested that the public invested too much time and money in it and called on Canadians to become concerned with other things. Finally, in a strange paradox in this individualistic business community, the editor decried the fact that a professional made so much money.[87] In 1882, another editorial made some revealing comments. First, it questioned whether anyone could ever beat Hanlan and then went on to state, "Of course, it is a question of very little importance."[88] Here was an editorial accepting the super-human qualities of Hanlan and then stating it was unimportant. In short, the value system underlying the educated elite was antithetical to recognition beyond the sport field. While the newspapers reported what the readers wanted – news of Hanlan – they rejected the value system that made him important. Here was a man, Ned Hanlan, more famous than any other Canadian, bringing honour and respect to his country, being castigated by men who, in retrospect, did little to develop Canadian identity among the *mass* of Canadian society. However, despite the efforts of various individuals and groups to disparage his achievements, throughout his lifetime he remained the "Boy in Blue" to Canadians everywhere and his death, in 1908, was greeted by an outflowing of eulogies and tributes from across the world that are usually reserved for the most prominent citizens. Historians may continue to disparage and ignore the contributions of Hanlan and other sportsmen, but to the average Canadian during his lifetime he was of far more importance than all the politicians and academics.

What emerges from this brief review of the commercialization and professionalization of sport is the centrality of money to all aspects of sport. It became increasingly important as the century progressed and organized sport spread throughout all segments of society. All sport, amateur and professional, private and commercial, was predicated on a sound financial base. Lack of financial resources was the main cause of the failure of so many sporting clubs and commercial enterprises. However, the role money played varied across the spectrum of sports and social groups. While money was important to the development of sport across the country, it was most central in the larger urban areas where conditions transpired to make money a necessity for any sporting venture. As towns and cities expanded, increased pressure on land forced up costs, which in turn affected the ability of groups to maintain exclusive facilities. For the wealthy, financial considerations allowed them to maintain the exclusiveness of their social sporting activities. While they denied that their activities had any commercial orientation, their involvement in the highly profitable thoroughbred racing suggests otherwise.

During the 1870's and 1880's, with increasing middle-class involvement, money became a visible and significant element in the growth of sport. Rising land costs and increased taxation forced the middle classes to open up their private facilities to public use. In this, they revealed their hypocritical stance: while vehemently condemning professionals they still rented their grounds to these same professionals. This position is most clearly revealed in the amateurs' use of money to differentiate between themselves and the professionals. Amateur sport, however, could not escape the need to generate money. As organized sport expanded, financial expenditures increased to meet rising costs of equipment, facilities, and travel. Amateur sport organizations, such as the OHA, soon recognized the commercial potential of their championship series and moved to promote them. In fact, they soon became the major source of income. For fully commercial professional sport, victory and championships, and money, became the reasons for existence. Sport had become truly capitalistic. Yet in a paradoxical fashion the consummate professional sportsman, Ned Hanlan, was decried because he made money. The full hypocrisy of Canadian intellectuals and sportsmen was thus revealed. While glorifying the making of money by businessmen, they condemned the making of money in sport. This irony lay at the heart of sport in Canada.

6

The History of Organized Sport: A Case Study of Lacrosse, 1834-1914

The previous chapters have focused on particular elements in the growth and development of organized sport in Canada. Each has dealt with an important aspect of the change from pre-industrial to industrial sport forms: the change in the competitive structure from challenge and exhibition games to a league structure, the complex growth of bureaucratic organizations, and the central importance of money in the development of all sport. In addition, we have seen the unique characteristics of Canadian sport and its relationship with Great Britain and the United States. In no one chapter, however, has a coherent view of all aspects been presented. Therefore, the function of this chapter is to provide a picture of the totality of Canadian sport in all its complexity. If one sport exemplified the uniqueness of the development of sport in Canada it was lacrosse, claimed, erroneously, by lacrossists to be Canada's national game.[1] The history of lacrosse illustrates the roots of the game in Montreal and Ontario, its particular patterns of development both within Ontario and across the country, and the development of the professional game out of amateur lacrosse. As well, its history pinpoints particular problems faced by Canadians in constructing their own sport culture, regional differences, the battle between the old and the new, the inability of middle-class Canadians to arrive at a consensus, and the pervasiveness of the British and American influence. Thus, lacrosse is an ideal case study of Canadian sport.

181

THE HISTORY OF LACROSSE, 1834-1885

The European Canadians had been aware of the Indian game of baggataway for many years before some young Montrealers recognized its potential as a game suitable for white men. Perhaps the first stirring of interest was evidenced in the Indian exhibition of lacrosse in Montreal in 1834. However, it was not until the summer of 1844 that white men first stepped onto the field to test their mettle against the Indians. On this occasion they lost. The real beginnings of organized lacrosse occurred in 1856 with the formation of the Montreal Lacrosse Club (MLC) by a group of socially prominent young Montrealers. This ushered in a period of expansion. By 1861, the city of Montreal had nine clubs. The highlight of these early years was the exhibition game played before Edward, Prince of Wales, on his visit to Montreal in 1860.

George Beers and the members of the MLC brought lacrosse into an era of real growth. During the summer of 1867, Beers and his colleagues sent an invitation to lacrosse clubs in Canada to meet in Kingston, Ontario, in late September for the purpose of forming a national lacrosse association. This initiative and the subsequent formation of the National Lacrosse Association (NLA) had far-reaching consequences for the game. The NLA became the sole arbiter in matters concerning rules, eligibility, and conduct on the playing field. Until 1886, the NLA remained the sole lacrosse association; its history provides the clearest view of the growth of the game, the men who created it, its penetration into Canadian life, the problems it faced, and the solutions adopted.

The National Lacrosse Association

Lacrosse was created, nurtured, and dominated by Montrealers. The first club, the MLC, was central to every development, dispute, and altercation until 1886. A group from the MLC, led by Beers, a Montreal dentist, promoted the idea of a national organization. With a characteristic sense of timing, a meeting of lacrosse clubs was called for September 26, 1867, at Kingston. Under Beers's leadership, forty-two representatives of twenty-seven clubs from Ontario and Quebec met to consider lacrosse affairs and, particularly, to "Systemize rules and establish a national association."[2] The result was the formation of the NLA. Its power and prestige were related to the circumstances of its formation. The rules of the game published by Beers in 1860 became the rules of all lacrosse. Therefore, it was not beset with the problem of different local rules that served to hinder the development of Canadian football and ice hockey. Also, as late as May, 1867, there were only eight lacrosse clubs in Canada, all located in or near Montreal. The other nineteen clubs that met at Kingston had been formed during the summer of 1867. More important than the increase in numbers was the expansion into Ontario. Toronto, which did not have a single club at the beginning of the year, by October counted thirteen with 600 players. In fact, by September of 1867 there were more clubs in Ontario than Quebec. By accident, therefore, the move to form a national association took place at exactly the right time. At the same time, the problems that were to beset the NLA and eventually lead to the destruction of its power were rooted in its origins: the reality of Montreal domination.

By 1871, the initial surge of interest in lacrosse had dissipated. Many teams had dropped by the wayside, problems had emerged, and basic differences in approach split lacrossists into several groups. In 1870, a championship game between the MLC and its archrival, the Montreal Shamrocks, ended in both player and spectator violence. As a result of this and other incidents the MLC withdrew from the association. The reasoning given for its withdrawal illustrated the nature of the problems facing these early lacrossists.

> A thorough determination to wipe all associations and con-
> nections with matches which attracted the rowdy elements was
> formed, and the sensational champion matches which had been
> a deep injury to the game, as experience had proved, disgusting
> good players as well as the respectable part of the public . . . .[3]

This pinpointed the nature of the problems that had emerged since 1867 – the presence of "rowdy" or undesirable elements and dissatisfaction with the competitive structure in lacrosse, in particular, the championship games. These factors were to remain central to the history of lacrosse and, in fact, to all organized sport.

The years 1871-76 were fallow ones for lacrosse. Only occa-sional games were played during the summers and a total of ten championship games were contested between 1872 and 1875. By 1876, there was a renewed interest in the game as it spread through Ontario and western Quebec. Throughout Canada interest was heightened by the successful tour of the MLC and Caugh-nawaga Indians to Great Britain, where a series of matches were played before enthusiastic crowds. The tour culminated with a game at Windsor Castle in front of Queen Victoria. More significant, in the long run, was the meeting held at the initiative of the Toronto Lacrosse Club (TLC) on May 6, 1876, "for the purpose of re-organizing the National Lacrosse Association of Canada."[4] This resulted in the revival of the NLA. The importance of this action lay both in the regeneration of the organization and in the commencement of a shift in control from Montreal to Toronto. Prior to 1876, the championship had been the exclusive preserve of Montreal area clubs, mainly the Montreal Shamrocks. The year 1876 saw the first successful challenge by the TLC – the base of power was shifting.

In reality, nothing had changed for the better during the intervening years, the newly constituted organization being confronted with the same problem that had plagued it in the five previous years: undesirable behaviour on the playing field, especially in the critical championship games. During this period the amateurs' explanation for violence and ungentlemanly conduct – professionalism – was first voiced. In ensuing years this became the explanation for all that was wrong with lacrosse. This concern culminated in strong action being taken at the annual convention of the NLA in 1880. The delegates voted to change the name of the organization to the National Amateur Lacrosse Association. The lacrossists believed that this action would solve all their problems. Once again the prestigious MLC withdrew, this time because the organization was not amateur enough for its liking. This move eventually forced the NALA to take action to meet the objections of the MLC, and the MLC rejoined in 1882.

The NALA had tried to solve the problems by removing the symptoms but nothing had changed. The result was its collapse as the sole controlling body for lacrosse in 1886 when the TLC led a mass breakaway of Ontario clubs and formed a rival association, the Canadian Lacrosse Association (CLA). Therefore, when lacrosse needed solidarity and a strong central organization to face the problems of mass sport, the sport was split into rival associations, neither of which had the power to control the major lacrosse clubs.

The failure of the NALA to solve the problems was related to factors germane to Canadian sport *per se* and not just to lacrosse. The answers lay in the origins of amateur sport in Canada and its particular developmental patterns. Montreal and Toronto dominance of nineteenth-century Canadian sport gave to the Canadian

Table 5
**Geographical Distribution of Lacrosse Clubs in the National
Lacrosse Association / National Amateur Lacrosse Association,
1867-84**

	Montreal		Quebec City		Rest of Quebec		Toronto		Rest of Ontario		Rest of Canada		Total
	No.	%	No.	%	No.	%	No.	%	No.	%	No.	%	
1867	12	44	1	4			5	19	9	33			27
1878	12	27	4	9	2	5	8	18	18	41			44
1879	12	21	5	9	5	9	6	11	28	50			56
1884	8	15	3	6	2	4	6	11	32	59	3	6	54

sporting scene its particular characteristics. Thus, the problems facing lacrossists were, in substance, the same as those faced by footballers and ice hockey players. The first problem area was the power structure of lacrosse, and this can be examined by identifying the sources of power and the methods of its exercise. Second, the problems facing sport administrators seeking to control sport can be examined by identifying the problems lacrossists faced and the solutions they adopted.

The sources of power within the NLA were related to four variables: the number and distribution of clubs, permanence of membership, dominance of the executive, and success on the playing field. Table 5 provides a picture of the geographical and numerical distribution of members of the NLA. It demonstrates the Ontario and Quebec monopoly of lacrosse, with three Manitoba clubs joining in 1883-84 giving bare substance to the national title of the organization. Contained within these figures are some interesting perspectives. First, despite the Montreal origin and promotion of the association, even at the outset it was dominated by Ontario clubs – 52 per cent in 1867. This dominance was to become more pronounced as the years progressed, with the imbalance between Quebec and Ontario reaching its highest level in 1884 when only 25 per cent of the clubs were located in Quebec. Perhaps of even greater significance was the decline in the position of Montreal itself. The origin of lacrosse was accurately reflected, in 1867, by the pre-eminent position of Montreal with twelve (44 per cent) of the twenty-seven clubs. By 1884, even though it still had the most clubs, both the number (eight) and the percentage (15 per cent) had decreased. More subtle, but just as important to the long-term development of the game, was the shift from large to small urban centres, a pattern that was to become more pronounced in the twentieth century. Taking Montreal and Toronto as representative of the larger urban complexes, their joint position in both clubs (seventeen to fourteen) and percentage (63 to 26) dropped significantly from 1867 to 1884. The real power, in terms of voting members, lay in the heartland of Ontario and particularly along the railways. Between 1867 and 1884, 79 per cent of the clubs were located on a railroad.[5] The picture that emerges from this brief analysis is of an increasingly Ontario-based organization with numerical power shifting from the two larger centres to the more broadly based membership in the smaller towns of Ontario.

In considering the sources of power, distribution of members is only one factor. The number and distribution masked another important factor – the permanence of clubs. It is logical to expect the clubs with continuous membership in the organization would wield more power than those without a continuous presence. Only four clubs were permanent members, two from Montreal and one each from Quebec City and Toronto. However, after the reorganization of the NLA in 1876, ten other clubs, nine from Ontario and one from Quebec, were constant members. Therefore, if continuity had any significance, the locus of power lay in Ontario.

There were two other sources of power – in the board room and on the playing field. The two were linked because of the correlation between executive membership and pre-eminence on the playing field. The majority of executive positions were held by representatives from the Montreal and Toronto clubs, with the Shamrocks providing a number of key executives. The other positions were filled by representatives of clubs that challenged for the prestigious senior championship of Canada – Cornwall, Prescott, Tecumsehs of Toronto, and Independent of Montreal. Noticeable by their absence from the executive, and after 1880 from the NALA, were the Indian clubs of Caughnawaga and St. Regis. The executive power lay with a small group of clubs – the MLC, TLC, and Shamrocks – who among them won sixty-three of the seventy-one championship games played between 1866 and 1884.[6] It is difficult to avoid the conclusion that the NLA was an organization run by Montreal and Toronto.

Analysis of distribution of clubs, permanency, executive, and playing success is a necessary prelude to a discussion of the reality of power. Despite the increasing presence of Ontario in the council and the success of Toronto on the field of play after 1876, the NLA/NALA remained a Montreal-controlled organization. In fact, it is not too much to say that the NLA, created by George Beers and the MLC, remained at heart an organization of the MLC with such individuals as Beers, William Maltby, Angus Grant, and Hugh Becket maintaining an active role throughout. From 1876 to 1885 there was a continual battle between the MLC and TLC for control; Toronto lost and eventually broke away and formed the rival CLA. What was surprising was the apparent ineffectiveness of the Shamrocks, on the playing field the most successful club.[7]

What, then, were the reasons for the success of the MLC in imposing its extreme views on an organization that could have rejected them? First, and foremost, was its espousal of pure, unsullied amateurism, an ideology that all accepted in principle but in practice frequently violated. The Montreal Lacrosse Club was the only one against whom accusations of using professionals was not levelled.[8] Allied to these strong principles was an inflexibility of purpose and will; the MLC would stop at nothing, even the destruction of the organization, to maintain its integrity. The Montreal club leaders effectively destroyed their own creation in 1871 over a matter of principle and attempted to do so again in 1880. These strong convictions and their ruthlessness stood them in good stead because they, along with the TLC and Shamrocks, were the only indispensable elements in the organization. Neither the Torontos nor the Shamrocks were, until 1885, willing to destroy the organization, and thus Montreal reigned as the absolute power in the NALA. It is true to say that the MLC created and, through its inflexibility, destroyed the organization – a sad day for lacrosse and the men who did so so much to promote sport in Canada. Events had overtaken them. Organized sport had arrived.

One of the central threads running through this history was the tripartite rivalry among the Toronto and two Montreal Clubs. The inability of these clubs to reach consensus was one of the basic reasons for the failure of the organization. This deep-seated antagonism was reflected in the newspaper reports on the games. In the case of inter-city games, the score and the presence of violence were the only commonalities, each paper accusing the other city of flagrant violations. The battle was often carried by representatives of the clubs from the field of play into the newspapers. In the case of the Montreal-Shamrock rivalry, the *Gazette* and the *Star* blamed the Shamrocks for the outbursts of violence. It is difficult to escape the conclusion that this was, in part, a class or ethnic distinction since the Shamrocks were Irish, Roman Catholic, and working-class. Despite protestations to the contrary, there was a deep and abiding antipathy among the three clubs. One club invariably would vote against another just because the motion was proposed by the other. In the 1880's there were instances of the three clubs reversing position within one year and taking diametrically opposed positions on issues such as the series system and two hours of play. This destroyed the NALA because it became impossible for the organization to solve real problems that had faced the game ever since the formation of the NLA in 1867.

The problems the game faced were complex and to solve them would have required the co-ordinated efforts of lacrosse administrators. They were, basically, the same problems that other sports faced. The fact that lacrosse was the first game to face this particular set of problems and did not have the benefit of past experiences increased the difficulties. Contemporaries recognized and identified the problems but several obstacles stood in the way of removing them successfully. First, there was considerable difficulty differentiating between cause and effect, symptom and disease. Second, because of the conflict between the three major clubs, there was difficulty in obtaining the two-thirds majority in the NLA council necessary to effect a change in the by-laws. Finally, if rules were passed with which they disagreed, the big three would ignore them. Since there was no effective method of punishment the rule changes had no impact.

The concerns facing the administrators fell into two categories, those dealing with the structure and those with the playing of the game. Structure involved questions of game length, methods of determining the victor, and the crucial problem of competition. Problems on the playing field were a concern from the initial championship game in 1866. Violence and unsportsmanlike conduct were perennial while the role of officials and the influence of spectators became of increasing concern during the late 1870's and early 1880's. From the late 1860's, players, administrators, and the general public were aware of serious questions facing lacrosse. The NLA took immediate steps, through legislation, to remove what was perceived to be the cause. Despite well-meaning efforts on the part of the legislators and extensive editorial comment in the newspapers, there was little to suggest that success attended these efforts to bring about structural changes or to reduce the violence and ungentlemanly conduct on the field. In most cases the symptoms were treated, not the real cause. The approach taken by the lacrossists was the same as that taken by other sports at a later date.

The changes in the structure of the game fell into two categories: the game as spectacle and the meaning of the contest. Central to both was the shift from pre-industrial to industrial forms of sport. The change from a loosely structured game form to one with clearly defined spatial and temporal boundaries is an accurate measurement of the shift from the past to the present. The reaction of the administrators, players, and public to these questions illustrated a basic inertia to change. Once the rules had been codified at the Kingston meeting in 1867, there was great reluctance to change the rules, changes only being made after lengthy discussion or when the problem was perceived to be so serious as to threaten the integrity of the game.

The factors affecting the game as a spectacle were the length of the game, the method of determining a winner, and the delays in starting the game. From the very beginning, lacrosse was a player-oriented game. The idea of spectators was foreign but became of interest as soon as large numbers of spectators flocked to the grounds. The main question was the length of the game. At the Kingston meeting it was passed that a match would be won by the best three out of five games (goals). By the mid-1870's, concern was being expressed over the shortness of some matches, one Montreal-Caughnawaga match being over in under ten minutes. Despite increasing recognition of the rights of spectators, this remained the rule for determining the outcome of the game. The first official expression of concern was at the NLA convention on August 3, 1877, when two prominent members of the MLC, Angus Grant and Hugh Becket, moved and seconded "That a match shall be decided by the winning of the greatest number of goals in two full hours of play."[9] This was defeated. The motion was reintroduced in 1881 by the Shamrocks but failed to get the two-thirds majority. The question was not finally settled until 1889, by which time the NALA had been split into two independent organizations. Another persistent problem concerning the rights of the public was the frequent delay in getting the game started. Delays of up to two hours were not uncommon and were not restricted to any single club, the Shamrocks, MLC, TLC, and Caughnawaga all being guilty of late appearances. Both of these problems reflected a pre-industrial value system; the idea of time limits, of starting times and schedules, basic ingredients of modern sport, were not yet accepted by players, administrators, and the public.

Perhaps the most important of the changes facing the early lacrossists was one that few observers recognized as such – the changing structure of competition. In 1885, at the annual meeting of the NALA, the old championship system was abandoned and replaced by what was, in effect, the first lacrosse league. The old challenge system, whereby the champions remained champions until challenged by another team, was replaced by a series system of four teams, two each from Montreal and Toronto, playing home-and-home games against each other. This apparently simple move was fundamental in launching lacrosse into the world of contemporary sport. The majority of games played between 1867 and 1885 were exhibition or challenge matches. There was a subtle difference between this type of game and a league game. Exhibition and challenge matches had no significance beyond the actual contest itself. The creation of a league gave meaning to each game beyond the boundaries of that contest, the standings at the end of the season being dependent on a cumulative point total. This is at the heart of modern sport and was at the core of the debate over competitive structure, which was irrevocably changed at the NALA convention in 1885. The change from exhibition games to a league is essential to modern sport and reflects, clearly, the perceptive insights of some of these lacrossists and the complete blindness on the part of the majority to the real consequences of their actions.

In 1866, the Caughnawaga Indians defeated the MLC in the first championship of Canada. Until the next challenge match the Indian team remained champion of Canada. The introduction of the championship game revolutionized lacrosse since each championship game took on a significance far outweighing the routine exhibition and challenge games. How important this was in affecting behaviour on the playing field was illustrated in the exhibition and championship games played by senior clubs from 1866 to 1885. Incidents of violence were significantly greater in championship matches than in the others, a clear indication of the effect of competitive structure on the behaviour of players.[10] As early as 1871 the MLC recognized that the initiation of championship games had changed the way the game was played, and in its view the change had not been beneficial. That the problems in lacrosse were attributed to the championship matches was supported by various letters to the *Montreal Star* and *Gazette* during the 1870's. At a meeting of the MLC in 1873, reference was made to "The sensational champion matches which had been a deep injury to the game."[11] Another observer of lacrosse in 1875 attributed the temporary decline in the game to "the championship contest between Montreal and the Shamrocks."[12] Perhaps the most perceptive observer of all was "Lacrosse," who wrote to the *Gazette* in 1877 recommending:

> That lacrosse in the future have no championship, but like cricket clubs promote a more kindly and friendly spirit among the clubs and players – the people are weary of these championship matches and the squabbles they produce.[13]

In spite of the obvious truth in these statements and the general condemnation of the behaviour generated by the championship games, there was never any serious attempt within the NLA or NALA to disband the system. It was universally accepted, despite the fact that its results were contrary to the most cherished beliefs of the majority of administrators. Less understandable was their reluctance to take the logical step and create a league. This reluctance only made sense within the confines of a certain value system, the ideology of amateurism.

The need to change to a league system was recognized in 1878 when James Hughes, president of the TLC, expressed the opinion that "It was a hardship that a club should retain the championship until the close of the season and then, losing one game – it should pass away from them until the next season."[14] It was not until 1883 that any motions for change were placed in front of the NALA. At that time the MLC, the bastion of pure amateurism and sportsmanship, introduced a motion that would, in effect, spell the end of lacrosse as its leaders believed it should be played. Inappropriately, it was W.L. Maltby, the purest of pure amateurs, who proposed an amendment:

> That the Championship be held from the 1st November in one year to the 30th October in the following year by the Club winning the majority of a series of matches held throughout the season between a certain number of clubs, which shall be recognized as "First Class Clubs."[15]

Just as inexplicable as the Montreal support of this motion was the Shamrocks' opposition to it. In fact, both clubs were supporting positions antithetical to ones that they had previously expressed.

Table 6
Number of Senior Lacrosse Championship Games
in Four-Year Periods, 1866-1885

Period	Number
1866-69	13
1870-73	10
1874-77	14
1878-81	18
1882-85	32
Total	87

The motion failed but was reintroduced in 1884 and passed after a "fiery debate," but without the required two-thirds majority. However, at the 1885 meeting, against strong Toronto opposition, it was decided that the championship for the 1886 season would be held by the overall winner of home-and-home series to be played between a select number of first-class clubs. Lacrosse had finally entered the era of modern sport.

One of the factors leading to the change to league competition was the increased popularity of the game. In the 1860's it was rare for the senior clubs to play more than two or three games a year; lacrosse was, in truth, an avocation. By the late 1870's these infrequent games had been replaced by a relatively full schedule of between fourteen and twenty games. This increase is illustrated by the increase in the number of championship games (Table 6).[16] The senior championship of Canada was played annually from 1866. However, not until the 1880's was there any expansion beyond this one level. In 1882 the NALA inaugurated an intermediate championship and by 1884 there were Ontario championships, local contests in southern, eastern, western, and central Ontario, championships of Quebec, western Quebec, Manitoba, and the Northwest. Lacrosse had moved into a new era.

The changing structure of competition and the increased popularity of the game brought myriad problems to players, administrators, and concerned observers.[17] The solutions provided a bench mark against which other groups, faced with similar problems, measured their own answers. The problems emerged both from the change from pre-industrial to industrial sport forms and from the particular characteristics of Canadian sport. These problems, at times threatening to destroy the game, were never solved conclusively. Some solutions had temporary success, but within a few years the same problem, sometimes in a different form, emerged once again to confront the administrators of lacrosse. These unsolved issues concerned violence, unacceptable conduct on the field of play, and disputes with the officials.[18] The existence and persistence of unacceptable behaviour were clearly evident in the games between first-class clubs. Throughout the years, 28 per cent of the games involved disputes, violence, and even rioting.[19] Obviously the issues were difficult to solve.

Perhaps the best way to illustrate the nature of the problems and the underlying causes for the failure to correct them is through two accounts of the Torontos-Shamrocks championship game played in Toronto on Saturday, July 9, 1881, which the Shamrocks won. The *Montreal Star* reported:

> The play throughout this game was very determined and the Torontos were anything but careful of their opponents, and as a consequence Butler was severely cut on the head, and Heelan was so injured that he had to leave the field. The Torontos played a rough game from the word go and it seemed as if they wanted to hold on to the Championship by brute force. Mr. Bernard Tansey stated "That he considered the Toronto men to be perfect butchers in their play, and their conduct throughout was anything but becoming gentlemen." The Toronto men showed their roughness in another manner – that is by running off the field without waiting to give the customary cheers to the opposing team.[20]

The *Toronto Globe* gave the same account of violence, but with a rather different bias. In the first place, blame was set squarely upon the referee: he "may be a successful businessman, but is in no sense a representative lacrosse man." The *Globe* went on to state that there was:

> Remarkably little roughin' on both sides considering the game at stake and the intense feeling caused by the claims of foul which were raised by both contestants. The victors (the Shamrocks) forgot to assemble and cheer the vanquished as is the usual custom. They were hissed by the crowd as they passed the grandstand.[21]

This game was by no means unusual for those involving the MLC, TLC, and Shamrocks. Violence and ungentlemanly conduct were endemic. The importance of these two accounts, however, is not so much in the content but in the insights provided for the failure of the NLA and lacrosse clubs to control the incidence of violence and disputes on the playing field. In the first place, the two accounts illustrate the tremendous rivalry between Toronto and Montreal. This rivalry was so intense that even the newspapers could not avoid extreme partisan support of their own teams. There was no effort to be objective even in the instance of handshakes. The fact that the teams did not shake hands was reported by both newspapers, but it was impossible to determine whose fault, if anyone's, it was. By 1881, the rivalry between the clubs had reached such a peak that there were continual disagreements and disputes over fouls, scoring goals, and officiating. Invariably, the loser claimed either foul play or biased, incompetent refereeing. This antagonism led to heated exchanges in both the newspapers and the NLA. Within the NLA council rule changes would have to be made, but this was rendered virtually impossible by the rivalry of the big three. Toronto would disagree with a recommendation made by the Shamrocks simply because it came from that source.

In addition to the antipathy between the major competitive clubs, there was never a strong impetus within the executive or council to legislate for behaviour. This was due to certain basic assumptions held by sportsmen and administrators relating to the way in which a game should be played. An examination of the attempts to legislate for the removal of violence and ungentlemanly conduct illustrates this. The actions taken were simple in the extreme: add new rules to meet the particular offence. By 1882, the list of rules governing play had increased to seven, each with several subsections. Thus, a complex set of rules, open to varying interpretations, governed the playing of the game. For example, Rule XVIII, governing rough play:

> No player shall grasp an opponent's stick with his hands, hold it with his arms, or between his legs, nor shall any player hold his opponent's crosse in any way to keep him from the ball until another player reaches it, no player with his crosse or otherwise, shall hold deliberately, strike or trip another, nor push with hand, nor must any player jump at, or shoulder an opponent from behind while running for or before reaching

the ball, nor wrestle with the legs entwined so as to throw an opponent.[22]

In fact, this was the extent of efforts to solve fundamental problems confronting lacrosse. The organizers failed to enforce the rules, to give power to the referees and officials, or to create a body of efficient officials. Their failure to remove the causes rather than the symptoms stemmed from the underlying value system with its assumptions of why men played lacrosse and how it should be played. This was clearly stated in an editorial in the *Montreal Star* on July 16, 1881, that discussed the critical condition of lacrosse:

> The papers are full of suggestions .... But all these suggestions only prove that the public is not satisfied with these constant disputes.... But there is one improvement that lies within the power of all players, and it is a necessary one if the game is to hold its own, and that is to play lacrosse in a gentlemanly way and not as becoming rowdies.[23]

Players were *expected* to play the game within the spirit and letter of the law. It was inconceivable that gentlemen would not play the game in such a fashion. Placing the onus of responsibility on the individual player explained attitudes to the referees and officials. Referees were to adjudicate disputes, not to see that fair play was done. It was the field captain's duty to call for fouls, not the referee's. This also explained the laissez-faire attitude to the appointment of officials. The appointment of the referee, which is taken out of the hands of the clubs today, was left up to the clubs to arrange before the game, even in the important championship games. The fact that before these games there were frequent acrimonious disputes only attests to the fact that the assumption was false and the administrators failed to recognize this.[24] The administrators were unwilling to legislate because it ran counter to their basic value system.

The logical conclusion for lacrossists was that the incidence of disputes, violence, and undesirable conduct on the field of play could mean only one thing – some players were not gentlemen. The truth of this observation was given substance by the presence of Indians, who always played for money and, by race alone, could not be gentlemen, and of the working-class Shamrock team. The Montreal and Toronto clubs probably did not see the problem simply along class lines, but this undoubtedly was part of their analysis. The incidence of violence, the Indians and Shamrocks, the increasing emphasis on winning were all linked together into one answer – professionalism. The advent of professionals was seen as the underlying cause of all the problems and thus their removal would remove the problem. In 1880, the renaming of the NLA as the National *Amateur* Lacrosse Association was seen as the answer. This excluded the Indian teams. Of course, once again, administrators had removed a symptom, not the cause. The cause was a complex set of circumstances: an increased emphasis on winning, the changing competitive structure, the widening base from which players were chosen, in other words, the move from pre-industrial sport to industrial sport, from sport for a select social group to mass sport. The central thread that ran throughout this era of change and instability was the amateur/professional question. Without an understanding of this, it is impossible to understand the genesis and development of sport.

The Montreal Shamrocks

The foregoing has traced the development of lacrosse in Montreal and its spread into Ontario. It has focused on the dominant role of Montreal and the emergence of problems that have persisted to the present. However, it has not explored the nature of the game itself, who played, and its importance within the community. The central importance of lacrosse in the lives of ordinary Canadians and the dangers of overemphasizing the role of the middle class are revealed most clearly in the history of one club, the Montreal Shamrocks.

As Table 7 illustrates, the Shamrocks were, without question, the most successful team prior to 1885.[25] Not only were they the most successful, they were also the most vilified. They were an anachronism, a team before their time, dedicated to winning when it was not considered "correct" to emphasize that aspect of the game, a team reflecting the ideology of modern-day sport before it had fully taken shape. The Shamrocks were out of place both socially and athletically. Social misfits on the middle-class playing fields, the Shamrocks were Irish, Roman Catholic, and working-class.[26] The Shamrock Lacrosse Club was formed in 1867 in the heart of Irish Montreal, Griffintown, along the Lachine Canal. They were, more than anything, Irish, with the membership crossing class and occupational boundaries. The management was in the hands of businessmen, bookkeepers, a Queen's Counsel, and a medical doctor. They received active support from Alderman

Table 7
Victories In Championship Lacrosse, 1866-1884

Teams	Games Won	Percentage	Comments
Montreal Shamrocks	39	52%	
Toronto	13	17	All after 1875
Montreal	11	15	Ten before 1870
Ontarios (Toronto)	2	3	Both in 1876
Caughnawaga	4	5	Three before 1870
St. Regis	2	3	All before 1870
	4 drawn	5	
Total	75	100	

James McShane, the mayor of Montreal. On the playing field they were represented by "horny handed sons of toil," the working class. Here was a club whose major identifying characteristic was ethnic rather than social homogeneity, very different from the upper-middle-class, English, Protestant Montreal and Toronto clubs.

From their origin, the Shamrocks came into conflict with the MLC and within three years a strong dislike, verging on enmity, developed between the two clubs. This embryonic rivalry came to a head in one of their first championship games in October, 1869. In a subsequent analysis, the *Montreal Star* commented:

> Last October, Moffat (S) received a cut on the head from Maltby (M) perfectly accidental, but a yell arose that he did it on purpose. From this we may trace the origin of an enmity on the part of the spectators who always follow the Shamrocks.[27]

The seeds laid in October came to fruition on June 18, 1870, when the Shamrocks won the first of many championship victories against the MLC. The account of the game in the *Star* illustrated features of Shamrock games that were to remain constant throughout their existence. "The ground was speedily swamped by inroads of the great unwashed who coolly dropped over the tall fences and took their stand several deep all around the field cursing and swearing, yelling and hooting . . . ." During the game,

Brady (M) objected to the conduct of Moffat (S) in throwing him head over heels backwards, but the play went on. The ball went into the crowd, the men were shamefully treated and greeted with the most insulting treatment from the rowdies.[28]

Subsequently, Hinton of Montreal was kicked when he fell near the crowd, and this incident soon developed into a mass fight involving spectators and players. This was the end of the game, Montreal refusing to continue after order had been restored. From this developed the intense rivalry between the two clubs, to the extent that exhibition games between the two clubs were more violent than championship games against other clubs.[29]

Even more illuminating were the characteristics associated with the Shamrocks. Invariably, championship games involving the Irish team were followed by accusations and counter-accusations of ungentlemanly conduct, outright violence, and harassment of the officials. Other teams were beset by the same problems but none to the same extent. The Shamrock supporters were different from those who flocked to the Montreal and Toronto lacrosse grounds. Many references to the "unwashed" and "denizens of Griffintown" attested to the different social origins of some of the spectators. The supporters used abusive language unfit for the ears of ladies, and therefore the "gentle sex" withheld their patronage, much to the chagrin of the reporters of the *Star*. The Shamrock supporters, drawn from working-class Griffintown, were the first real fans in Canadian sport. Certainly there is an affinity between them and modern-day sporting spectators. As well, the Shamrocks were followed by success – they had that Midas touch that enabled them to grasp victory from defeat. This is not to say that other teams were not dedicated to winning, but the Shamrocks were more committed to victory even though lip service was paid to how the game was played.

The victory of June 18, 1870, ushered in five years of unprecedented triumph for the Irishmen. Their main rival, Montreal, posed no real threat and the Torontos had not yet managed to assemble a team that came close to beating them. Despite their overwhelming success, they were nearly forced to disband in 1872. Although the movement for dissolution was actively supported by the *Montreal Star*, a complete reorganization was undertaken at a well-attended meeting in St. Ann's Church Hall, Griffintown, and the club was saved.[30] From this moment, the Shamrocks went from strength to strength, invariably to the accompaniment of accusations of dirty play and ungentlemanly conduct. At the same time, the Torontos were gaining strength. In the early years of the Shamrock-Toronto rivalry there was a lack of disputes and confrontations, perhaps because the Shamrocks usually won 3-0! After the games, the two teams dined together at either the St. Lawrence Hall, Montreal, or the Queen's Hotel, Toronto. By 1874 this aspect of the game disappeared and was replaced by accusations and counter-accusations of dirty play and ungentlemanly conduct. Coincidentally, these were the first games that were close enough to be considered contests.[31]

On October 9, 1875, the impossible happened – victory by the Torontos in Montreal. The Shamrocks were, for the most part, graceful in defeat, admitting that the Torontos thoroughly deserved the victory, but at the same time they claimed that "overweening confidence" was the true cause of defeat. Whatever the real cause, the end result was the same, the termination of friendly competition and the beginning of a heated and sometimes violent rivalry between the Shamrocks and Toronto. During the next nine years the Shamrocks won twenty-seven championship games, Toronto twelve, and the other teams four. Clearly the Shamrocks were the true champions. However, the results of the games against Toronto showed that this judgement was premature and masked the real intensity and equality of the rivalry between the two teams. Of the fourteen games played against Toronto, the Shamrocks won five, lost six, drew three, and had one further victory due to a Toronto forfeit in 1877. Despite the overwhelming superiority of the Irish team against all challengers, the real champions of the 1876-1880 period were the Torontos, who beat their rivals consistently except for 1877. Thirty-four championship games were played during these four years; thirty of these were won by the two teams but only six involved direct confrontations. Most of these were won by Toronto and were accompanied by protests from the Shamrocks against unfair refereeing (1876), disputed goals (1878), and roughness and lack of practice (1880).

The 1881 season ushered in one of the greatest eras in the history of the Shamrocks. Playing twenty-nine games in 1881 and 1882, they only lost one. More importantly, they beat their archrivals, the Torontos, four times in 1881 in a series of games that revealed both the good and bad sides of lacrosse. The era began with their victory in Toronto on July 9, 1881, in one of the most violent and bloody contests in the history of the rivalry. In stark contrast to this bloody battle was the game played in

Montreal on September 3, 1881, in front of 9,000 spectators. The teams shook hands before the game and proceeded to give what newspaper reporters claimed to be one of the greatest exhibitions of sportsmanlike lacrosse. After the Shamrock victory the team and supporters accompanied the Torontos to the railway station from whence the losers departed amid a storm of cheering. In these two seasons, the Shamrocks reached heights that the club was not to reach again until the great team of 1901-05. Undoubtedly, this fine team of Irish Canadians was the true champion of the first seventeen years of organized lacrosse. Although there was dissension among the other clubs, the Shamrocks were the focal point of the disputes, disagreements, and accusations that plagued the lacrosse world. The question is why?

After the inaugural game to open the new Shamrock Lacrosse Grounds in 1878, won incidentally by Montreal, 3-0, the Irishmen hosted their rivals to dinner. In 1881, after the great September game against Toronto, they once again played host at the Windsor Hotel. Despite this evidence of a degree of bonhomie between the clubs, the reality was that the other two teams despised the Shamrocks. This was clearly illustrated in 1882, the year following the Shamrocks' greatest triumphs. Six weeks into the season the Shamrocks had not received any challenges for the championship. This caused certain individuals on the club to accuse the other first-class clubs of boycotting the champions in an attempt to force them into financial difficulties. Strenuous denials were issued by the three major teams, but the pro-Montreal and anti-Shamrock *Montreal Star* felt called upon to state: "It cannot be denied that there is a dearth of challenges for the 'trophy' this season, when in past seasons it was found difficult for the champions to answer all challenges."[32] Dr. Guerin, vice-president of the Shamrocks, stated it more emphatically in an interview published on July 15, 1882. "The fact remains that we are shunned most scrupulously, the Independents, Montreal, and Toronto clubs are constantly playing amongst themselves."[33] The justice of the accusation is open to question but the reality of the enmity between the clubs is not. The reasons for this cast interesting light on early lacrosse.

As with so many problems facing sport, the causes are to be found in a complex set of factors that are impossible to separate completely. At the root of the continuing conflict were some fundamental differences that served to separate the Shamrocks from the others. First were the ethnic and class differences. In addition, success could account for the antagonism between Montreal and the Shamrocks – in championship contests from 1870 to 1884, the Montreal team only won once. Also, religious differences separated the teams, the Shamrocks being Roman Catholic and the others Protestant. While it is difficult to prove, there appear to have been antithetical value systems underlying the philosophies of the clubs. Despite claims to the contrary, the Shamrocks were more dedicated to winning than some of the other clubs. This different emphasis led to different interpretations of acceptable and unacceptable behaviour, which was at the root of much of the dissension between the clubs.

The division between the Shamrocks and the other teams was at heart the difference between "sport" (amateur) and "athletics" (professional); between a game in which things other than victory or defeat are to be gained from participation and one in which victory is everything; in short, between the amateur sport of the 1870's and sport today. This difference is critical to an under-standing of the emergence of modern sport and the problems facing it. The Shamrocks represented modern sport. What, then, was the value system of the Shamrocks? In the first place, there were consistent indications that they were more committed to winning. A greater commitment to winning meant a tendency to stretch the boundaries of acceptable behaviour. This was accentuated by the physical nature of the game, which resulted in the varying interpretations that frequently resulted in violent and bloody physical battles. Second, the Irish were not averse to playing for money, and this was anathema to the amateurs. The championship and $500 were at stake in the game against Caughnawaga in September, 1875.[34] After the first defeat by Toronto, the Shamrocks responded with a challenge with stakes of $1,000 a side – needless to say, this challenge was not accepted. Associated with this was the unsavoury association with betting that seemed to cling to the club. In the 1870's the Shamrocks promoted betting by selling pools. As late as the 1880's, Bernard Tansey, one of the officers of the club and owner of the Tansey House, sold pools at his tavern. In 1881, the *Star* estimated that Shamrock supporters collected over $15,000 in bets as a result of the victory over Toronto. Any association with money was rejected by the exponents of pure amateurism.

The concern over money led to the most important differen-tiating factor – professionalism. This was the catalyst for all the problems facing the game in the 1870's. The pure amateur clubs attributed all the ills that beset the game to the money element and professionalism and there is little doubt that the Shamrocks were regarded as the primary team that fell under this rubric. However, the Irishmen were certainly not professionals in the full sense of the word. They were an amateur team that paid expenses and sometimes found jobs for the players. Some of the players, such as Giroux and Moffat, were professional runners, and it was only at this level that charges of professionalism could be maintained against the team. But this sufficed, in 1880, to cause them to lose some players because of the definition of amateurism accepted at the 1880 annual meeting of the NLA. The Shamrock representative, Hoobin, spoke to no avail against the new definition, stating that: "It was a hardship not to allow a man to play lacrosse because he had run a race for money against a professional."[35] The fact that the Shamrocks remained members of the NALA was concrete evidence that, in spite of all the accusations, they were not professionals because if they were they would have been expelled. The answer then must be sought in the acceptance of a different value system and in the social origins of the players.

In 1874, after a rough game with the St. Regis Indians, the Shamrocks were strongly castigated by the press for conduct unbecoming white men. Morgan O'Connell, captain, replied to this censure with a letter querying the attitude of the Montreal newspapers. "I hope this is not because we are only mechanics and Irish Catholics at that."[36] This suspicion was given further substance on two occasions when Toronto and Montreal balked at playing because of two players. In the first instance, on June 9, 1877, the team and supporters had travelled to Toronto to play a championship game. On arriving at the grounds they were greeted by the Toronto team, who refused to play because one of the Shamrocks had served time in a penitentiary.[37] On the other occasion, in July, 1884, Montreal threatened to default the game because Green had been convicted of a serious criminal offence. Montreal played the game under protest. Thus, there appeared to be some substance to the claim that the enmity was, in part, due to social origins and conflicting value systems.

The Shamrock Lacrosse Club was different from any of the other major clubs, especially as it related to the community. The club's support was based in Griffintown, the Irish enclave, and came from "the great unwashed," "rowdies," and "scallywags." This conglomeration of society gave to the Shamrocks the kind of unwavering, partisan support associated with present-day sport.

Spectators entered fully into the game, infringing on the field of play, hurling abuse at the officials and opposing players. Support was vocal and loyal, with crowds of 8,000-9,000 cheering on their heroes in championship matches. Yet it was not just on the playing field that the club served a community function. The team was the focal point of many other community events. The club often gave concerts in the St. Ann's Parish Hall in the middle of Griffintown.[38] In 1873, an impromptu torchlight procession was held and they paraded through the streets to the music of the Hibernian Band. After successful trips to Toronto, they were greeted by enthusiastic throngs at the station. Nowhere was the role of the club demonstrated more clearly than in the reception accorded the players after the battle of Toronto on July 9, 1881. After the game the Shamrocks had to rush to catch the train. The train was decorated throughout its length with green boughs. Thus started the triumphal procession to Montreal. En route, the team was greeted by crowds at Whitby, Cobourg, and Cornwall. These receptions were simply a foretaste of what awaited them in Montreal. They were greeted at Bonaventure Station by "an immense crowd" that escorted them to the Grand Central Hotel, where a reception was held.[39] Although both the MLC and the TLC were greeted by enthusiastic crowds, neither could rival the Shamrocks in support. They were truly a community team, a vehicle of religious and ethnic pride.

This has been the unfinished story of the Montreal Shamrocks, a team before its time, a modern team in a pre-industrial setting. The sole representatives of the working class in senior lacrosse, the Shamrocks catch the imagination as a colourful team capable of hard play but with an underlying fairness that brought them popularity and support throughout the world of lacrosse. Perhaps even more important are the insights their history provides into the role and function of lacrosse in the lives of the inarticulate segments of society. It was, as sport is today, central to the lives of many Canadians, providing a vehicle for the demonstration of ethnic, religious, and class identity and pride. Sport was not merely a frivolous diversion divorced from the mainstream of life. Rather, it played a central role in the developing urban areas.

LACROSSE, 1886-1914

The creation of a lacrosse league in 1885 and the breakaway of the Ontario clubs in 1887 marked a new era in lacrosse, one in which the game was confronted directly by the spectre of professionalism. The professionalization of the game and the resultant problem of differentiating between amateurs and professionals provided the dominant theme in the history of lacrosse and, in fact, of other popular sports. The professional question was further exacerbated by the spread of the game across Canada. This came at a time when lacrosse was rent by dissension and disunity. No single group could claim to represent the interests of lacrosse. Lacking a strong central organization, inter-provincial and regional differences were accentuated and the problems intensified. It is necessary, therefore, to outline the spread of lacrosse across Canada before moving to an examination of the growth of professionalism and the problems it created.

The Spread of Lacrosse

In the thirty years after 1885, lacrosse spread across Canada. However, its distribution was by no means uniform and was related to several factors. First, the spread of the game was closely tied to its origins – its birth in Montreal and its early years in Ontario. It was never able to break its ties with Ontario and western Quebec, which remained the lacrosse centres of Canada. The game was taken by young Canadians emigrating from Montreal and Ontario to the West and East. Thus, after 1885, the game's expansion was closely tied to the movement of Canadian-born anglophones. The strength of its development was linked to the ethnic composition of the population in different parts of Canada. On the Prairies its dominance was strongly contested by British sports, while on the East Coast the central role of the British garrisons ensured strong ties with British sports. In addition, the game failed to gain a firm foothold in two major institutions, the schools and churches. In fact, only in the three strongholds of the game was it incorporated to any degree within the educational system. Toronto public schools inaugurated a league in 1894 that did not survive for many years. Winnipeg was the only city where it gained a permanent place in the schools' sports program. The league, founded in 1901, was still flourishing in 1914.[40] On the West Coast the game was adopted by the Victoria schools by 1915. Elsewhere, schools did not embrace the game to any significant degree. The churches, which became involved in promoting sport among youth in the early 1900's, were notable in their rejection of the Canadian game, their reason being the same as that given by newspapers and other sportsmen for its failure to gain more support – violence on the playing field. Finally, the organizers of lacrosse failed to develop a strong national association, and consequently the game was unable to face with a united front the severe problems that emerged during the early 1900's. It was not until 1912, when the game was in serious trouble, that the AAUC led the way in the formation of the Canadian Amateur Lacrosse Association (CALA), a case of bolting the door after the horse had gone. Thus the spread of lacrosse from its base in Ontario and western Quebec was characterized by distinct local variations with each region exhibiting a different pattern of development.

Lacrosse was introduced into the Maritimes during the late 1880's. Often, as was the case with the game in Saint John, increased interest was related to the arrival of enthusiasts from Ontario or Quebec. Frank Dowd, a leading player from the MLC, arrived in Saint John in 1889 and immediately introduced the game to the young men of the city.[41] In July, during the Carnival week, the famous Caughnawaga Indian team from Montreal played a match against Saint John AAA.[42] This was followed by attempts, in 1890, to promote the game in Halifax.[43] These initiatives did not flourish and by the mid-1890's lacrosse was a rarity on the playing fields of the Maritimes. The game, however, did not disappear entirely; periodically, initiatives were undertaken to promote the game, but all were to no avail. In 1895, two Halifax teams and one from Truro formed a short-lived league.[44] Ten years later Westville, Pictou, and Truro formed the Maritime Provinces Amateur Lacrosse Association – again, it failed. Lacrosse never gained a foothold in the larger cities of Halifax, Saint John, Fredericton, and Moncton. Without a base in these cities it was bound to fail. Perhaps the most important reason for its failure to take root was the strong British presence. By the mid-1880's, cricket was firmly established as the summer game of middle-class Maritimers. This strong British orientation retarded the success of lacrosse.

In 1885, the Montreal-dominated NALA had total control of affairs in the world of lacrosse. The Shamrocks and the MLC were among the premier competitive clubs in Canada. All in all, lacrosse – and Montreal – could look to the future with optimism. But within three years the world of lacrosse had disintegrated into fragments. No one organization could claim jurisdiction over the game. Ontario and Quebec had separated, and the five major clubs had formed a small independent organization. This fragmentation took place because of growing dissatisfaction with Montreal domination and, on the part of the major clubs, with the increasing power of the junior clubs. Toronto unrest came to a head in 1886 when the Toronto club was denied the senior championship of the NALA on a technicality. It withdrew from the NALA in 1887 and formed a rival organization, the Canadian Lacrosse Association (CLA). Except for eastern Ontario, all the Ontario clubs joined the new organization. Lacrosse was now ruled by what were, in effect, two provincial organizations. The position of these two organizations was undermined in 1889 when the five leading clubs, drawn from both organizations, created a league independent of either body. The Shamrocks and the principal lacrosse clubs from Montreal, Toronto, Cornwall, and Ottawa formed an independent Five-Team League. This created an elite group of five clubs playing the highest level of lacrosse, and in these circumstances top-level lacrosse, not subject to the two organizations, lost its contact with the grassroots. Therefore, when lacrosse faced the problems of increasing violence and professionalism there was no one body ready and able to meet the challenge.

The destruction of Montreal's power parallelled the expansion of the game to other areas of Quebec. Prior to 1885, the game in that province was primarily limited to the immediate environs of Montreal except for a few teams in Quebec City. It was an exclusively anglophone game. During the 1890's lacrosse gained a following among French Canadians in Montreal and Quebec City. While it is difficult to pinpoint the exact date when French Canadians became involved it is possible to identify when they became a real force in the game. The first French team to reach premier status was Le National of Montreal, formed in 1894.[45] That they took to the game was illustrated by the fact that in May, 1895, just one year after their formation, they became the first French-Canadian team to beat one of the premier lacrosse clubs, Cornwall.[46] Although the game spread to other French-Canadian communities in the ensuing twenty years – to Grande Mère, Trois-Rivières, Montagny, Villeray – its strongholds remained Montreal and Quebec City. Unlike Ontario, where it was a small-town game, it remained associated with the larger urban areas in Quebec.

The creation of the CLA in 1887 represented the shift in numerical strength from Montreal to Ontario. Ontario was now the centre of the game in Canada and it retained its pre-eminence until the war. The period between 1887 and 1895 witnessed a significant expansion in the number of clubs. In fact, by 1895 lacrosse had reached the limits of its geographical expansion. In the ensuing years the number of clubs increased from eighty-two to 115 but much of this was due to the inauguration of a junior championship in 1901 (players under age twenty) and a juvenile championship in 1909 (under eighteen).[47] This meant an increase in the number of teams in small towns but little increase in its geographical spread. Lacrosse was played in specific locations and was notably absent in others. The game maintained a presence in the Ottawa Valley but did not experience significant growth. Like most other areas, the smaller towns, such as Carleton Place, Almonte, and Renfrew, maintained single teams. The only place with intra-city leagues was Ottawa. The CLA focus was on Toronto but it did not derive its power from the city. Of the twenty-eight senior championships contested betwen 1887 and 1914, only three were won by Toronto teams. The real champions of this era were the Athletics of St. Catharines, who won the coveted trophy ten times.

An even clearer picture of the distribution of the CLA comes from the seventy-two teams that won the various championships – all came from within a 100-mile radius of Toronto. The CLA was essentially a small-town organization, and few of the Ontario cities (six of twenty-eight) played lacrosse on a consistent basis. The strongholds of lacrosse were the rural towns around Peter-borough and Belleville, Simcoe County to the north of Toronto, the St. Catharines area, and the small towns to the west of Toronto. Noticeable by their absence from the lacrosse scene were the cities of Hamilton, Berlin, and Guelph and the smaller towns in the heart of the Golden Horseshoe. Lacrosse never gained a foothold in this area where baseball reigned supreme. Only in Brantford, with the Six Nations Reserve, was the game played to any extent. The champions of lacrosse came not from Hamilton, London, Windsor, Sarnia, or Chatham but from Seaforth, Fergus, Orillia, Markham, Orangeville, and Brampton.

The foundations of lacrosse in Ontario were weak indeed. The game never found fertile ground in the larger cities, a necessary condition for the growth of organized sport; it never gained support from the schools and churches; and lacrossists failed to develop a feeder system in the CLA. Lacrosse was always on shaky ground, the high-profile professional teams being rooted in shifting ground. Unlike baseball, soccer, and ice hockey, extensive intra-city leagues failed to develop except in a few locations, notably Toronto and Ottawa. Outside of these cities, few intra-town leagues existed for more than a few years. The contemporary perceptions of the strength of lacrosse were illusory, based on a view of the high-profile spectator lacrosse and not on the degree to which it had penetrated the whole of Ontario. In fact, for a majority of Ontarians opportunities to play and watch lacrosse were strictly limited. Lacrosse, claimed by some to be Canada's national game, was not even the most popular game in Ontario, the supposed heartland of the game.

As young Ontarians moved west into Manitoba in the 1870's and 1880's, they took lacrosse with them. Soon after the first settlers moved in, lacrosse clubs were organized. Winnipeg had semi-permanent clubs by 1876. Brandon, first settled in 1881-82, had a club in 1883.[48] By 1888, there was sufficient interest to form a Manitoba Lacrosse Association. In 1896, eleven clubs banded together to form the Western Canada Lacrosse Association (WCLA). By 1905, the WCLA intermediate series contained five districts with twenty-one teams. Of course, the centre of the game was Winnipeg, which by 1901 contained seven leagues and thirty-two teams. Yet, the strength of lacrosse must not be overemphasized. In particular, it faced strong opposition from British and American sports. Like their Ontario counterparts the British immigrants brought with them their own games, in particular cricket and soccer. Unlike ice hockey, lacrosse faced strong opposition for players and spectators. At the same time, it did maintain a presence in Manitoba.

Organized lacrosse was a relative latecomer in what were to become Saskatchewan and Alberta. Although there is evidence of teams in Edmonton as early as 1889 and in Regina and Calgary in the 1890's, the competition was irregular. The game was placed on a more stable footing in the early 1900's when inter-city leagues developed. Invariably these leagues embraced the larger towns – Regina, Medicine Hat, Lethbridge, Calgary, and Edmonton. By 1907 Regina entered the professional game, importing such players as "Newsy" Lalonde from the East. There were also a few short-lived leagues involving small towns and villages. The game had developed some roots. This was reflected in the formation of provincial associations in Saskatchewan and Alberta in 1907. However, the hold of lacrosse was always weak, and it never really went beyond maintaining a presence in the larger towns. Perhaps its position is most clearly illustrated by Edmonton, where in 1915 only two teams took to the playing fields.

If one area did threaten the domination of Ontario and Montreal it was the West Coast, in particular the cities of Vancouver, New Westminster, and Victoria. As early as 1887, occasional games were played between Victoria and Vancouver. These competitions were formalized early in the 1890's with a three-team league. Like the Prairies, much was owed to the immigrants from the East, such as A.E. McNaughton from the MLC. Within a few years the West Coast teams were the equal of the Five-Team League. This was demonstrated in 1899 when the New Westminster Salmonbellies toured the East, beating all the teams in the Five-Team League except for Toronto, with whom they drew. From that date, British Columbia teams moved to the top rank. In 1908 the Salmonbellies wrested the Minto Cup, symbolic of the national championship, from the Montreal Shamrocks and thus began an era of western dominance. The West was not to lose hold of the Minto Cup before competition was suspended in 1914. In addition to this success, after an initial victory by the Young Toronto Club in 1910, the Mann Cup, symbolic of the amateur championship of the Dominion, became the exclusive property of West Coast clubs prior to the war. Thus, in the years immediately preceding the war, British Columbia teams were the undisputed champions of Canada.

Yet the game was not in a healthy condition on the West Coast. In the first place, the highly visible and successful senior teams were not founded on a solid infrastructure. Lacrosse never expanded outside the three cities and even there it was never the popular game it was in the East. In 1905, Vancouver, the centre of lacrosse, contained only four leagues and sixteen teams. By 1915, the number of teams had diminished to eleven. In order to field competitive professional teams, the West Coast cities were forced to raid the East in an attempt to attract the best players. Also, the West Coast experienced the same problems of professionalism and violence as Manitoba and the East. The violence escalated to such an extent that a newspaper that had loyally supported the New Westminster team made the following statement after the New Westminster team had set upon and beaten up Alderman Fred Lynch after a game with Vancouver: "Died in New Westminster, on Saturday, October 4, 1913, professional lacrosse."[49] While this pronouncement was made in the heat of the moment, it was, in fact, an accurate assessment of the state of lacrosse in Canada. The malaise was so deep-rooted that the now familiar effort to save the game, the formation of the British Columbia Amateur Lacrosse Association in 1915, was doomed to failure. The heyday of lacrosse had passed, never to return.

The distribution of lacrosse across the country was characterized by local peculiarities. As an amateur game it was only played with any degree of continuity in Ontario, Manitoba, and British Columbia. The game was characterized by its lack of permanence in the Maritimes, most of Quebec, Alberta, and Saskatchewan. Even in the areas of strength there were distinct, isolated strongholds of the game: the city of Montreal and eastern Ontario; the area within a 100-mile radius of Toronto; Manitoba, with a strong concentration around Winnipeg; and the three West Coast cities. This particular pattern was reflected in the emergence of autonomous local and provincial bodies that fought each other as strongly as they attempted to stem the tide of professionalism. The lack of a truly national amateur body was a continuing weakness that was only addressed seriously in 1913 when steps were taken to create a strong national amateur organization under the aegis of the AAUC. Unfortunately for lacrosse, this was too little too late.

The question remains as to why lacrosse, undoubtedly the most popular game in Canada in 1885, failed to live up to its expectations and become a truly national game. Contemporary verdicts that pervasive violence in the amateur and professional games was the root cause of its demise, while containing a grain of truth, were an oversimplification. In addition to the violence, the cause of which was never really understood, were other more basic weaknesses. Lacrosse failed to develop a truly national following. Its claim to being the national game was propagated by its most zealous supporters and was never reflected in reality. The game developed where the enthusiasts from Montreal, Toronto, and eastern Ontario took it, especially to Winnipeg and Vancouver. For the most part, it remained an Ontario game with many of the leading players in all parts of the country learning their lacrosse in that province. In addition, the absence of a strong national body to co-ordinate competition and solve the myriad problems that faced the game was a real hindrance to the spread of lacrosse. Perhaps most important of all was its lack of a solid foundation in the large cities. As we have seen, even on the West Coast there was little lacrosse outside a few cities and no base of junior and intermediate clubs. In the East, although it had been created and nurtured in Montreal and Toronto, the game was popular as a spectacle but not so widespread as a participant sport. The great era of lacrosse in Montreal and Toronto was the 1890's. Its strength lay in the small towns of Ontario; such towns as Brampton, Elora, and St. Catharines, which still boast teams today, were the real home of the game. No modern sport can become a true mass sport without having a strong foundation in the large cities. Lacrosse, created in pre-industrial Canada, remained an essentially pre-industrial game in an increasingly industrialized society. Whether any action could have saved it is, indeed, a moot point.

This brief overview of the spread of lacrosse across the country indicates that the foundations were not strong, that the base of support was always weak. However, few contemporaries recognized the importance of the infrastructure, turning instead to the highest level of the sport, the senior clubs. Invariably, the professionalization of the game was held accountable for its demise along with the perceived increased violence and the resultant decline in the number of spectators. As Sir Henry Pellatt stated in 1931, "I think the entering into lacrosse of the professionals has been the means of lessening the interest of the amateurs and the public."[50] To complete our view, then, we must turn to the rise of professional lacrosse.

THE GROWTH OF PROFESSIONAL LACROSSE

The history of lacrosse between 1885 and 1914 encompassed the rise of the game to its greatest heights in numbers of players and public interest and the beginnings of its precipitous decline in prestige and popularity. The origins of professionalism lay, not with entrepreneurs or organizations that had a marketable product, recognized its worth, and attempted to sell it, but with amateur teams vying with each other for the championship of the city, province, or nation. It was not limited to the highest level of the game but permeated all organized lacrosse at the junior, intermediate, and senior levels. Inducements, in one form or another, were offered at different levels of the game in an attempt to win particular championships. It became virtually impossible to identify and punish all culprits. This was, in part, responsible for the decline of the game – the question of the hidden professional was never solved. However, the development of professional teams, as opposed to individual players, occurred in its clearest form only at the highest level of the game – in the prestigious Five-Team League, the senior series of the CLA, and the West Coast League of Victoria, Vancouver, and New Westminster. There was one other brief venture on the Prairies in the first decade of the twentieth century, but this failed to survive. The road to professionalism was neither straightforward nor clear cut. It is possible, however, to identify three main eras. The first, from 1885 to 1899, was the era of pseudo-amateurism, when players were hired to bolster the teams but were not "officially" paid to play lacrosse. The period 1900-06 witnessed a battle between the lacrosse organizations and the CAAU over the mingling of amateurs and professionals on the lacrosse fields. Finally, the years 1907 to 1914 saw the rise of the fully professional game to its greatest heights and its sudden decline.

The problem of player payment did not spring to life in 1885. Prior to that date the leading teams made frequent accusations and counter-accusations about the presence of professionals. The creation of a league in 1885 brought about important changes, the significance of which was illustrated, after the 1886 season, by the players themselves. When asked by a reporter from the *Montreal Star* about the effect of the new series system, the comments added up to a recognition that the game had changed from an avocation to a vocation. The season was now too long, the players were required to give up too many Saturdays and had to practise four nights a week; in other words, the game had changed from "sport" to "athletics." In the words of one of the players, "The first and greatest [change] is that it is too much work for amateur teams and occupies too much of their time, therefore professionalism will be hard to keep out."[51] These most perceptive comments identified many of the basic characteristics of sport today.

Perhaps more important was the conscious recognition of the basic changes in the game – the difference between an avocation and a vocation. As though the players, spectators, and organizers recognized this fundamental shift, the 1886, 1887, and 1888 seasons were crucial to the history of lacrosse and did, in fact, ensure the growth of the professional game. The 1886 season ended on a sour note when the MLC was awarded the championship over Toronto on a technicality. As a result, Toronto withdrew from the Senior Series and from the NALA early in 1887. In 1888, the NALA Senior Series collapsed amidst a cacophony of accusations over foul play, ungentlemanly conduct, use of professionals, and the bribing of players and referees.[52] Lacrosse was in disarray, the two organizations fighting for members, the highest level of lacrosse shattered, and the problem of professionalism growing. By 1889, both the NALA and CLA spent most of their annual meetings dealing with the question of professionals. Interestingly, the clubs were never held accountable for paying players; rather, the players were blamed for accepting money. In 1889, the five leading clubs in the country took an irrevocable step toward professionalism by creating the independent Five-Team League. There were now two major leagues, the Five-Team League and the Senior Series of the CLA. The clearest illustration of the growth of fully professional teams lay with the Five-Team League, which remained stable except for the addition of the Montreal Nationals in 1897 and the Toronto Tecumsehs in 1906. On the other hand, the composition of the Senior Series of the CLA changed frequently, but by 1900 it had reached the same position as its rivals.

The history of the Five-Team League from 1889 to 1899 illustrates the process and nature of the change from amateurism to professionalism. One question dominated the councils of the league – professionalism. From the outset, however, it was not simply a matter of money, although this was the central issue, but also of the changing social status of the players. Amateurism implied for some a certain social class that could afford to play without recompense. The entrance of other segments of the population was predicated on payment in one form or another – travelling expenses, payment for time off work, etc. One of the clearest indications of a shift is to be seen in the social composition of the Ottawa Capitals team of 1893: a manager, a railway company employee, a storeman, an electrician, and seven post office workers.[53] The offer of employment had become one of the major methods used by clubs to induce players to join. In 1894, Quinn, one of the star players for the Ottawa Capitals, moved to Brockville because the team there offered a better and more permanent job.[54] The extent of this was evident, as early as 1889, when the Ottawa team included players from Richmond Hill, Montreal, Quebec City, Brockville, and Toronto.[55] In each instance, the clubs avoided breaking the strict letter of the law but certainly did not live up its spirit. This was the great age of the pseudo-amateurs.

Throughout the last decade of the nineteenth century a continual internal battle raged in the councils of the Five-Team League between the dedicated amateurs and those advocating a more liberal interpretation of the term "amateur." At the same time, it should be noted, all teams considered themselves amateurs and were strong opponents of professionalism. The differences lay in the rigidity of the definition as to who was or was not an amateur.[56] The first major confrontation occurred at the meeting preceding the 1890 season over the question of who should make the decision in disputes over professionals. The majority, Ottawa, Cornwall, and the Shamrocks, voted that the Five-Team League establish its own body to make the decisions. Montreal and Toronto threatened to resign unless the jurisdiction was given to the Amateur Athletic Association of Canada. Incidentally, Montreal and Toronto were the only clubs that were also members of the AAAC. Such was the power and prestige of the two clubs that the majority backed down and allowed the AAAC to become the arbitrator, but this was not the end of the affair. The question was reintroduced in 1891. This led the MLC and the TLC to withdraw and set up a separate schedule to "Endeavour to promote the interests of purely amateur lacrosse."[57] Despite claims of outstanding success by the rival leagues, a compromise was reached prior to the 1892 season when the majority capitulated to the MLC and the TLC. The proponents of pure amateurism had apparently won the battle, and the AAAC reigned supreme. In fact, it was a Pyrrhic victory, for by 1900 all teams had accepted the presence of professionals. During the years 1892 to 1896 there was increased evidence of inducements, of buying players, and of professsionals at all levels of lacrosse. A continual barrage of accusations filled the newspapers, and the only club whose reputation remained unsullied was the MLC.

Unable to accept the hypocritical practices of its opponents and thus becoming less competitive on the field of play, the MLC made one final effort to save the amateur game. In 1897 it withdrew from the Five-Team League and sponsored intermediate and junior competitions:

> The reasons which led up to this action consisted primarily of the fact that being unable to adopt methods now in vogue by the other clubs to secure players, the committee felt that they could not continue to place in the field teams with prospects of successful competition.[58]

Clearly the MLC was caught in a bind – unwilling to condone unacceptable practices but trapped in the reality of all sport, the need for success. The only action open to the club was withdrawal.

In 1898, in order to promote its concept of amateur lacrosse, the MLC formed the Inter-provincial Lacrosse League of Canada, all to no avail. Prior to the 1900 season, the lone outpost of purely amateur lacrosse in the Big Five capitulated to the inevitable by applying for readmission to the league and by so doing gave support to the practice it had fought against for so long. The Five-Team League, now the Senior Lacrosse Union, was ready to step into the era of full professionalism. Coincidentally, in the same year, the Athletics of St. Catharines of the Senior Series of the CLA became openly professional while continuing to play against so-called amateur teams. Thus, both leagues were ready for the next stage, the playing of open professionals on the same teams and fields as amateurs.

By 1900, professionalism in lacrosse had developed to such a degree that money was being paid openly to players on various teams. As far as can be ascertained, though, there were no fully professional teams or players who made their living solely from playing lacrosse. The period 1900-06 witnessed a vain effort on the part of the three senior leagues to reach a compromise with the Canadian Amateur Athletic Union over the playing of amateur and professional players on the same teams.[59] The final battle to maintain high-level amateur lacrosse took place in the East in the vain attempts of the CLA and SLU to persuade the CAAU to accept the playing of amateurs and professionals on the same team.

Perhaps goaded by the arbitrary action of the St. Catharines team in 1900, the CLA was the first organization to express official dissatisfaction with the actions of the CAAU. It began to exert pressure on the so-called national organization to accept the principle of professionals and amateurs playing together. At the annual meeting of the CLA in 1901 the delegates voted to recognize officially the presence of professionals. During the next year, Brantford and the Toronto Tecumsehs provided statements of payments to players – weekly payrolls of $60.[60] The size of the payrolls demonstrated the level of professionalism. They provided neither a living wage for an individual nor enough money for all team members. What the CLA wanted was that the amateur bodies recognize this reality and thus not penalize all the amateur players who played with or against the few professionals. The CAAU refused to accept the requests of the CLA and, in 1904, brought matters to a head by professionalizing the five senior teams plus Orillia.[61] In 1905 the CLA tried to salvage the situation by clearly differentiating between the professionals in the Senior Series and the others, thus saving the amateur status of the majority of teams in the CLA. In other words, the actions of the CAAU had ensured the all-or-nothing principle. This, in fact, relegated the Senior Series to obscurity. The only way the Senior Series could maintain a high standard and attract players that brought in the crowds was by playing amateurs and professionals together. Brantford, St. Catharines, Guelph, and Brampton, the strongholds of the Senior Series, were small towns that could support semi-professional teams but were unable to pay the salaries for teams of full-time professionals. The Senior Series consequently deteriorated into a secondary league in 1906 when the Toronto Tecumsehs, the only team with real spectator potential, abandoned the CLA for the more prestigious and lucrative Senior Lacrosse Union, now renamed the National Amateur Lacrosse Union.[62]

Despite evidence of payment of players and ongoing evasions of the rules, the senior league steadfastly maintained the facade of amateurism. A suggestion in 1901 "That clubs will be allowed to play both amateurs and professionals" was greeted with universal condemnation.[63] At the same meeting, in order to emphasize the character of the organization, the name was changed to the National Amateur Lacrosse Union. This pretence was systematically stripped away in the next five years. In 1904, twenty-one of the twenty-four players on the Toronto team were declared to be professionals. As a result, the NALU terminated its affiliation with the CAAU. All pretence was dropped in 1906 when the word "amateur" was removed from the title. Thus, except for the MLC, the National Lacrosse Union accepted the fact that amateurs and professionals could play together; it was now a fully professional league. The Montreal club, as it had in the past, continued to fight a rearguard action after all was lost. Through its parent body, the MAAA, it managed to split the CAAU over the question of amateurs and professionals playing together.[64] It lost this fight as it had lost all previous fights, and the stage was now set for fully professional lacrosse teams.

The era of professional lacrosse was brief indeed, covering eight years from the 1907 season to the end of 1914. There were many reasons for its failure; violence on the playing field and an inadequate base were undoubtedly contributing factors, but these do not explain a failure that was to be repeated in other sports in the 1920's and 1930's. From the outset, professional leagues were rooted in the large urban areas, in particular Montreal,

Toronto, and Vancouver. The other teams were drawn from small cities such as Ottawa, Cornwall, and Victoria. These towns found it increasingly difficult to provide the financial support necessary for successful franchises. Even the three larger centres had difficulty providing adequate funding. Professional sport depends on spectators, and Canada could not provide large enough pools of spectators to support increasingly expensive teams. This problem was exacerbated by a buying war between the West and the East, which caused a serious and severe escalation in the cost of running a team. In 1908, the yearly salaries of the MLC, one of the least successful clubs, totalled $3,261.70. This was a significant increase over the $60 a week paid by Brantford six years earlier.[65] And it was only the beginning.

By 1912, meeting expenses had become such a problem that the new Dominion Lacrosse Association sought to place a lid on salaries by imposing a team limit of $8,000, over twice the amount paid by Montreal only four years earlier. The main reason for this escalation in player salaries was the buying war that erupted between the West and the East. There is little doubt as to who won: the West held the Minto Cup, symbolic of the professional championship, from 1908 to 1914. The war reached is apogee in 1911, when Con Jones of Vancouver "bought" the Minto Cup by bringing two of the best players in the country to Vancouver. "Newsy" Lalonde and Billy Fitzgerald were attracted to Vancouver with the astounding sums of $6,500 and $5,000, respectively.[66] The battle for players was intensified in 1911 and 1912 when two professional organizations, the NLU and the DLA, were formed. Conflict over players was ensured. Lacrosse, weakened by violence on the field, an inadequate base, and excessive salaries, was unable to meet the challenge with a united front and thus it was doomed to fail. And fail it did in the years leading to the war.

This abbreviated history of lacrosse illustrates basic elements in the development of organized sport in Canada. In particular, it highlights the central role of Montreal in the development of sport to 1914. This role is seen in the importance of small groups of middle-class Canadians, in Montreal and other cities, in developing the structures and ideology that were fundamental to all amateur sport. As well, the spread of the game to Ontario, Manitoba, and British Columbia demonstrates some common patterns of growth: the importance of urban areas and the central role of the larger cities. However, we also find that, even from its earliest days, sport found fertile ground outside the dominant middle class. The history of the Shamrocks offers a fleeting glimpse of sport's potential importance among less affluent Canadians. As early as 1870, working-class Canadians were eager participants in organized sport, albeit within the boundaries imposed by a dominant middle class.

Perhaps most important of all were the problems faced by administrators, players, and the public at large with the massive expansion of sport in the late nineteenth century. That contemporaries collapsed the causes of the problems into the one basic evil of professionalism only guaranteed that the real problems would never be solved. They failed to recognize that the emergence of industrial capitalism had changed society and that the ideology of a small, select social group was inappropriate to a new society where victory and money were the most sought-after rewards. Sport was no longer a diversion or amusement of no import to the meaning of life; rather; it had become the centrepiece of the lives of many young male Canadians and reflected the dominant cultural values. As the *Columbian* reported on the reception accorded the New Westminster Salmonbellies on their return from Montreal after wresting the Minto Cup from the Montreal Shamrocks:

> Greater than any political demonstration that ever happened, greater than anything of its kind which has ever been recorded in days gone by was the reception that awaited the boys in their triumphant home-coming last night. To that great moment when the team stepped from their private car to the station platform, from the multitudes came a truly British Columbian cheer that will go down in history and linger longer than the memories of those who were privileged "to be there."

Lacrosse, indeed all organized sport, had moved to centre stage in the lives of young, and not so young, male Canadians. It was important to the community and to the individual. But perhaps even more significant, it had become big business.

7

Conclusion: Of Sport and Canada

The present work has had three objectives: to describe the changes in the form of sport resulting from the shift to an industrial economy; to explain how the new forms emerged and the role that individuals and groups played in the process; and to examine the particular characteristics of Canadian sport. It is in our examination of *Canadian* sport that the various threads finally are brought together. Yet, what does the word "Canadian" mean when applied to the history of sport? Was there anything that transcended provincial, educational, religious, and gender boundaries? Could a Canadian from Sherbrooke, Quebec, move to Barriere, British Columbia, and find anything that was familiar in the world of sport? For male Canadians, the answer was yes. By 1914, organized sport had spread to every corner of the Dominion and had become a visible part of life to all Canadians, although access and choice were limited by local conditions, in particular one's proximity to an urban centre. The larger the urban centre the more deeply had organized sport penetrated. The choice of games, levels of competition, availability of commercial and professional sport, and involvement of various institutions epitomized Toronto and Winnipeg but not Digby, Nova Scotia, and Oxbow, Saskatchewan. Rural sport remained closer to the rhythm of the seasons and the necessities of farming life. In the rural areas, sport was more of a communal concern and did not serve to accentuate the social differences to the degree that it did in the cities. Thus, while organized sport had spread to all corners of Canada, its particular characteristics varied across the country.

Bringing a sense of unity and coherence to sport across the country was the ideology of amateurism. From the Abegweit Athletic Association of Charlottetown to the James Bay Amateur Athletic Association of Victoria, organizations committed to the propagation of amateurism flourished and provided leadership in the development of amateur sport. However, amateurism was associated most strongly with a particular social group, the anglophone middle classes of the urban centres. Even in such smaller towns as Minnedosa, Digby, and High River, the doctors, lawyers, and businessmen took the lead in organizing sport. But the strength of amateurism's influence was related to the size of the urban area. Amateurism, with its implicit class discrimination, found its most fertile ground in the larger cities and towns. Its hold was directly related to the size of the urban area and the degree to which a British middle-class influence had penetrated. There is little to suggest that native Canadians, French Canadians, and the working class were at all enamoured of the amateur ideology. Certainly they were not present in the executive councils of amateur sport and their presence on the playing fields and ice rinks was tolerated only under certain clearly defined conditions. Nonetheless, organized sport spread to these groups, albeit outside the confines of amateur sport. The transitory nature of their teams, the attachment to money prizes, and the escalating problems of behaviour suggest a strongly rooted alternate value system. There was, in fact, a growing resistance to the dominant amateur sport organizations. While this resistance was ongoing, it never seriously threatened the hegemony of amateurism prior to World War I.

The AAUC victory of 1909 was the victory of the middle class in imposing its view of sport on all organized sport. This reflected the ideology of industrial capitalism. Increasingly, the attainment of local, provincial, and national championships became the ultimate aim of amateur teams. Thus, in a strange paradox, amateurism, an ideology that denied the ultimate importance of victory, gained its greatest power by making victory the most desirable end product. This, in turn, led to increased expense in the form of facilities and travel and consequently placed money, which in one sense the amateurs abhorred, on centre stage and ensured that amateur sport would remain firmly under the control of those who had the financial resources – the middle class. Amateur sport, in other words, became a vehicle for the establishment and maintenance of the hegemony of the middle class.

One feature that characterized the Canadian sporting scene was the development of social sporting clubs with expensive facilities that were limited to certain segments of the community. Once again finding the most fertile ground in the larger urban centres, these clubs were created with the basic objective of institutionalizing social inequality. While it was most visible and clearly defined in the largest cities, institutionalized discrimination permeated down to the smaller towns. The various elites in the Canadian towns and cities created a system of clubs with entrance based on clearly defined criteria to exclude undesirables. The rhetoric of equality, which is a basic tenet of North American society, was not translated into the experience of living. There was no pretence that all Canadians should have access to the good things in life. Canadian sport reflected the reality of Canadian life – institutionalized, structured social inequality.

Finally, in terms of the commonalities of Canadian sport, two games, ice hockey and baseball, were available to all male Canadians. The harshnesss of the Canadian winter ensured the success of ice hockey, for it had no rival for the affection of robust young Canadians. Thus the climate placed its imprint on the history of sport and ensured the success of the game that Canadians, even today, identify as their own. Certainly more interesting in terms of what it tells us about Canada was the phenomenal success of baseball in the face of concerted efforts by various groups to promote lacrosse, soccer, and cricket. Its success was concrete evidence of the pervasive influence of the United States upon Canadian life.

While organized sport, amateurism, social inequality, the climate, and the United States affected all Canadians, certain attributes of Canadian sport bespoke of differences rather than similarities. These differences were so great that the word "Canadian," in some senses, ceased to have any real meaning. The reality of Canada, therefore, must also take into account these differences. However, the history of sport does allow for some generalizations that take us deep into the complexity that is Canada.

The various games played across Canada had strong ethnic overtones: cricket, soccer, and English rugby were always associated with Britain, baseball with the United States, and lacrosse, ice hockey, and Canadian football with Canada itself. If these games are regarded as symbolic of the cultural orientation of the groups playing them, the cultural mosaic of the country takes on a particular character. The pervasiveness of baseball suggests the dominant influence of the United States across the country. Perhaps more important to our understanding of Canada was the distribution of the Canadian games. In examining the areas where all three were played, we find a distinct pattern emerging. Lacrosse, ice hockey, and Canadian football only found root in Ontario and the city of Montreal. Even in Ontario, it was in particular areas, the larger urban areas within 100 miles of Toronto, that all three were popular. In the twentieth century these games spread to Manitoba and by the war were beginning to take root in the cities of Alberta and Saskatchewan. They were never, as a group, popular in British Columbia, the Maritimes, or francophone Quebec. Thus, the areas of Canadian sport were clear and by no means widespread. In another sense, the developing metropolitan areas – Toronto, Montreal, Winnipeg, and, by the mid-1920's, Vancouver – were the repository of a strong Canadianism. At the same time, the game of ice hockey served to create a sense of Canadianism since it had, by 1914, spread from coast to coast. The popularity of particularly Canadian games was characterized by distinctive patterns of distribution. If this can be taken as a measure of the strength of a "Canadian" presence then the centrality of the large urban centres, and in particular the province of Ontario, is clear.

It is impossible to understand nineteenth-century Canada without considering the British influence. The history and distribution of soccer, cricket, and English rugby highlight some different perspectives. Unlike the Canadian games, there was only one small area where all three were popular – Victoria and Vancouver. In fact, the popularity of British games was characterized by a continuing but often weak presence. They frequently appeared to be in danger of disappearing but always managed to survive. The presence of soccer was directly related to the flow of immigrants from the old country. What success cricket had was based on its adoption by the prestigious private schools. English rugby, on the other hand, depended on an ongoing British presence in the form of garrisons and on its adoption by the public school systems of the Maritimes and British Columbia. If the adoption of British games reflected a tendency to look outside Canada, the distribution and location of these games is indeed suggestive. The strength of the British connection in the upper segments of Canadian society was clear, and the private schools and prestigious clubs were concrete examples of this. At a more popular level, though, the British presence was transitory, depending to a large extent on recent immigrants. Soccer did begin to develop roots, particularly in parts of Ontario, Manitoba, and British Columbia, and by 1914, it was beginning the process of institutionalization in some areas. Thus, the British presence was uneven and complex, rooted as much in class as ethnicity.

Not surprisingly, the history of organized sport in francophone Canada is significantly different from that in the rest of the country. Still, by 1914, it had spread through the towns and villages of Quebec. In those areas where the francophones were in close proximity to anglophones – Montreal, Quebec City, and the Eastern Townships – organized sport developed. However, the French accepted neither English games nor English values. The two sports that gained significant French involvement were baseball and ice hockey. At the same time, the French maintained their attachment to challenge and exhibition games as opposed to leagues. The admittedly fragmentary evidence suggests strong and deliberate resistance to both anglophone sport and ideology.

The ideology of amateurism appears to have reached into all areas of the country, although, as has been suggested, the strength of the influence diminished with the size of the urban area. This ideology was derived from Britain, but in a Canadian context it was unequivocally Canadian. Young Canadians from Montreal, Toronto, and Ottawa developed the Canadian approach to amateurism. Lacrosse and hockey players, not the organizers of soccer and baseball, were at the forefront in articulating the ideology. Canadian amateurism therefore was distinctly Canadian, albeit of a small minority drawn from the middle class of the larger urban areas.

Professional sport, in some respects, was not available to all Canadians. If the definition of an amateur adopted by the AAUC in 1909 is used, then professional sport pervaded Canada, from the prize money at baseball tournaments on the North Thompson` River to the Montreal Canadiens hockey team. In fact, it would not be too much to say that money games were the most popular; certainly, they were outside the major amateur strongholds in the larger towns. Yet, inevitably, it was in the larger towns that fully professional teams developed. Professional sport became a marketable commodity, and it soon became dependent on the American market. Professional Canadian sport was, in some ways, a contradiction, in that Canada had not developed the population necessary for successful professional sport. Thus, Canadian sport was inexorably drawn within the orbit of the United States and it is doubtful if, even today, it would be possible to support a fully professional Canadian league. (The Canadian Football League is, on the surface, a notable exception. However, it is dependent on a flow of players and coaches from the United States, and so, in some respects, is not an exception at all. The recent financial difficulties of some CFL franchises – notably Montreal, Calgary, and Saskatchewan – also point to the problem of maintaining a Canadian league without an American market.)

Sport was an essential part of the cultural mosaic and reflected the predominant societal influences. It was not just a diversion or amusement divorced from the mainstream of life. Rather, it was a site for the propagation of systems of domination and subordination, and dominant groups tried to impose their view of the world on the whole society. Through its domination of the media, government, and institutions of learning, the middle class successfully imposed its view. Yet the ongoing problems faced by amateur sport and the success of professionalism suggest that middle-class control was always contested. Indeed, in the final analysis, the history of sport presented here has, of necessity, been filtered through the eyes of the dominant hegemony. What we have at present is an incomplete picture of the growth of sport in Canada. To be sure, organized sport was an upper- and middle-class creation, but to gain a more complete view of sport in Canadian society as a whole we will have to look outside the world of amateur sport and into areas that, up to now, have remained hidden from view.

Bibliographic Note

The theoretical underpinnings of the work at hand are to be found in four different areas. The most important of these is represented by E.P. Thompson, *The Making of the English Working Class* (New York, 1966). With respect to the importance of urban growth, L. Wirth, "Urbanism as a Way of Life," in A.J. Reiss, ed., *On Cities and Social Life* (Chicago, 1964), is a classic essay that has lost little of its relevance in the forty-three years since it was written. In a Canadian context, John Porter's *The Vertical Mosaic* (Toronto, 1965) provides a different approach to the analysis of Canadian society. Notwithstanding the importance of these three writers and others (R. Williams, A. Giddens) to the theoretical structure underlying this book, another source reflects more clearly the underlying assumptions of this book: Richard Gruneau, "Class, Sports and Social Development: A Study in Social Theory and Historical Sociology" (PH.D. dissertation, University of Massachusetts, 1981).

It is my contention that the history of sport, a social phenomenon, cannot be isolated from the mainstream of social history. Therefore it must be placed within the context of Canadian social history. It is impossible to list the corpus of available material, but the following examples provide a focus. Fundamental to any introduction to Canadian social history is A.R.M. Lower, *Canadians in the Making* (Toronto, 1958). Providing a different background are J.M.S. Careless and R. Craig Brown, eds., *The Canadians, 1867-1967* (Toronto, 1968) and J.M.S. Careless, ed., *Colonists and Canadiens* (Toronto, 1971). From another perspective, Peter G. Goheen, *Victorian Toronto, 1850 to 1900* (Chicago, 1970), affords a view of the growth of Canadian cities. Important to any social history of Canada are the articles in *Histoire sociale/ Social History* and *Labour/Le Travail*.

Of course, more than anything, this book is concerned with sport. The recency of sport history has meant that the secondary sources reflecting different approaches are missing. In fact, few of these sources reflect a clear thesis. Anyone writing sport history in Canada must start with the same central core of sources. Any bibliography of Canadian sport must start with Henry Roxborough's *One Hundred – Not Out* (Toronto, 1966). Unfortunately, this work includes no notes or bibliography. More important in providing a wealth of factual material is N. Howell and M.L. Howell's *Sports and Games in Canadian Life, 1700 to the Present* (Toronto, 1969). From a different perspective, providing biographies of over 150 Canadian "hall-of-famers," is S.F. Wise and D. Fisher, *Canada's Sporting Heroes* (Toronto, 1974). This book goes a step further in providing some penetrating insights into the growth of Canadian sport.

More important for readers interested in specialized, in-depth studies on Canadian sport are a number of PH.D. dissertations and Master's theses written at Canadian universities. Master's theses have been written principally at Alberta, Western Ontario, Dalhousie, and Windsor. Most important are the PH.D. dissertations from the University of Alberta. Of special value among these are Peter Lindsay, "A History of Sport in Canada, 1807-1867" (1969); Allan E. Cox, "A History of Sports in Canada, 1868-1900" (1969); Kevin G. Jones, "Sport in Canada, 1900-1920" (1970); Ian F. Jobling, "Sport in Nineteenth Century Canada: The Effects of Technological Changes on Its Development" (1970); Keith L. Lansley, "The Amateur Athletic Union of Canada and Changing Concepts of Amateurism" (1971); and Gerald Redmond, "The Scots and Sport in Nineteenth Century Canada" (1972). For anyone researching sport history these dissertations and theses provide an invaluable source. One of the most significant recent dissertations is M.K. Mott, "Manly Sports and Manitobans: Settlement Days to World War One" (PH.D. dissertation, Queen's University, 1980).

The periodical literature is spread across a variety of journals, particularly in the last five or six years. Two journals, however, provide a substantial number of articles, albeit of varying quality. These are the *Canadian Journal of History of Sport and Physical Education* (1970-), which is now *Canadian Journal of History of Sport*, and the *Journal of Sport History* (1974-).

Any book claiming to do more than collate existing material must be rooted in primary sources. An invaluable source for the growth of Canadian sport in the nineteenth century is the papers of the Montreal Amateur Athletic Association, which are housed in the Public Archives of Canada in Ottawa. These papers provide an outline of the growth of sport in anglophone Montreal. The most useful source in the MAAA collection is a number of scrapbooks collected by Hugh W. Becket that cover the periods

1872-76, 1877-1880, and 1886-1890. In addition, the history of the pioneering sporting club, the Montreal Snow Shoe Club, can be gleaned from the Minute Books of the Montreal Snow Shoe Club, 1861-1885, and from Hugh W. Becket's *The Montreal Snow Shoe Club: Its History and Record* (Montreal, 1882). Further information on the activities, structures, and composition of various clubs is available in the Minute Books of the Montreal Bicycle Club, 1872-1882, 1885-1891, 1891-1894, 1895-1909; Montreal Football Club, 1872-1895; and the Montreal Lacrosse Club, 1882, 1886-1893, 1893-1899, 1904-1911. Invaluable for providing quantifiable data were the Reports of the Directors of the MAAA, 1882-1896.

Despite the importance of the MAAA papers in providing information on the emergence of modern sport, the most important sources in determining the development of sport in Canada are newspapers. Because of the centrality of Montreal and Toronto in the history of Canadian sport, greater attention has been given to the papers of these cities. For Montreal, the *Montreal Transcript*, *Montreal Gazette*, *Montreal Star*, and *La Presse* were used to cover the period 1840-1915. The *Toronto Globe* was used for Toronto. In order to provide a broader Canadian perspective, the following newspapers were used for 1889, 1895, 1905, and 1915: *Halifax Herald*, *Saint John Daily Sun*, *Digby Courier*, *Le Moniteur Acadian* (Shediac), *Progres du Valleyfield*, *L'Etoile* (Joliette), *Le Progress du Saguenay* (Chicoutimi), *Le Soleil* (Quebec City), *Norfolk (Simcoe) Reformer*, *Peterborough Examiner*, *Exeter Times Advocate*, *Sault Daily Star*, *Ottawa Citizen*, *Windsor Evening Record*, *Minnedosa Tribune*, *Winnipeg Free Press*, *Brandon Daily Sun*, *Grenfell Sun*, *Oxbow Herald*, *Qu'Appelle Progress*, *Regina Leader Post*, *High River Times*, *Calgary Daily Herald*, *Edmonton Bulletin*, *Kamloops Sentinel*, *Vancouver Province*, *Victoria Daily Times*.

Notes

Introduction

1. C.L.R. James, *Beyond a Boundary* (London, 1963), p. 157.
2. S.F. Wise and D. Fisher, *Canada's Sporting Heroes* (Toronto, 1976); S.F. Wise, "Sport and Class Values in Old Ontario and Quebec," in W. Heick and R. Graham, eds., *His Own Man: Essays in Honour of A.R.M. Lower* (Montreal, 1974).
3. Bryan D. Palmer, *A Culture in Conflict: Skilled Workers and Industrial Capitalism in Hamilton, Ontario, 1860-1914* (Montreal, 1979), pp. 52-54.
4. For example, P. Bailey, *Leisure and Class in Victorian England: Rational Recreation and the Contest for Control, 1830-85* (London, 1978); K.A.P. Sandiford, "The Victorians at Play: Problems in Historiographical Methodology," *Journal of Social History*, 15 (Winter, 1981), pp. 271-87; M. Mott, "The British Protestant Pioneers and the Establishment of Manly Sports in Manitoba, 1878-1886," *Journal of Sport History*, 7, 3 (Winter, 1980), pp. 25-36.
5. For discussions of the change to modern sport, see Allen Guttman, *From Ritual to Record: The Nature of Modern Sports* (New York, 1978), pp. 15-55; M.L. Adelman, "The First Modern Sport in America: Harness Racing in New York City, 1825-1870," *Journal of Sport History*, 8, 1 (Spring, 1981), pp. 5-6.
6. For discussion of the relationship between play and culture, see Johan Huizinga, *Homo Ludens* (Boston, 1950), and Roger Callois, *Man, Play, and Games* (New York, 1961).

Chapter 1, The Roots of Organized Sport

1. Data on birthplace of population in *Census of Canada*, 1861.
2. See R.W. Malcolmson, *Popular Recreations in English Society, 1700-1850* (Cambridge, 1973).
3. E. Guillet, *Pioneer Days in Upper Canada* (Toronto, 1967), p. 188.
4. See G.M. Craig, ed., *Early Travellers in the Canadas, 1791-1867* (Toronto, 1955).
5. R. Day, "The British Army and Sport in Canada: Case Studies of the Garrison at Halifax, Montreal and Kingston to 1871" (PH.D. dissertation, University of Alberta, 1981); P. Lindsay, "The Impact of the Military Garrisons on the Development of Sport in British North America," *Canadian Journal of History of Sport and Physical Education*, I, 1 (May, 1970), pp. 33-44.
6. *Toronto Patriot*, July 13, 1836.
7. This is reflected in the appointment of Mr. G.A. Barber from England, who was central to the growth of cricket in Canada.
8. Wise and Fisher, *Canada's Sporting Heroes*, p. 8.

9. *Ibid.*, p. 10.
10. *Ibid.*
11. P. Lindsay, "A History of Sports in Canada, 1807-1867" (PH.D. dissertation, University of Alberta, 1969).
12. See G. Redmond, "The Scots and Sport in Nineteenth Century Canada" (PH.D. dissertation, University of Alberta, 1972), pp. 77-78.
13. For an excellent history of the first curling club, see Robert W. Simpson, "The Influence of the Montreal Curling Club on the Development of Curling in the Canadas, 1807-1857" (M.A. thesis, University of Western Ontario, 1980).
14. *Ibid.*, p. 71.
15. Redmond, "Scots and Sport," p. 129.
16. Simpson, "Montreal Curling Club," p. 46.
17. Lindsay, "The Impact of the Military Garrisons."
18. H.W. Becket, *The Montreal Snow Shoe Club: Its History and Record* (Montreal, 1882), pp. 15-16.
19. *Montreal Transcript*, December 15, 1849.
20. See Chapter 2 for the development of these clubs.
21. *Montreal Transcript*, August 20, 1844.
22. PAC, MAAA Papers, Becket Scrapbook, 1877-1880, p. 348.
23. *Ibid.*
24. *Montreal Transcript*, December 23, 1847.
25. A. Metcalfe, "The Evolution of Organized Physical Recreation in Montreal, 1840-1895," *Histoire sociale/Social History*. XI, 21 (May, 1978), p. 146.
26. W. Humber, "Cheering for the Home Team: Baseball and Town Life in 19th Century Ontario, 1854-1869," *Proceedings of 5th Canadian Symposium on the History of Sport and Physical Education*, University of Toronto, August 26-29, 1982.
27. *Ibid.*, pp. 192-195.
28. Lindsay, "History of Sports," p. 82.
29. Data for the discussion on Victoria is taken from the *Daily Colonist*, 1865.

Chapter 2, The Growth of Social Sporting Clubs

1. M.K. Mott, "Manly Sports and Manitobans: Settlement Days to World War One" (PH.D. dissertation, Queen's University, 1980), p. 252.
2. A. Metcalfe, "Sport and Social Stratification in Toronto, 1870-1920," manuscript.
3. See Becket, *The Montreal Snow Shoe Club*. This system was generally used in nineteenth-century sporting clubs.
4. *Montreal Daily Star*, September 27, 1884.
5. *Qu'Appelle Progress*, January 25, 1889.
6. *Victoria Daily Times*, January 30, 1905.
7. *Halifax Herald*, August 26, 1905.
8. *Digby Weekly Courier*, October 20, 1905, January 15, 1915.
9. *Halifax Herald*, August 28, 1905.
10. D. Pethick, *Summer of Promise. Victoria, 1864-1914* (Victoria, 1980), p. 126.
11. *Vancouver Daily Province*, September 2, 1905.
12. Robert A.J. McDonald, "'Holy Retreat' or 'Practical Breathing Spot'?: Class

Perceptions of Vancouver's Stanley Park, 1910-1913," *Canadian Historical Review*, LXV, 2 (June, 1984).

13. Redmond, "Scots and Sport," p. 280.
14. K. Jones, "Sport in Canada, 1900-1920" (PH.D. Dissertation, University of Alberta, 1970), p. 133.
15. Redmond, "Scots and Sport."
16. *Peterborough Examiner*, April 8, 1905.
17. Mott, "Manly Sports and Manitobans."
18. Metcalfe, "Sport and Social Stratification."
19. Redmond, "Scots and Sport."
20. *Ibid*.
21. Mott, "Manly Sports and Manitobans," p. 76.
22. Redmond, "Scots and Sport," pp. 156-57.
23. *Ibid*., p. 159.
24. *Ibid*., p. 167.
25. *Ibid*.
26. See A. Metcalfe, "Organized Sport and Social Stratification in Montreal 1840-1901," in R. Gruneau and J. Albinson, eds., *Canadian Sport: Sociological Perspectives* (Toronto, 1976), pp. 77-101.
27. *Toronto Globe*, 1905.
28. *Norfolk Reformer*, February 14, 1889, February 28, March 14, 1895; *Peterborough Examiner*, October 2, 1889, July 6, October 5, 1895.
29. *Toronto Globe*, January 9, 1895.
30. *Ibid*., February 27, 1895.
31. Mott, "Manly Sports and Manitobans," pp. 84, 86.
32. *Minnedosa Tribune*, May 30, 1895, December 9, 1915; *Grenfell Sun*, January 10, 1895.
33. See D. Howell, "The Social Gospel in Canadian Protestantism, 1895-1925: Implications for Sport" (PH.D. dissertation, University of Alberta, 1980).
34. *Vancouver Sun*, April 17, 1915.
35. Metcalfe, "Sport and Social Stratification."
36. Metcalfe, "Organized Sport"; Mott, "Manly Sports and Manitobans."

Chapter 3, The Emergence of Organized Team Sport

1. See A. Metcalfe, "The Changing Concept of Time" (M.A. thesis, University of Wisconsin, 1968); E.P. Thompson, "Time, Work Discipline and Industrial Capitalism," *Past and Present*, 38 (1967).
2. See R.W. Malcolmson, *Popular Recreation in English Society, 1700-1850* (Cambridge, 1973).
3. T. Williams, "Cheap Rates, Special Trains and Canadian Sport in the 1850's," *Canadian Journal of History of Sport*, XII, 2 (December, 1981), pp. 84-95.
4. I. Jobling, "Urbanization and Sport in Canada, 1867-1900," in Gruneau and Albinson, eds., *Canadian Sport: Sociological Perspectives*, p. 67.
5. See P. Rutherford, *The Making of the Canadian Media* (Toronto, 1978).
6. Leroy O. Stone, *Urban Development in Canada* (Ottawa, 1967), pp. 67-80.
7. Lacrosse, the first organized Canadian game, is dealt with in Chapter 6.
8. Wise and Fisher, *Canada's Sporting Heroes*, p. 34.

9. *Montreal Daily Star*, February 9, 1884.

10. There is some question as to the type of football. In all probability it was a local form of the English game. The Canadian form was not adopted until 1897.

11. See A. Metcalfe, "Sport and Athletics: A Case Study of Lacrosse in Canada, 1840-1889," *Journal of Sport History*, 3, 1 (Spring, 1976), pp. 1-19.

12. See P.D. Routledge, "The North-West Mounted Police and Their Influence on the Sporting and Social Life of the North-West Territories 1870-1904," (M.A. thesis, University of Alberta, 1978).

13. PAC, MAAA Papers, Report of Directors of the MAAA, 1895, pp. 121-22.

14. *Ibid.*, 1892.

15. T.A. Reed. *The Blue and the White* (Toronto, 1944), p. 92.

16. *Montreal Daily Star*, November 24, 1897; *Toronto Globe*, November 25, 1897.

17. Professionalism is considered in Chapters 4, 5, and 6.

18. Reed, *The Blue and the White*, p. 95.

19. For a full discussion of this, see J.W. Myrer, "The Canadianization of Intercollegiate Football in Ontario and Quebec from 1897 to 1921" (M.H.K. thesis, University of Windsor, 1977), pp. 172-75.

20. Wise and Fisher, *Canada's Sporting Heroes*, p. 44.

21. *Montreal Daily Star*, February 26, 1891.

22. Although the Victoria Club was the first formally constituted club, there is evidence that a Metropolitan-Montreal club existed from 1877.

23. Wise and Fisher, *Canada's Sporting Heroes*, p. 48.

24. *Ibid*.

25. *Montreal Daily Star*, December 15, 1892.

26. The SOHA was formed in December, 1894, with four teams and expanded to eight by 1895.

27. *Halifax Herald*, February, 1895.

28. *Oxbow Herald*, January, 1905.

29. *Peterborough Examiner*, January 4, 1905.

30. *Progres du Saguenay*, March 16, 1905; *La Presse*, November 30, 1895, February 3, 1905.

31. *Peterborough Examiner*, March 1, 1905; *Sault Daily Star*, February 23, 1905; *Simcoe Reformer*, February 6, 1896.

32. Mott, "The British Protestant Pioneers," pp. 22-30.

33. Mott, "Manly Sports and Manitobans," p. 8.

34. Wise and Fisher, *Canada's Sporting Heroes*, p. 49.

35. *Ibid*.

36. *Saint John Daily Sun*, February 18, 1905.

37. *Halifax Herald*, February 27, 1915.

38. Mott, "Manly Sports and Manitobans."

39. *Peterborough Examiner*, February 5, 1895.

40. *Toronto Globe*, November 18, 1912.

41. See Chapter 4.

42. *Toronto Globe*, December 5, 1904.

43. *Ibid*.

44. See Chapter 5.

45. Mott, "Manly Sports and Manitobans."
46. See D.A. Swain, "The Impact of the Royal Navy on the Development of Sport in British Columbia," *Proceedings of the 4th Canadian Symposium on the History of Sport and Physical Education*, University of British Columbia, June 24-26, 1979, pp. 1-18; R.D. Day, "The British Garrison at Halifax: Its Contribution to the Development of Sport in the Community," *ibid.*, pp. 1-14.
47. See *Halifax Herald*, 1885, 1895; *Victoria Daily Times*, 1885, 1895.
48. *Halifax Herald*, November 16, 1895.
49. *Vancouver Daily Province*, October 13, 1905.
50. Mott, "Manly Sports and Manitobans."
51. *Minnedosa Tribune*, 1929.
52. Swain, "The Impact of the Royal Navy," p. 9.
53. Interview with D. Forsyth published in *Toronto Globe*, June 7, 1930.
54. *Toronto Globe*, June 7, 1930.
55. Reed, *The Blue and the White*, p. 129.
56. *Ibid.*
57. *Ibid.*, p. 130.
58. Mott, "Manly Sports and Manitobans," p. 100.
59. *Exeter Times*, 1895.
60. *Grenfell Sun*, 1895; *Qu'Appelle Progress*, 1895.
61. *Sault Daily Star*, 1905.
62. *High River Times*, 1915.
63. *Peterborough Examiner*, March 25, 1905.
64. Interview with D. Forsyth published in *Toronto Globe*, June 7, 1930.
65. See Redmond, "Scots and Sport."
66. Wise and Fisher, *Canada's Sporting Heroes*, p. 10.
67. Mott, "Manly Sports and Manitobans," p. 96.
68. *Digby Courier*, July 26, 1889.
69. *Norfolk Reformer*, July 4, 1889.
70. *Exeter Times*, July 25, 1889.
71. *Ibid.*, August 15, 1895.
72. *Edmonton Bulletin*, June 12, 1905.
73. *Peterborough Examiner*, October 14, 1889.
74. *Grenfell Sun*, 1889, 1905; *Qu'Appelle Progress*, 1889.
75. *Toronto Globe*, January 25, 1895.
76. *Halifax Herald*, September 2, 1885.
77. Mott, "Manly Sports and Manitobans," p. 100.
78. *Toronto Globe*, April 23, 1895.
79. *Ibid.*, May 7, 1895.
80. Jones, "Sport in Canada, 1900-1920," p. 86.
81. Data from *Halifax Herald, La Presse, Edmonton Bulletin, Toronto Globe*, 1915.
82. Humber, "Cheering for the Home Team."
83. John Staley, "History of Sport in Essex County, Ontario" (M.ED. thesis, Wayne State University, 1971), p. 119.
84. Humber, "Cheering for the Home Team," p. 196.
85. *Montreal Daily Star*, April 18, 1873.

86. *Victoria Daily Times*, 1875; Mott, "Manly Sports and Manitobans," p. 68.
87. Staley, "Sport in Essex County," p. 122.
88. Mott, "The British Protestant Pioneers," p. 31.
89. Data from *Halifax Herald, Saint John Daily Sun, Toronto Globe, Winnipeg Free Press, Victoria Daily Times*, 1899.
90. *Oxbow Herald*, 1915; *Kamloops Standard*, 1915.
91. *Le Moniteur Acadian*, July 15, 1915; *Grenfell Sun*, June 30, 1895; *High River Times*, July 20, 1915; *Progress du Saguenay*, July 22, 1915.
92. Mott, "Manly Sports and Manitobans," p. 68.
93. *Calgary Herald*, August, 1905.
94. Taken from *Simcoe Reformer*, 1915.
95. *Kamloops Standard*, June 22, July 16, August 24, August 31, 1915.
96. *Victoria Daily Times*, 1889.
97. *Saint John Daily Sun*, 1895; *Winnipeg Free Press*, 1905; *Montreal Daily Star* and *La Presse*, 1915.
98. See Chapter 5.
99. Data from *Halifax Herald, Montreal Daily Star, Toronto Globe, Winnipeg Free Press, Edmonton Bulletin*, 1895, 1905, 1915.
100. *Montreal Daily Star*, August 24, 1872.
101. *Acadian Reporter*, July 18, 1874. Clipping in PAC, MAAA Papers, Becket Scrapbook, 1872-1875, p. 116.
102. *Toronto Globe*, May 8, 1877.
103. *Halifax Herald*, May-August, 1889; *Saint John Daily Sun*, May-August, 1889, May-August 1895.
104. *La Presse*, August 2, 1895.
105. *Victoria Daily Times*, May 25, 1889.
106. *Ibid.*, June, 1889.
107. *Sault Daily Star*, May 11, 1905; Staley, "Sport in Essex County," p. 125.
108. *Saint John Daily Sun*, August 7, 1905; *Digby Weekly Courier*, August 18, 1905; *Le Soleil*, September 11, 18, 1905; *Peterborough Examiner*, September 19, 1905.
109. *Edmonton Bulletin*, May 31, 1905.
110. *Grenfell Sun*, June 25, 1914.
111. *Ottawa Citizen*, September 3, 1915.
112. *Kamloops Sentinel*, June 15, 1915.
113. See Chapters 4 and 5.
114. Humber, "Cheering for the Home Team," p. 195.
115. Jesse E. Middleton, *The Municipality of Toronto, A History* (Toronto, 1923), II, p. 749.
116. *Halifax Herald*, August 17, 1889.
117. *Saint John Daily Sun*, October, 1889.
118. *Ibid.*, June 12, 1905.
119. *Halifax Herald*, June 21, 1915.
120. *Victoria Daily Times*, July 2, 1889.
121. *Ottawa Citizen*, June 24, 1889.
122. *Peterborough Examiner*, July 20, 1895.
123. *Ottawa Citizen*, July 3, 1915.

124. *Sault Daily Star*, May 11, 1915.
125. *Exeter Times*, August 20, 1889; *Victoria Daily Times*, May 6, 1889.
126. *La Presse*, March 27, April 15, 1905.
127. Data from *Victoria Daily Times, Edmonton Bulletin, Calgary Daily Herald, Regina Leader Post, Winnipeg Free Press, Ottawa Citizen, Peterborough Examiner, Montreal Daily Star, La Presse, Le Soleil, Joliette L'Etoile, Halifax Herald, Saint John Daily Sun, Toronto Globe, Vancouver Sun, Vancouver Province, Le Progress du Valleyfield*.
128. Mott, "Manly Sports and Manitobans," p. 179.
129. *Edmonton Bulletin*, August 23, 1915.
130. Humber, "Cheering for the Home Team," p. 191.
131. Palmer, *A Culture in Conflict*, pp. 52-54.
132. Metcalfe, "The Evolution of Organized Physical Recreation in Montreal, 1840-1895," p. 150.
133. *Ottawa Citizen*, July 31, 1915; *La Presse*, May 4, 1915.
134. *Montreal Daily Star*, April 30, 1884.
135. *Ibid.*, June 24, 1876.
136. *L'Etoile Du Nord*, December 5, 1889; *Progres du Valleyfield*, August 29, 1895; *La Presse*, June 17, 1895.
137. *Montreal Daily Star*, August 13, 1869.
138. *Saint John Daily Sun*, March 30, August 19, 1889.
139. *Halifax Herald*, July 1, 1895.
140. *Saint John Daily Sun*, July 29, 1905.

Chapter 4, The Growth of Organizations

1. K.L. Lansley, "The Amateur Athletic Union of Canada and Changing Concepts of Amateurism" (PH.D. dissertation, University of Alberta, 1971), p. 80. The data presented in this thesis have been invaluable, although my interpretation is different.
2. *Ibid.*, p. 17.
3. Maltby, Becket, and Paton were part of a small group of Montrealers, about nineteen in all, who had an influence on the growth of sport out of all proportion to their numbers.
4. Montreal Lacrosse Club and Montreal Snow Shoe Club were founding members of the MAAA.
5. Minute Book, AAAC, 1883-1888.
6. *Ibid.*, April 11, 1884.
7. 1st Annual Report of the AAAC, September 27, 1884, p. 6.
8. Lansley, "Amateur Athletic Union of Canada," pp. 39-40.
9. Annual Reports of AAAC, 1886-1888.
10. AAAC, Letter Book, 1890-1894.
11. *Montreal Star*, September 10, 1892.
12. AAAC, *Constitution, By-laws and Laws of Athletics*, November, 1896 (revised edition).
13. Lansley, "Amateur Athletic Union of Canada," p. 62.
14. *Ibid.*, p. 55.
15. *Ibid.*, p. 64.

16. *Ibid.*, p. 62.
17. The NALU dropped its amateur title in 1906.
18. Lansley, "Amateur Athletic Union of Canada," p. 67.
19. Jones, "Sport in Canada, 1900-1920," p. 437.
20. Lansley, "Amateur Athletic Union of Canada," p. 67.
21. *Ibid.*, p. 68.
22. *Ibid.*, p. 74.
23. *Toronto Globe*, October 26, 1908.
24. Lansley, "Amateur Athletic Union of Canada," p. 81.
25. *Ibid.*, p. 62.
26. *Ibid.*, p. 300.
27. Jones, "Sport in Canada, 1900-1920," p. 155.
28. *Montreal Star*, March 30, 1901.
29. PAC, MAAA Papers, Becket Scrapbook, 1877-1880, p. 270.
30. *Montreal Gazette*, January 22, 1870.
31. PAC, MAAA Papers, Becket Scrapbook, 1872-1876, p. 115.
32. *Ibid.*, p. 106.
33. *Ibid.*
34. This famous definition of an amateur adopted in England in the 1870's is one of the clearest pieces of evidence for the aristocratic origins of amateurism.
35. This paradox pervades middle-class attitudes to sport.
36. Lansley, "Amateur Athletic Union of Canada," pp. 290, 295, 300.
37. *Montreal Star*, November 29, 1890.
38. Quoted in J. Purcell, "English Sport and Canadian Culture in Toronto, 1876-1911" (M.P.E. thesis, University of Windsor, 1974), pp. 41-42.
39. See Metcalfe, "Organized Sport," pp. 87-88.

Chapter 5, The Growth of Professional and Commercial Sport

1. Robert W. Simpson, "The Influence of the Montreal Curling Club on the Development of Curling in the Canadas, 1807-1857" (M.A. thesis, University of Western Ontario, 1980), p. 105.
2. *Montreal Star*, November 26, 1873.
3. *Ibid.*, January 13, 1880.
4. These data reflect only those rinks that advertised in the *Montreal Star*.
5. A notable exception to this is contained in the work of M. Adelman on New York City, 1820-1871. See Introduction, note 5.
6. Sabbath desecration was the subject of editorial comment in the *Montreal Star* on thirty-five occasions between 1870 and 1894.
7. *Montreal Star*, August 15, 1869.
8. *Ibid.*, May 25, 1870.
9. *Ibid.*, October 15, 1870.
10. *Ibid.*, March 27, April 10, June 19, 1871.
11. *Ibid.*, November 18, 1875.
12. *Ibid.*, May 15, 1878.
13. *Ibid.*, January 12, 1880.
14. *Ibid.*, March 19, 1891, March 17, 1892.
15. The prosecutions, I believe, reflect only the tip of the iceberg; in fact,

cockfighting was far more widespread.

16. Material taken from the *Montreal Gazette* and *Montreal Star*.
17. *Brandon Daily Star*, April 11, 1889.
18. *Peterborough Examiner*, 1889.
19. *Ottawa Citizen*, March 11, 1889.
20. *Saint John Daily Sun*, February 13, 1895.
21. Mott, "Manly Sports and Manitobans," pp. 80, 86.
22. *Ibid.*, p. 102.
23. *Vancouver Daily Province*, 1905.
24. *Digby Weekly Chronicle*, November 15, 1895.
25. B. Schrodt, G. Redmond, and R. Baka, *Sport Canadiana* (Edmonton, 1980), p. 95.
26. Wise and Fisher, *Canada's Sporting Heroes*, p. 189.
27. *Toronto Globe*, January 17, 1867.
28. Mott, "Manly Sports and Manitobans," p. 80.
29. *Halifax Herald*, 1885.
30. Mott, "Manly Sports and Manitobans," p. 102.
31. *Edmonton Bulletin*, November 11, 1895.
32. *Grenfell Sun*, October 18, 1906; *Halifax Herald*, February 13, 1915.
33. *House of Commons Debates*, speech by Mr. Miller, April 6, 1910, p. 6413.
34. *Ibid.*, p. 6411.
35. E. "King" Dodds, *Canadian Turf Recollections and Other Sketches* (Toronto, 1909), p. 73.
36. See D. Guay, "Problems De l'integration Du Sport Dans La Sociale Canadienne 1830-1865: Le Case Des Courses de Chevaux," *Canadian Journal of History of Sport and Physical Education*, IV, 2 (December, 1973), pp. 70-92.
37. Mott, "Manly Sports and Manitobans," p. 40.
38. *Montreal Transcript*, June 28, 1849.
39. Dodds, *Canadian Turf Recollections*, p. 165.
40. *Ibid.*
41. Mott, "Manly Sports and Manitobans," p. 83.
42. *Victoria Daily Times*, July 3, 1889.
43. *Halifax Herald*, June 17, 1895; *Toronto Globe*, May 23, November 18, 1895.
44. *House of Commons Debates*, speech by Mr. McColl, April 6, 1910, p. 6433.
45. *Ibid.*
46. *Ibid.*
47. *Ibid.*, p. 6431.
48. *Ibid.*
49. *Ibid.*, p. 6413.
50. *Ibid.*, p. 6419.
51. Dodds, *Canadian Turf Recollections*, p. 208.
52. Data from *Toronto Globe*, *Ottawa Citizen*, *Exeter Times*, *Simcoe Reformer* for 1895; thus, the data for harness-racing and trotting represent a minimum figure.
53. See p. 139.
54. *House of Commons Debates*, speech by Mr. Crosby, April 7, 1910, p. 6560.

55. *La Presse*, January 4, 1895.
56. *Ibid.*, February 2, 1895.
57. *Halifax Herald*, September 2, 1905.
58. *Montreal Daily Star*, March 12, 1884.
59. *Saint John Daily Sun*, September 14, 1889.
60. *Ibid.*, March 2, 1905.
61. *Montreal Daily Star*, July 12, 1870.
62. *Ibid.*, August 26, 1870.
63. *Ibid.*, August 29, 1870.
64. *Ibid.*, May 18, 1882.
65. *Ibid.*, April 17, 1882.
66. Humber, "Cheering for the Home Team," pp. 195-96.
67. *Toronto Globe*, October 2, 1895.
68. *Saint John Daily Sun*, September 5, 1889.
69. *Ottawa Citizen*, January 24, 1889.
70. *Calgary Herald*, May, 1889.
71. M. Mott, "The First Pro Sports League on the Prairies: The Manitoba Baseball League of 1886," *Canadian Journal of History of Sport*, XV, 2 (December, 1984), pp. 7-21.
72. Mott, "Manly Sports and Manitobans," p. 234.
73. *Toronto Globe*, August 27, 1908.
74. *Ottawa Citizen*, April 10, 1915.
75. *Sault Daily Star*, March 3, 1905.
76. Mott, "Manly Sports and Manitobans."
77. B. McFarlane, *50 Years of Hockey* (Toronto, 1969), p. 13.
78. See J. Key, "Socio-Cultural Characteristics and the Image of the Urban Anglo-Canadian Athletic Hero, 1920-1939" (M.H.K. thesis, University of Windsor, 1982).
79. Until recently, any attention given to the lives of the working class was written from a middle-class perspective. This has been remedied in the work of a group of historians of the working class who approach the question from a different perspective. This approach is most clearly demonstrated in the work of Greg Kealey and Bryan Palmer.
80. Since 1969, I have asked every class in sport history if they had heard of Ned Hanlan. Out of over 1,000 students, less than ten had heard of him.
81. The following section is heavily dependent on Wise and Fisher, *Canada's Sporting Heroes*, pp. 112-14; F. Cosentino, *Ned Hanlan* (Don Mills, 1978); A. Brown, "Edward Hanlan, The World Sculling Champion Visits Australia," *Canadian Journal of History of Sport and Physical Education*, XI, 2 (December, 1980), pp. 1-44.
82. Wise and Fisher, *Canada's Sporting Heroes*, pp. 97-98.
83. *Halifax Herald*, 1925.
84. Wise and Fisher, *Canada's Sporting Heroes*, pp. 104-105.
85. *Montreal Star*, August 6, 1878.
86. Wise and Fisher, *Canada's Sporting Heroes*, p. 88.
87. *Montreal Star*, May 14, 1880.

Chapter 6, A Case Study of Lacrosse

1. This is one of the myths surrounding lacrosse. There was no evidence in the parliamentary debates or Acts to support the contention that it was proclaimed Canada's national game.
2. *Daily Globe*, September 30, 1867.
3. *Montreal Gazette*, May 8, 1876.
4. *Ibid.*
5. Data from reports of the annual meetings of the NLA and NALA in *Montreal Star*, *Montreal Gazette*, and *Toronto Globe*.
6. Data from the *Montreal Star*, *Montreal Gazette*, *Toronto Globe*, 1866-1885.
7. The Shamrocks, winners of 52 per cent of championship games, 1866-85, were grossly underrepresented on the executives of the NLA and NALA.
8. This remained true until 1900.
9. *Montreal Gazette*, August 6, 1877.
10. Metcalfe, "Sport and Athletics: A Case Study of Lacrosse in Canada, 1840-1889," pp. 1-19.
11. *Montreal Star*, April, 1873.
12. *Montreal Gazette*, July 6, 1875.
13. *Ibid.*, August 1, 1877.
14. *Montreal Star*, December 18, 1878.
15. *Ibid.*, April 14, 1883.
16. Data from *Montreal Daily Star*, 1866-1885.
17. Metcalfe, "A Case Study of Lacrosse," p. 2.
18. These are the fundamental problems facing sport today.
19. Metcalfe, "A Case Study of Lacrosse," p. 5.
20. *Montreal Star*, July 11, 1881.
21. *Toronto Globe*, July 11, 1881.
22. *Montreal Star*, September 30, 1882.
23. *Ibid.*, July 16, 1881.
24. It is difficult to understand how administrators were so blind, but their failure to recognize the real problems is beyond dispute.
25. Data from *Montreal Star*, *Montreal Gazette*, *Toronto Globe*, 1866-1884.
26. Evidence of the working-class nature of the team can be found in *Montreal Star*, October 9, 1874; PAC, MAAA Papers, Becket Scrapbook, 1877-1880, pp. 315-24.
27. *Montreal Star*, June 20, 1870.
28. *Ibid.*
29. Metcalfe, "A Case Study of Lacrosse," p. 17.
30. *Montreal Star*, September, 1874.
31. *Toronto Globe*, October 11, 1875.
32. *Ibid.*, July 11, 1882.
33. *Ibid.*, July 15, 1882.
34. *Montreal Gazette*, September 11, 1875.
35. PAC, MAAA Papers, Becket Scrapbook, 1877-1880, p. 315.
36. *Ibid.*, newspaper, September, 1874.
37. *Toronto Globe*, June 9, 1877.

38. *Montreal Star*, May 28, 1873.
39. *Ibid.*, July 11, 1881.
40. Mott, "Manly Sports and Manitobans," p. 197.
41. *Saint John Daily Sun*, April 9, 1889.
42. *Ibid.*, July 22, 1889.
43. N.K. McDonald, "The Wanderers' Amateur Athletic Club of Halifax 1882-1925. Its Contributions to Amateur Sport" (M.S. thesis, Dalhousie University, 1974), p. 43.
44. *Halifax Herald*, June 22, 1895.
45. *La Presse*, March 18, 1895.
46. *Ibid.*, May 25, 1895.
47. *Official Lacrosse Guide, 1931* (Toronto, 1931), pp. 23-24.
48. Mott, "Manly Sports and Manitobans," p. 77.
49. Jones, "Sport in Canada, 1900-1920," p. 140.
50. *Official Lacrosse Guide, 1931*, p. 11.
51. *Montreal Star*, October 5, 1886.
52. Metcalfe, "A Case Study of Lacrosse."
53. *Montreal Star*, September 25, 1893.
54. *Ibid.*, May 11, 1894.
55. *Ibid.*, August 13, 1889.
56. See Chapter 4.
57. Report of Directors of Montreal Amateur Athletic Association, 1892.
58. *Ibid.*, 1898.
59. The AAAC changed its name to the Canadian Amateur Athletic Union in 1898.
60. This is the first example of lacrosse clubs issuing official statements of payment.
61. Jones, "Sport in Canada, 1900-1920," p. 144.
62. In 1906 the NALU dropped the word "amateur" from its title. *Ibid.*, p. 147.
63. *Montreal Star*, July 18, 19, 1901.
64. This was the critical moment in the history of amateur sport. It effectively spelled the end to Montreal power.
65. Minute Book of Montreal Lacrosse Club, 1904-1911.
66. Wise and Fisher, *Canada's Sporting Heroes*, p. 66.

Index

Alberta, 64, 77, 82, 142–45, 157, 208–09

Amateur Athletic Association of Canada (AAAC), 104–10, 128, 214

Amateur Athletic Union of Canada (AAUC), 85, 102, 116–18, 220

Amateurism, and professionalism 111–14, 118–19, 130, 184, 196, 201–03; definitions, 103–05, 112, 117, 123–24; origins, 45–46, 119–20; philosophic bases, 119–27; role of Montreal, 104–10; societal foundations of, 124–28

American influence on: baseball, 85–95, 164–68; Canadian football, 55–56, 60; horse racing, 159; ice hockey, 168

Armaindo, Louise, 161

Artificial ice rinks, 67, 171

Athletic war, 114–16

Baseball, 85–93, 164–68; origins, 26, 85–86, 164; professional, 88–89, 164–68; relationship to United States, 88–89, 164–68

Becket, Hugh Wylie, 107, 128, 189

Beers, George, 24, 31, 182

Billiards, 138

Brandon, Manitoba, 142

British Columbia, 90–91; *see also* Vancouver; Victoria

British influence, 15–21, 30, 73–85

Brown, George, 175

Calgary, sport in, 37, 57–58, 156, 208

Canadian Amateur Athletic Union (CAAU), 110–16

Canadian Amateur Hockey Association (CAHA), 72, 118

Canadian Amateur Lacrosse Association (CALA), 117

Canadian football, 54–59; origins, 54; professionalism, 59; role of educational institutions, 55–56, 58; spread of, 56–59

Canadian identity, 13, 30–31, 47, 52, 96–98, 219–24

Canadian Intercollegiate Rugby Football Union (CIRFU), 56

Canadian Jockey Club (CJC), 149–50

Canadian Lacrosse Association (CLA), 206–08, 213, 215–16

Canadian Rugby Union (CRU), 56

Church and sport, 41, 44, 59, 65, 84

Class, middle class, 20, 41, 44, 64–65, 68, 82–83, 98–100, 129, 220, 233; upper class, 17, 29, 32, 43–45, 56, 82–83, 135, 150; working class, 29, 31, 65, 79, 85–86, 92–94, 139–41, 196–203

Coloured Canadians, 64, 95

Commercialization, 133–59; amateur sport, 136; causes of, 133–34, 142; definition, 133;

facilities, 134–39; horse racing, 145–59
Cricket, 80–84
Curling, 20, 39–43

Dalhousie University, 74, 78
Deerfoot, 160

Edmonton, 40, 57–58, 156, 208
English rugby, 73–74

Fitzgerald, Billy, 217
Forsyth, David, 76
French Canadians, 67, 86, 94, 223

Gambling, 150–52
Golf, 37–38
Grey Cup, 59

Halifax, 35–36, 37, 43, 70, 73, 80–83, 85, 86, 88, 91, 145–46, 154–56, 205
Hamilton, 18, 26, 37–38, 44, 59, 63, 86, 93, 149–50, 164–67
Hanlan, Edward (Ned), 136, 172–79; feats, 175–77; as a Canadian hero, 177–79
Horse racing, 147–59; commercialization, 152, 154–55; thoroughbred racing, 148–52; trotting and pacing, 153–59
Hunt clubs, 33–34

Ice hockey, 61–71, 168–72; artificial ice, 67, 171; expansion of, 63–65, 72; origins, 61–63; problems facing, 69–70; values attributed to, 68–69
Industrialization, 21, 49–50

James, C.L.R., 9

Lacrosse, 24, 182–215; National Lacrosse Association (NLA), 24, 182–96; problems facing, 183–84, 189–96; professional, 211–15; origins, 211–12; Five-Team League, 213–15; reasons for failure, 204–05, 210–11, 217–18; Shamrocks Lacrosse Club, 196–203; spread of, 204–11; British Columbia, 209–10; Manitoba, 208; Maritimes, 205; Ontario, 206–08; Quebec, 206
Lalonde, "Newsy," 217
Lawn tennis, 43–44
Leagues, emergence of, 50–51; baseball, 86, 164; cricket, 84; ice hockey, 63–65, 67; lacrosse, 203; professional, 169; soccer, 76
Lower Canada, 20–21, 147–50

Maltby, William L., 107, 128
Manitoba, 39, 74, 76–77, 86–89, 142–45, 157, 208; see also Winnipeg
McGill University, 55, 63, 79, 128, 134, 136
Merrick, J.G., 116, 128
Middle class, 20, 41, 44, 64–65, 68, 82–83, 98–100, 129, 220, 223
Money, 87, 89–92, 133–59, 179–80; role of, 133, 179–80; commercialization, 133–59
Montreal, 20–26, 33–35, 37–38, 41, 44, 54–56, 61–63, 65, 76–77, 80–81, 88, 94, 104–10, 146–50, 154–56, 159–64, 182–87, 213–15; birthplace of organized sport, 22, 54–55, 61–63; commercialization,

case study of, 134–41; emergence of organized sport, 21–26; lacrosse, 24–25, 182–83; role of, 52, 72, 104–10

Montreal Amateur Athletic Association (MAAA), 104–10, 114–15, 131–32

Montreal Curling Club, 20

National Hockey Association (NHA), 169

National asssociations, 101

National Lacrosse Association (NLA), 24, 182–96

New Brunswick, 64, 82, 86–89, 93, 156–57, 205; see also Saint John

Nova Scotia, 44, 64, 69, 82, 86–87, 142–45, 153, 156–57, 205; see also Halifax

Ontario, 38–42, 70, 74–77, 80, 82, 85–87, 93, 142–45, 153–55, 156, 163–65, 168, 185, 206–08; see also Hamilton; Ottawa; Toronto

Ontario Hockey Association (OHA), 63, 69, 70–72, 168–69

Ontario Rugby Football Union (ORFU), 56–57, 59

Organized sport, definition, 11–13; origins, 16, 22; spread, 26–29

Organizations: AAAC, 104–10, 128, 214; AAUC, 85, 102, 116–18, 220; CAAU, 110–16; CAHA, 72, 118; CALA, 117; CIRFU, 56; CJC, 149–50; CLA, 206–08, 213, 215–16; CRU, 56; NLA, 24, 182–196; MAAA, 104–10, 114–15, 131–32; NHA, 169; NLA, 24, 182–96;

OHA, 63, 69, 70–72, 168–69; ORFU, 56–57, 59

Ottawa, 34, 55, 63, 83, 155, 213–15

Paris crew, 174–75

Pre-industrial sport, 15

Professional sport, 70–71, 159–72, 211–17, 223; conditions for, 160–63, 166, 223; definition, 163–64; team sport, baseball, 89–92, 164–68; ice hockey, 70–71, 168–72; lacrosse, 211–17; touring professionals, 159–62

Quebec, 80, 86, 93–94, 153–55, 185–86, 205–06; see also Montreal

Queen's University, 58, 60

Regina, 44, 57–58, 208

Robertson, James Ross, 69, 71–72, 83

Rowing, 136, 172–79; professional, 174–77; Hanlan, Ned, 136, 172–79; Brown, George, 175; Paris crew, 174

Rural sport, 76–77, 82, 86–87

Saint John, New Brunswick, 36, 37, 43, 63, 65, 70, 80–83, 88, 91, 93, 143–45, 154–56, 165, 174–75, 205

Saskatchewan, 44, 64, 76–77, 82, 86–89, 142–145, 156–157, 208; see also Regina

Scottish influence, 20, 39–40, 78

Shamrocks Lacrosse Club, Montreal, 196–203; professionalism, 201; relation to community, 203; record, 197–98;

social origins, 196, 202
Soccer, 74-78
Social sporting clubs, 32-46;
   curling, 39-43; golf, 37-39;
   hunt, 33-34; lawn tennis, 43-
   45; yachting, 35-36
Sport hero, definition, 173-74;
   attitudes to, 172
Stanley Cup, 69
Structure of competition, 190-92

Technological changes, 51
Time, 49-50; concept of, 49-50;
   relation to sport, 50
Toronto, 17-18, 26, 35, 37-38,
   41, 44, 55-56, 63, 65, 71, 74-
   76, 80-85, 88, 90-93, 102-
   04, 143-45, 148-50, 159-67,
   171, 175-76, 184-88, 193-
   94, 199-200, 213-17; baseball, 26, 85, 88, 90-93, 164-
   67; Canadian football, 54-56;
   cricket, 17-18, 80-84; facilities, 143-45; horse racing,
   148-50; ice hockey, 63, 65,
   71, 171; lacrosse, 184-88,
   199-200, 213-17; rowing,
   103, 175-76
Transportation, 51-52

Universities: Dalhousie, 74, 79;
   McGill, 55, 63, 79, 128, 134,
   136; Queen's, 58, 60; Toronto,
   55, 59-60, 76

University of Toronto, 55, 59-60,
   76
Upper Canada, 17-20, 147-50
Upper Canada College, 16-17,
   56, 81, 84
Upper class, 17, 29, 32, 43-45,
   56, 82-83, 135, 150
Urbanization, 32, 45, 47-48, 53,
   219; definition, 48; relation to
   organized sport, 47-48; role of
   urban centres, 32, 45, 53, 219

Vancouver, 35-37, 44, 67, 73,
   76-77, 91, 92, 143, 150, 165-
   67, 209-10, 217; baseball,
   90-92, 165-67; lacrosse, 209-
   10, 217
Victoria, 26-29, 34-37, 44, 67,
   73, 76-77, 82, 86, 90, 146,
   150, 154, 165-67, 171, 209-
   10, 217; baseball, 86, 90,
   165-67; lacrosse, 209-10, 217

Winnipeg, 33, 37-39, 43-45, 53,
   58, 63, 64-65, 68-70, 76, 83,
   85-88, 92, 142-43, 146, 154,
   167-68, 208; baseball, 86-88,
   167-68; ice hockey, 63, 65,
   69-70, 170
Women, 32, 38, 43, 67, 161
Working class, 29, 31, 65, 79, 85-
   86, 92-94, 139-41, 196-203

Yachting, 35-36

THE CANADIAN SOCIAL HISTORY SERIES

Terry Copp,
*The Anatomy of Poverty: The Condition of the Working Class
in Montreal 1897-1929*, 1974.

Gregory S. Kealey, Peter Warrian, Editors,
Essays in Canadian Working Class History, 1976.

Alison Prentice,
*The School Promoters: Education and Social Class
in Mid-Nineteenth Century Upper Canada*, 1977.

Susan Mann Trofimenkoff and Alison Prentice, Editors,
*The Neglected Majority:
Essays in Canadian Women's History*, 1977.

John Herd Thompson,
The Harvests of War: The Prairie West, 1914-1918, 1978.

Donald Avery,
*"Dangerous Foreigners": European Immigrant Workers
and Labour Radicalism in Canada, 1896-1932*, 1979.

Joy Parr, Editor,
Childhood and Family in Canadian History, 1982.

Howard Palmer,
*Patterns of Prejudice:
A History of Nativism in Alberta*, 1982.

Tom Traves, Editor,
Essays in Canadian Business History, 1984.

Alison Prentice and Susan Mann Trofimenkoff, Editors,
*The Neglected Majority:
Essays in Canadian Women's History*, Volume 2, 1985.

Ruth Roach Pierson,
*"They're Still Women After All":
The Second World War and Canadian Womanhood*, 1986.

Bryan D. Palmer, Editor,
*The Character of Class Struggle: Essays in Canadian Working-Class
History, 1850-1985*, 1986.

Angus McLaren and Arlene Tigar McLaren,
*The Bedroom and the State:
The Changing Practices and Politics of Contraception and
Abortion in Canada, 1880-1980*, 1986.

Alan Metcalfe,
*Canada Learns To Play: The Emergence of
Organized Sport, 1807-1914*, 1987.